FLUTES
OF FIRE

California Indian Languages

FLUTES
OF FIRE

ESSAYS ON
CALIFORNIA INDIAN
LANGUAGES

Leanne Hinton

Heyday Books • Berkeley, California

Publisher's Cataloging in Publication
   (Prepared by Quality Books Inc.)

Hinton, Leanne
   Flutes of fire : essays on California Indian languages / by Leanne Hinton.
   Includes bibliographical references and index.
   ISBN 0-930588-62-2

   1. Indians of North America–California–Languages. 2. Indians of North America–California–Languages–Revival. 3. Indians of North America–California–Languages–Study and Teaching. 1. Title.

PM501.C3H55 1994   497'.09794
                                      QB193-22508

Interior design and graphics: Jeannine Gendar
Cover design: Diana Howard
Typesetting and production: Jeannine Gendar and Wendy Low
Cover painting by Frank Day, courtesy of Norm Wilson
Printing by Hignell Book Printing, Winnipeg, MB

Printed in Canada

10 9 8 7 6 5 4

Dedication

To my parents

Acknowledgements

My thanks, first of all, to Dave and Vera Mae Fredrickson, in general for all the years of friendship and inspiration, and in particular for inviting me to dinner when I first joined the faculty at U.C. Berkeley in 1978, to introduce me to Malcolm Margolin. As for Malcolm—well, how can I list all the things there are to thank him for? Without him, this book would certainly not exist.

Along this wild and wonderful ride into the joy of California languages, I have met other language lovers who have helped me travel further along the road: Mary Bates Abbott, whose funding and organization efforts are helping Native Californians in their quest for language preservation and renewal; Jeannine Gendar, gentle editor; and the many people whose devotion to their languages of heritage has been such an inspiration: Loren Bommelyn, Julian Lang, Bun Lucas, L. Frank Manriquez, Ernestine McGovran, Nancy Richardson, Darryl Wilson, and Linda Yamane, just to name a few of those I have gotten to know best.

Many people were consulted during the writing of the essays here: besides those mentioned above, my heartfelt thanks for their contributions go to Brian Bibby, Gene Buckley, Catherine Callaghan, Victor Golla, Margaret Langdon, Sue Lobo, Herb Luthin, Jack Marr, Marianne Mithun, Pamela Munro, Bev Ortiz, Jean Perry, Alice (Schlichter) Shepherd, Shirley Silver, Ernest Siva, Ken Whistler, and Akira Yamamoto. John Sporich, Rina Margolin and Pam Morgan all read drafts of this volume and gave me insightful suggestions for the final editing. Thanks to Robert Oswalt and Vera Mae Fredrickson for their contributions to this book in Chapters 9 and 17, and to Yolanda Montijo, who spent the many hours on the phone that allowed us to give a best guess of how many people now speak the California languages. Special thanks go also to Laura Buszard-Welcher, who researched the quotes from linguistic and narrative literature that enliven this book. And my gratitude for many things to my husband, Gary Scott—for helping in various ways throughout the years on these essays, and for helping make life in general warm and worthwhile.

Finally, a salute to the first Master-Apprentice language teams, who are beginning work as I write this, on an intensive language learning project to transmit six California languages to the younger members of the teams. My best wishes go to Parris Butler and Claude Lewis (Mojave); Melodie Carpenter, Ray Baldy and Winnie George (Hupa); Carole Korb and Jessie Exline (Yurok); Terry Supahan and Violet Super (Karuk); Matt and Agnes Vera (Yowlumne); Caleen Sisk-Franco and the great spiritual leader Florence Jones (Wintu). May you have joy in your learning, and may the languages of Native California live on!

82593   L. Frank

Arrived home, Mouse sat on top of the assembly house, playing his flutes and dropping coals through the smokehole. Coyote interrupted him, however, before he was finished, and so it is that the people who sat in the middle of the house received fire. Those people now cook their food and talk correctly. The people who sat around the edge of the room did not get any fire and today when they talk their teeth chatter with the cold. That is the way the languages began. If Coyote had not interrupted and Mouse had been able to finish playing all his flutes of fire, everyone would have received a share of fire and all would have spoken one language.

Indians today talk many different languages for the reason that all did not receive an equal share of fire.

—a Maidu origin tale from Gifford and Block, *Californian Indian Nights*, p. 136

CONTENTS

As in many things Californian, the superlative applies to the number of languages spoken within the borders of the state in aboriginal times. One hundred and four languages and dialects were spoken by the aborigines of the state when Caucasians first settled within its boundaries. This vast aggregation of languages within so limited an area is not found anywhere else in the world.

—Gifford and Block, *Californian Indian Nights*, p. 15

Introduction

The California Mosaic

California is a mosaic of overlapping cultures; there are practices performed and words uttered every moment of every day from Africa, Asia, Latin America, Polynesia, the Middle East, and of course dominantly from Europe.

Embedded in this complex pattern of people and traditions and ways of thought are the state's first people, the many communities of California Indians. Before the rest of the world arrived here, Native California was already one of the most diverse areas on Earth, culturally and linguistically, and had been for thousands of years. Over a hundred languages were spoken here, representing five or more major language families and various smaller families and linguistic isolates.

In a land of great and varied resources, people could maintain healthy populations and lead very different sorts of lives from each other. People along the coast had access to shellfish and the nutritious aquatic plants; some went out in boats to hunt the great sea mammals. A few miles inland were those whose staples were the acorn and pinenut. Along the Sacramento and San Joaquin river systems people could fish for the abundant salmon, while their upslope neighbors hunted deer or pronghorn. Ways of living varied greatly, but being geographically close to each other, people could interact often and develop close trading relationships and ceremonial ties. Because of these interactions, people were often multilingual, but each community could nevertheless be independent enough to maintain its own variety of speech.

Even today, there are about fifty different California Indian languages still spoken, each with its own particular genius. There is so much to learn from all these different languages, about the amazing choices humans have in organizing and talking about the world around them. There are so many ways to construct language itself, many ways to play with it or to use it to powerful effect. The elders who speak these languages have so much to tell us about the vocabulary of different kinds of knowledge and activities, about the world views expressed in

*Some California languages have only one fluent speaker
left, and some have none. Above: Mary Jones, the last
fluent speaker of her Konkow Maidu language. 1992
photo by Mary Bates Abbott.*

the way utterances are put together, the infinite number of ways people
have of constructing their lives. At a time when these languages (along
with over half of the languages in the rest of the world!) are endangered,
it is more important than ever to learn the lessons they can teach us.

California Indian languages are indeed in the ultimate crisis in a life-
and-death struggle. After decades of social change and of attempts by
authorities to eradicate native language use, Native California languages
are rarely spoken at home, so children do not learn them. Most languages
are spoken only by a few elders. Some languages have only one fluent
speaker left, and, as has already happened to so many, some have none.
During the drafting of this manuscript, half a dozen or so of the last speakers of California languages have died. We may see ninety percent of these
languages, or perhaps all of them, disappear in our lifetimes.

No one feels this impending loss more strongly than the Native
Californians themselves. Many concerned people are making enormous
efforts to keep the languages and cultural practices alive. All over
California, from the Oregon border to the Mexican border, from the
Pacific Ocean to the Sierra, Native Californians carry on the cultures of
their pre-Columbian heritage, even while they participate in the cultures
and intercultures more recently derived from Europe and elsewhere.

*Laura Somersal, one of the last native speakers of Wappo,
died in 1990. Photo by Scott Patterson.*

Elders such as Ray Baldy (Hupa) are teaching the languages in the
schools; others, such as Villiana Hyde (Luiseño) and Katherine Saubel
(Cahuilla) are working with linguists to make sure there is a record for
the future. Young adults like Loren Bommelyn (Tolowa), Julian Lang
(Karuk) and Parris Butler (Mojave) are making every effort to learn the
languages of their heritage, to keep them alive for another generation.
Some people, such as L. Frank Manriquez (Tongva/Ajachmem) and
Linda Yamane (Ohlone), whose ancestral languages ceased to be spoken
at all a generation or more ago, are gathering together all the written
materials and recordings they can find, to study and to treasure. Linguists and anthropologists and archivists, too, have worked to preserve the
California languages, in their own ways and for their own varied reasons,
often simply because they hate to see languages and cultures die.

Katherine Saubel, a Cahuilla scholar who has worked with linguists for years to record the Cahuilla language for future generations. 1992 photo by Mary Bates Abbott.

This is a book about the languages of California and about the people who are striving to keep them alive. It is a book about the joy of languages, the wonderful ways they are put together and the ways they express human thought—the sacred, the scientific, the practical, and the humorous. It is about how these languages change through time, and how they survive and influence other languages, including English.

My own journey to the languages of California has been long and full of detours, and most of the way I never guessed where I would arrive, even though looking back, it seems a predictable enough destination. My initial interest in ethnomusicology led me one summer to Supai, Arizona, the beautiful Grand Canyon home of the Havasupai Indians. That was 1964, and I was 22 years old, full of all the confusions of youth. The

Violet Super and Terry Supahan are part of a special "Master-Apprentice" program to develop fluency in younger speakers of California languages, in this case Karuk. 1993 photo by Mary Bates Abbott.

Havasupais took me in and molded my character and my career. Supai has always been and still is the most constant learning place in my life.

Having gone to Supai to study music, I soon found that I needed to know the language to understand the song. So linguistics started to become a major interest, and with the help of my friend Margaret Langdon, I eventually entered graduate school in that field with her as my mentor. My dissertation was a linguistic study of Havasupai songs.

My first university job took me far from California to the University of Texas at Dallas. I did not adjust easily to the academic world, and the only thing that kept me sane was a fulfilling project with the Havasupais— designing a writing system with them and helping them establish a bilingual education program. I also consulted with the nearby Hualapai language program and did much of the same kind of work there. This was, and still is, the sort of linguistics in which I find the most meaning.

My work with the languages of California began after I arrived at the University of California at Berkeley in 1978. Besides basic teaching and research duties, I was given the job of Co-director, and later Director, of the Survey of California and Other Indian Languages. I continued my interest in writing systems and bilingual education here in California, doing consultant work for programs around the state. I also taught a field methods class with Kashaya Pomo speaker Bun Lucas, working with graduate students to analyze the grammar of his language. With Alice Shepherd I have been studying Wintu songs, based on a series of tapes by singer Grace MacKibben. Most importantly, I have been spending time with a growing number of Native Californians whom I am honored to know and to learn from.

In 1987, Malcolm Margolin invited me to start a regular column on language in *News from Native California*, a quarterly devoted to California Indian history and culture. That was the actual beginning of this volume. This book is derived from a series of essays that originally appeared in that journal. The essays have all been edited at least slightly, and some significantly. Most have been expanded and some consist entirely of new material. This book is not intended to be an exhaustive analysis of the California languages; such is not possible anyway. There are many more things to write about, which will appear in future columns. But these essays were selected because they go well together and give, I hope, a good overview of some of the important issues and interesting characteristics of California languages.

California itself is of course a recent political construction, whose borders in no way match the borders of Native American linguistic or cultural groupings. I do not hesitate to cross these borders when there is a good story just on the other side. Chapters 2 and 3, especially, wander freely into Baja California, Arizona and the Northwest. In the same spirit of denying boundaries, I am loath to leave an excellent essay out of this book just because I am not its author, so there are a couple of columns from *News from Native California* by other people that seemed to me to go well here. I have incorporated a delightful essay by Robert Oswalt on Russian loan words in the Kashaya Pomo language (Chapter 9), and I have adapted some powerful oral histories transcribed by Vera Mae Fredrickson as the main part of the essay "Languages Under Attack" in Chapter 17. The first chapter, "Living Languages of Native California," is co-authored with Yolanda Montijo.

In Chapter 1 we will survey the Indian languages spoken in California and show how many people (how few, now!) speak each one. I follow immediately with a set of portraits of California language and culture, to show the richness of the heritage we may be about to lose. These are four essays on language creativity and playfulness: an essay on song, one on storytelling, and two about the structure of California languages and what that shows about world view.

Part II is a series of essays on what languages tell us about the history of their speakers; and in Part III, we explore some of the interesting aspects of the vocabulary and grammar of California languages. In Part IV, we examine the ways in which prejudice and oppression have led to the decline and death of languages in California; and Part V is a set of chapters on how the people who speak and study these wonderful languages are fighting to keep them alive.

I conclude the volume with an examination of how linguistics can and should relate to the needs of the communities being studied. As a linguist, I believe that the fascinating but often esoteric scholarly pursuits of professional linguistics can only gain meaning and validation by what they can provide to the rest of the world. This means maintaining a close relationship to and awareness of the needs of the communities that linguists study. The language issues that are important to the California Indians are not always the same ones that are important to academics. Yet linguists have a unique ability to address community language needs. Linguists must not allow academic institutions to be the sole source of their values, but must instead constantly endeavor to balance the priorities and demands of the two places where they do their work: the university and the speech community.

Therefore, I intend this book for a broad audience—for linguists, for Native Americans, and, for folks in general. Any book about language must also be about the lessons in humanity that we learn through language. Through this book I seek to bring to the reader a sense of urgency about the impending loss of our great linguistic treasure, and a sense of the priceless value the languages have, not only to the first Californians and to linguists, but to *all* of us.

Mulidom maʔu ʔul- šiba·ma· bakʰe ʔama· qan ʔt̓o cahno cóʔdoqon dubíhladuʔ̓ mu·
ʔemˇ ya maʔu haʔdíʔdi qan ʔt̓o lowa·c̓am ʔul men- ʔama· mu·kinʔ c̓óc̓qaw iñ
mulidom cahno cóʔdoqon- mílhqʰaʔ dubíhladuʔ̓ hadu· cahno lowá·c̓al mul šiba·
dubíhladuʔˆ heʔen ʔacaʔ mul ku tol men lowaʔ ʔíʔkʰe tʰin nihcénʔba꞉ mens̓iba yal
pʰala men cahno díhqaba ya bíʔamatol- be·li ʔiwñ maʔú ya cahno lowa·c̓al mul ya
lówaʔ̓ hadu· ʔel má·caʔ pʰala pʰalahá mens̓in ya heʔen bayatáʔkʰe tʰin ma·caʔkʰe ya
kúʔmul s̓iʔí ʔnatiñ*

He gave them languages for different places and sent them off. That's why we talk in
different ways—he created things that way. Giving [one group a certain] language,
he sent them off [to one place]. Those speaking another language he sent elsewhere, saying that the people can't all be together when they speak [differently] like
that. We, too, having been given a language, stayed here at this place. We spoke the
language that we are speaking now. Other people have different languages and we
can't understand theirs even though we are of one flesh.

—Herman James in Robert Oswalt's *Kashaya Texts*, pp. 42–43

---

* See Appendix for general discussion of symbols.

I

Living California Indian Languages

by Leanne Hinton and Yolanda Montijo

The continued existence of about fifty Native Californian languages,* with their alternately rollicking and beautiful linguistic creativity as characterized in the following essays, is an indication of the great cultural strength of California Indian communities. Their survival is especially amazing when we realize that it is now over two centuries since the deeply disruptive establishment of the Spanish missions, and nearly a century and a half since the Gold Rush and its tragic aftermath. But despite their endurance, the California languages are at the brink of extinction. The fifty living languages are what remain of around a hundred spoken here in 1800. And it appears that there is not a *single* California Indian language that is being learned by children as the primary language of the household. Even those who know the languages rarely use them: they may have no one to talk to, and the habits of native language use may wither. In a recent interview, Chemehuevi elder Gertrude Leivas talked about the last time she made full use of her native tongue, ten years before at her brother's funeral. "I surprised myself," she said. "The words came out like a string of beads." (*Los Angeles Times* article by Paul Feldman, 1993).

With no new speakers, most California languages are spoken now only by the elders. When the elders die, the languages will likely vanish from the face of the earth.

Still, people have a tenacious loyalty to their languages. Although no one is learning the California languages natively any more, there are many young people around the state who are trying to learn them as second languages. If these community and individual efforts succeed, the California languages may be around much longer than predicted. To paraphrase Mark Twain—reports of their death might be [we hope!] greatly exaggerated.

---

* Exactly how many there are depends on whether we define some varieties as separate languages or as dialects of a single language.

It would seem reasonable to try to inform readers exactly how many speakers there are of each California language, but this is not at all an easy thing to do. For one thing, what do we mean by "speaker"? Take Yurok, for example, a language spoken in the northernmost part of California. Yurok has only about fifteen fluent speakers, but there are many "semi-speakers" who have a large vocabulary in Yurok and may be able to carry on a simple conversation. There are also some who speak Yurok as a *second* language— people who learned the language as teenagers or young adults. Do we count second-language learners as speakers or not? And even if there were no fluent speakers at all, the language would not be completely "dead"—for there are many who don't speak the language of their heritage, but do know some phrases and words; some have a passive knowledge of the language that could be awakened into active usage with some work.

A second problem is that most surveys are by necessity based on casual estimates given by linguists or community members. Such estimates are rarely accurate, as the people forced to make them usually point out. A good case in point is a story told by linguist Marianne Mithun about her work with Cayuga people in Ontario, Canada. She kept asking people in the community how many there were that still spoke the language, and people generally estimated that there were around thirty speakers left. However, when she asked who the speakers were, the names were often different. Finally, a Cayuga man she told about this discrepancy decided to do a house-to-house survey on his own. He found that there were 376 Cayuga speakers!

A survey of speakers of Native American languages was made in the 1960s by Wallace Chafe, but the situation of endangered languages changes very rapidly, and this survey is now thirty years old.

We conducted a telephone survey in July and August, 1993 to determine as closely as possible how many fluent speakers there are *now* for California languages. We spoke to seventy tribal officers, native scholars and linguists to get the closest possible guess for each language.

Another source of information, but a highly questionable one, is the 1990 U.S. census. In 1990 these language questions were included in the census survey:

Does this person speak a language other than English at home? ( ) yes ( ) no
What is this language? (for example: Chinese, Italian, Spanish, Vietnamese)

This wording is slightly wrong for our own inquiry, for two opposing reasons. First, since speakers of endangered languages often do *not* speak their language at home, they might not report it. Second, the question does not ask about fluency—a person who knew only a few words and phrases, but tried to use them around the house, might report using another language. The first problem could lead to under-reporting the number of speakers of a language, and the second could lead to over-reporting.

Another difficulty is the fact that the questions about language were only on the "long form" of the census survey, which was given out to an average of one in seven households (the actual percentage of households surveyed with the long form differs from place to place). Thus, for each area, the number of responses was multiplied by seven or some other constant. This sort of statistical procedure can give reasonable results for large populations; but if, for example, there is only one speaker of a given California language, the census would state that there are none, or seven, depending on whether or not that particular household got the long form. As the Census Bureau pointed out to us, there are various other sources of error as well: for example, people may write down language names that the census tabulators can't recognize, and may put in the wrong categories.

It turns out that the census reports considerably *more* speakers of California languages than our telephone survey indicated. It would be wonderful to think that this is due to the Cayuga syndrome—that there are more speakers around than a casual estimate by informed people is likely to disclose. But it is much more likely that the discrepancies are due to sampling and statistical errors by the Census Bureau, coupled with the nonoptimal (for our purposes) wording of the question.

With the information from these sources, we created a table of all Native Californian languages which have at least one living speaker, and some of those with no living speakers. The extinct languages that we show here have been included for one of several reasons: either the last speakers died just recently, or the language has some fame and is therefore of general interest (such as Yahi, the Yanan language spoken by Ishi), or most importantly, the descendents of the speakers are studying the language and possibly attempting to revive it.

It is important to reiterate that all of these numbers involved some guesswork and none can be taken as unquestionable. Even the people most closely involved with a language may not know if a certain person speaks it fluently or not. There may well be people who know the language but have never been heard to speak it by their associates. In some instances where members of a tribe live far away from each other, people may not know for sure if a speaker is still alive. People also have different ideas of what constitutes "fluency," or even what language is spoken. For example, Modoc and Klamath people are on the same reservation, and there is disagreement among the people we spoke to as to whether some individuals counted as Modoc or Klamath speakers. (The two languages are closely related, so it hardly matters, except that we count Modoc as a California language and Klamath as a language of Oregon!)

Because of the various sources of uncertainty that are built into this task, we include three sorts of estimates in the table in this chapter:

Conservative estimate: People's best estimate of the number of *fluent speakers*. When more than one number is given, it means either that informed people differ in their estimates or that one person guesses the number falls between these two extremes. For example, in Cahuilla, "7–20" is a combination of estimates by two people, one of whom estimated "7 or more," and the other "around 20."

Liberal estimate: This is an estimate that may include less fluent individuals—semi-speakers and second-language speakers. Alternatively, it may include situations where the language spoken is a matter of interpretation.

1990 census figure: These numbers are taken from Series CPH-L, #133, Table 1 ("Detailed language spoken at home and ability to speak English for persons 5 years and over: 1990 United States") and Table 10 ("Detailed language spoken at home and ability to speak English for persons 5 years and over: 1990 California), Bureau of the Census. Sometimes this figure is dramatically different from the best estimates of knowledgeable people, for the reasons described above.

The census figure for California differs in some instances from the figure for the United States as a whole. In that case, we list both figures. This can sometimes be interpreted as meaning that there are Native Californians living outside of California who report themselves as speakers of these languages. However, sometimes the differences seem improbable and may be due instead to some error or difference in interpretation.

Note that we say nothing in this table about population size: for example, there are no fluent Chumash speakers, but there are of course many Chumash people. The number of people on the tribal rolls always exceeds the number of speakers by far.

There are many Native American languages spoken in California besides Native Californian languages. The census reports more speakers of Navajo in California than all Native Californian languages combined! Here is a list, from the 1990 census, of the other Native American languages spoken in California by people who have migrated from other parts of the country: Aleut 40, "American Indian" 1995, Apache 297, Arapaho 34, Arikara 20, Blackfoot 41, Chasta Costa 61, Cherokee 478, Cheyenne 63, Chiricahua 21, Choctaw 183, Comanche 8, Cree 60, Crow 61, Dakota 447, Eskimo 109, Fox 18, French Cree 7, Han 16, Hidatsa 17, Hopi 76, Inupik 18, Iroquois 9, Jicarilla 16, Kansa 5, Keres 139, Kickapoo 6, Kiowa 76, Menomini 55, Micmac 9, Mohawk 22, Muskogee 259, Navajo 1834, Nez Perce 5, Ojibwa 94, "Other Athapascan-Eyak" 10, Ottawa 2, Picuris 3, Pima 138, Potawatomi 29, Puget Sound Salish 5, Sahaptian 25, Salish 2, Tewa 111, Tiwa 35, Tlingit 22, Towa 40, Ute 28, Yavapai 5, Zuni 39.

Cocopa is spoken almost entirely in Arizona and Mexico, but we include it here because the tribe was originally on both sides of the Colorado River, and so partly in California. (The tribe has about 700 members in Arizona; our contact says about 60% speak or understand the language, with a third of those being fluent speakers.) Children have passive knowledge of Cocopa and can use some words and phrases; and a few may be learning fluently, but most fluent speakers are middle-aged or older. There are also about 700 Cocopas in Mexico who are not affiliated with the tribe on this side of the border. Little is known about their linguistic status, although we are sure there are many speakers.

The number of speakers of California languages might seem depressingly low, and it is sad to note that the speakers of these languages are almost all elders—as was noted at the beginning of the chapter, not a single California language is being learned by children as the primary language of the household. But Native Californians are waging a battle to keep their languages alive. In the table, we have included short notes about language preservation and restoration activities taking place within the California Indian communities.* We also note when we know that traditional singing, an activity closely related to language usage, is occurring. Many singers have begun to learn their languages as adults because of their commitment to singing. We include this column as evidence that California is in the midst of a great language revival, indeed a general cultural renaissance. If these "community-based language activities" efforts succeed, the California languages may be around much longer than the low numbers shown here indicate.

Our deepest thanks for their willingness to share their knowledge with us in this survey go to Cindy Alvitre, Craig Bates, Margaret Baty, Lowell Bean, David Belardes, Gordon Bettles, Brian Bibby, William Bright, Parris Butler, Catherine Callaghan, Linda Charles, Michelle Cisco, Gilbert Cordero, Betty Cornelius, Alan Daugherty, Eric Elliott, Kay Fowler, Hector Franco, Geoffrey Gamble, Lillian Garcia, Jeannine Gendar, Victor Golla, Ron Goode, Marlene Greenway, Bill Jacobsen, Albert James, Louise Jeffredo-Warden, Darrell Johnston, Michael Krauss, Paul Kroskrity, Jean LaMarr, Cindy Lamebull, Julian Lang, Margaret Langdon, Mel Lavato, Michael Lincoln, Frank Lobo, Sue Lobo, Mark Macarro, Martha Macri, Malcolm Margolin, Helen McCarthy, Ernestine McGovran, Wick Miller, Marianne Mithun, Pamela Munro, Angie Osbourne, Robert Oswalt, Pauline Owl, Lillian Parra, Victoria Patterson, Jean Perry, Stephen Quesenberry, Susie Ramirez, Nancy Richardson, David Robinson, Noel Rude, Alice Shepherd, Florence Shipek, William Shipley, Shirley Silver, Ernie Siva, George Somersall, Terry and Sarah Supahan, Julie Tex, Bernice Torrez, Kathy Turner, Norma Turner, Agnes Vera, Matt Vera, Ron and Carol Wermuth, Ken Whistler and Darryl Wilson.

---

* We do not include mention of works by linguists on these languages, since that would increase the size of this table a hundredfold! References to linguistic publications on these languages are readily available elsewhere. But both published works and linguistic field notes are playing a very useful role in community language restoration and preservation efforts.

Speakers of California Indian Languages

Shown here are conservative estimates of the number of fluent speakers of close to fifty Native Californian languages. In addition to those shown here, some of which have no fluent speakers, there were probably at least fifty other languages in California when Europeans arrived. A more detailed chart follows.

FLUTES OF FIRE

LANGUAGE	NUMBER OF SPEAKERS		
	CONSERVATIVE ESTIMATE	LIBERAL ESTIMATE	1990 CENSUS FIGURES
Achumawi	5–10	15–17	California: 70 U.S.: 81 —
Atsugewi	3	—	—
Cahto	0	1	—
Cahuilla	7–20	50	California: 32 U.S.: 35
Chemehuevi	Colorado River Reservation: 10 or less Chemehuevi Res.: 3	approx. 20	3
Chumash	0	—	—
Cocopa	approx. 150	approx. 400	"Delta River Yuman:" California: 15 U.S.: 321
Cupeño	1–5	—	9
Diegueño	Kumeyaay: 50 Ipai: 25; Tipai: 200	Kumeyaay: 75 —	Diegueño: 97 —
Esselen	0	—	—
Gabrielino (Tongva)	0	—	—
Hupa (Whilkut, dialectally related to Hupa, may have 2–3 speakers)	12–25	35–40	93
Juaneño (Ajachmem)	0	1	—
Karuk	10–12	40–60	California: 59 U.S.: 26
Kawaiisu	8–10	20	—
Luiseño	30–40	—	43

COMMUNITY-BASED LANGUAGE ACTIVITIES	COMMENTS
Singing is being revived; work is being done with old anthropological field notes.	
Work is being done with old anthropological field notes.	
Some individual language learning efforts.	
A group at Colorado River is working on a dictionary.	As is true of many California languages, there were hundreds of Chemehuevi speakers a mere twenty years ago.
The daughter of the last Chumash speaker is working with her mother's notebooks.	The Chumash languages include Obispeño, Barbareño, Puriseño, etc.
Introductory college course on Cocopa at nearby college; summer youth program with some language retention activities.	Most U.S. Cocopa speakers live in Arizona.
Language materials have been made; singers, including young people.	Our contact said Cupeño has "a handful of speakers."
Language program in Barona; some language revival activity elsewhere; singers.	The Tipai figure includes Baja California.
Language revival group.	
Some individuals are collecting and studying language materials.	Gabrielino is also known as Tongva. The last speaker died in the 1970s.
Adult and school language classes, including language immersion camps; many singers; Hupa education committee deals with language issues; Master-Apprentice team summer 1993.	The Master-Apprentice program is being piloted in summer 1993. Teams of elders and younger tribal members are working intensively together so that the apprentices can learn the language.
Some individuals have collected tapes and done other language preservation work. In 1992, part of a mass at San Juan Capistrano was conducted in Juaneño for the first time.	Juaneño is also known as Ajachmem. In the 1960s there were four speakers left; now there is one.
Many singers; Language Restoration Committee; language materials and programs, including summer immersion camps; official writing system taught in schools. Master-Apprentice team summer 1993.	
Language preservation work (dictionary, grammar, narratives, lessons) and language learning by some individual adults; singers.	Juañeno and Luiseño are very closely related.

	NUMBER OF SPEAKERS		
LANGUAGE	CONSERVATIVE ESTIMATE	LIBERAL ESTIMATE	1990 CENSUS FIGURES
Maidu languages	Konkow: 3–6 Nisenan: 1 Northeast Maidu: 1–2	Konkow: up to 15 — —	Northeast Maidu ("Mountain Maidu") California: 74; U.S.: 108
Miwok languages	Coast Miwok: 1 Lake Miwok: 1–2 Bay Miwok (Saclan): 0 Plains Miwok: 1 Northern Sierra Miwok: <6 Eastern Central Sierra : 6 Western Central Sierra : 6 Southern Central Sierra : 7	— 4–6 — — 6–8 — 7 —	"Sierra Miwok:" California: 65 U.S.: 105
Modoc	1–3	5	The census lists 88 Klamath speakers in the U.S., which would include Modoc.
Mojave	Fort Mojave Reservation: 30–35 Colorado River Reservation: 35–50	— —	California: 53 U.S.: 234
Mono	North Fork: 10–12 Auberry: about 15 Big Sandy Mono: 7–8 Dunlap Mono: 5–6 Waksachi: 0	North Fork and Auberry: 50-100 — —	California: 184 U.S.: 193
Ohlone languages	0	—	—
Paiute languages			"Paiute:" California: 317 U.S.: 1631
	Owens Valley Paiute: 50	—	
	Northern Paiute: Calif.: 25–40 U.S.: approx. 1000	—	California: — U.S.: 27
	California Shoshoni: 20	40	California: 58 U.S.: 2284

COMMUNITY-BASED LANGUAGE ACTIVITIES	COMMENTS
Instructional language materials; singers.	
Some singers among Northern, Central and Southern Sierra Miwok; Northern Sierra Miwok have some teaching materials. Computerized Miwok language program with schools being developed.	
Active language programs and materials development for Modoc/Klamath.	The Modocs originally lived in California, but were sent to a reservation in Oregon. Led by the famous Captain Jack, they resisted this move, but eventually the government prevailed. All Modoc speakers now live in Oregon with the Klamath tribe. The two languages are closely related and have become more similar during their 100 years of close association.
Language materials, active language programs for children; both communities have writing systems; Master-Apprentice team summer 1993; singers.	Mojave people live along the Colorado River, with the majority in Arizona.
North Fork Mono: informal language classes; dictionary under development, audiotapes and videotapes being made for preserving aspects of verbal and nonverbal culture. Big Sandy Mono: language classes; collection of word lists.	Linguistically, closely affiliated with Owens Valley Paiute. Our contact says there are about a hundred North Fork Mono speakers with "some command of the language."
Some Ohlones are collecting and studying language materials.	The 8 Ohlone, or Costanoan, languages, most of which had several dialects, were Karkin, Chochenyo, Tamyen, Ramaytush, Awaswas, Rumsen, Mutsun, and Chalon. All lost their last fluent speakers in the 19th or early 20th centuries.
Owens Valley Paiute: informal language programs; singers. Northern Paiute (Gidutikad band): language classes, written language materials.	Linguistically, the Owens Valley Paiute are most closely related to the Mono. The 1000 Northern Paiute speakers are in Nevada, Oregon, Idaho and California, with the majority in Nevada and Oregon. California Shoshoni people are also known as Panamint. A handful of speakers live in Nevada, but the rest are in California. The large U.S. Census figure includes other Shoshoni languages too.

FLUTES OF FIRE

LANGUAGE	NUMBER OF SPEAKERS		
	CONSERVATIVE ESTIMATE	LIBERAL ESTIMATE	1990 CENSUS FIGURES
Pomo languages	Kashaya Pomo: 45 Southern Pomo: 1 Central: 8; Northern: 1 Eastern: 5; Southeastern: 5 Northeastern Pomo: 0	Kashaya: 65 Central: 10–12 — —	"Pomo" California: 118 U.S.: 165
Quechan (Yuma)	150	400–500	California: 249 U.S.: 343
Salinan	0	—	—
Serrano	2	8	2
Shasta	0	1	"Shastan" California: — U.S.: 12
Tolowa	4–5	—	—
Tubatulabal	3–5	up to 12	—
Wappo	2	4–5	—
Washo	approx. 25	—	California: — U.S.: 111
Wintun languages	Wintu: 6 Nomlaki: 0–1 Patwin: 1–2	— — Patwin: 3 or more	"Wintun" California: 9 U.S.: 10
Wiyot	0	—	—
Yanan languages	0	—	—
Yokuts languages	Choynumni: 8–10 Chukchansi: approx. 12 Dumna: 1 Tachi: 3 Wukchumne: 10 Yowlumni: 25–27 Gashowu: 1	up to 20 approx. 18 — — — 30–40 —	"Foothill Northern Yokuts:" 78 Tache: 25
Yuki	0	2	6
Yurok	20–30	approx. 100	California: 152 U.S.: 160

COMMUNITY-BASED LANGUAGE ACTIVITIES	COMMENTS
Several active Pomo singing groups. Eastern Pomo and Kashaya have some teaching materials. Intermittent Central Pomo language teaching at Hopland. Kashaya has strong ceremonialism with lots of singing.	
No language program yet, but developing interest; singers.	
Developing interest in language revival.	
Lots of language teaching; language materials development; active scholarship, including recent book on Tolowa language.	Tolowa straddles the California-Oregon border. It is strange that the census does not list Tolowa. There is a general "Athabascan" listing for the U.S. (but not California), but since there are many Athabascan languages, we have no way of knowing if Tolowa was lumped in with them.
Informal language classes taught by elder; a group of Washo parents is making plans for a pre-school.	Most Washo speakers live on the Nevada side of the border.
Singers; Master-Apprentice team summer 1993.	
	These included the closely-related languages of Northern Yana, Central Yana, Southern Yana and Yahi. The last speaker of Yahi was Ishi, who died in 1917. Robert Oswalt recently interviewed a woman of Yana ancestry who remembers a few words she learned from her mother.
Chukchansi: trying to start language programs; singers. Tachi: headstart language program; grammar book; singers. Yowlumni: Master-Apprentice team summer 1993; singers; tribal education committee deals with language issues.	Dumna is considered a dialect of the Chukchansi language. Gashowu is considered to be a dialect of Yowlumni, heavily influenced by the "Foothill" languages, such as Wukchumne.
Master-Apprentice team summer 1993; many singers.	

PART I

California Languages at Work and Play: Four Portraits

So Coyote made people. He shut himself in his house while he carved people of wood. He used all kinds of wood: white oak, redwood, fir, pine, black oak, sugar-pine, buckeye, maple, live-oak. He carved them like sticks and stuck them in the ground all around the house. Then he sang and danced the rest of the night.

"In the morning you will be people," was what he sang.

Next morning they were people.

Then Coyote proceeded to give them names.

"You are Bluejay, and you, you are Deer, and you, you are Dog," he said, as he named every one of the sticks.

But these people did not know how to talk. So Coyote made a big dance. He made these people dance all night, while he was singing.

"Tomorrow, you will talk," he said.

When they awoke the next morning, the people were all talking.

"The fleas were terrible last night," they were saying to each other. "Those fleas nearly finished us."

Then Coyote spoke: "Good morning."

But the people were still talking about the fleas. Coyote was vexed at this.

—a Lake Miwok origin tale from Gifford and Block,
Californian Indian Nights, pp. 99-100

The "pattern number" of European and European-American lore is three: fairy tales have three brothers, or three sisters, or three good fairies; a hero makes three attempts before reaching his goal. "The third time's the charm," we say in English, or, "Bad things come in threes." But in most of Native California, the pattern number is four. It is the fourth try that succeeds; characters and episodes come in fours. So in keeping with California style, I introduce this book with four portraits of language in action, four essays that show how the use of language helps people make their way in the world of nature and society and values.

We begin at the edges of language: an investigation of the use of song in intertribal gatherings, as a way of removing the barriers to communication across languages. Second, I write about how storytellers represent animal talk, to demonstrate how California languages are used to have fun.

While the first two essays show how people construct their social world through language, the third shows how Native Californians use language to make sense out their *physical* world. I present an essay on how Californians speak of location and direction, and finally, we examine how language and thought relate to each other, and show how the structure of language reveals and influences the world view of California Indians.

Together, these four linguistic portraits give a glimpse into the culture of language in Native California.

"Now then, enough!" said Earthmaker.
"There will be songs—
there will always be songs,
and all of you will have them."

And after that, he sang—and sang—and sang;
then he stopped singing.

"These are the songs that you human beings will have,"
he said.
And then, he sang some other songs;
singing some other songs, he started off.

He went a long way
until he finally came to the middle of the world.
When he got that far,
he sat down and stayed there.

But, telling about the world,
Meadowlark sang very beautifully.
He was the first being created,
the first being to go across the meadows.
He was the being who saw the dry land,
very beautiful;
singing from the beginning—
a being who sang songs.

—William Shipley, *The Maidu Indian Myths and Stories of Hanc'ibyjim*, pp. 29-30

2

Song

Overcoming the Language Barrier

In California, the border between the United States and Mexico is clearly visible in satellite photographs. You can see a startling boundary line between the green crops of Imperial County, watered by the mighty canals that empty the Colorado River, and the brown fields of Baja California where, due to the barriers of international politics, the canals never reach. From the ground, barbed wire fences and armed guards make the location of the border obvious.

From the point of view of Native America, this boundary is arbitrary and alien. It clearly defines the division between the dominance of Anglo and Hispanic peoples, and the English and Spanish languages, but it simply runs right through the middle of American Indian linguistic and political divisions. Diegueño is spoken on both sides of the border, and so is Cocopa. Relatives are separated from each other by that border. It is not possible to write about the native languages of California and ignore Baja California.

Once, years ago, I went with a group of Diegueños and other friends from San Diego to visit the Kiliwas in Baja California. The Diegueño group included such illustrious people as Rosalie Pinto, singer and medicine woman, and Delfina Cuero, narrator of the book *Delfina Cuero: Her Autobiography* (Shipek 1991). It was Rosalie who was the motivating force for this trip—energetic and intense, full of intellectual curiosity, she wanted to visit the Kiliwa because she had heard they spoke a language related to Diegueño, and was interested in their isolation and traditionalism.

The Kiliwas live in the Arroyo Leon, located in the foothills south of Valle Trinidad in the heart of northern Baja. Nowadays, the paved peninsular highway goes through Valle Trinidad, cutting away its previous solitude. But back then, the Kiliwas were very isolated, both geographically and socially. Their dealings with Mexican institutions had not been particularly happy. It was a constant battle to keep their land base from being completely eroded away by the surrounding interests. During the Mexican Revolution, Kiliwa men were known as great fighters; but over half died in a massacre, and since they had fought with a radical fringe group that never gained any power in the new government, their families received neither recognition nor reparation. Embittered, ignored by the rest of Baja California, the tribe was alienated both socially and economically from the Mexican mainstream.

Some people left to work in the towns, but those who stayed lived almost completely without money—they built thatch homes, depended largely on wild foods, and for the most part, spoke no Spanish. At the time of our visit, there were only nineteen Kiliwas in Arroyo Leon, and only a few spoke Spanish fluently. From the vantage point of our over-populated cities here on the other side of the border, it boggles the imagination to think what it must be like to have only eighteen other people in one's entire social universe to communicate with.

But wait. Did I say communicate? One of the many things I learned on that wonderful journey was how many different ways there are to communicate. And what I learned most stunningly was how important *music* is as a form of communication.

The Kiliwa village in Arroyo Leon, in the early 1970s. Photo courtesy of Margaret Langdon.

*Song is an ancient form of intertribal commu-
nication, here between Kiliwa and Diegueño
people. Photo courtesy of Margaret Langdon.*

Speaking presented an interesting translation problem. None of the
Diegueños knew Spanish; none of the Kiliwas knew English. Some of the
Kiliwas and one or two of the English speakers spoke some Spanish.
When the Diegueño elders wished to say something, they spoke in the
Diegueño tongue; one of the younger Diegueños translated it into
English; someone else translated that into Spanish; and one of the
Kiliwas would then say it in their language. Who knows how many
meaning transformations a given speech went through!

But maybe the mishaps of translation through four languages weren't
all that important, for most of the talk was formal and polite, and the
main message was surely understood: I respect you, I feel kinship with
you, I am glad to be here with you.

People didn't spend all that much time trying to talk to each other. Most
of the time together was taken up with other forms of communication:
gesture, smiles, touch, eating and drinking together, dancing and singing.

Singing *together*. These two tribes shared no language in common,
and most of the individuals who were at this gathering had never seen

each other before. Yet they all knew the same songs. And the songs that weren't known to both tribes nevertheless belonged to genres known to both, so singing along was easy.

All night long the singers from the two tribes sang the Bird Songs—songs that tell of the migration at the beginning of time. All night long the party formed their opposing lines and danced back and forth beside the fires and lanterns out there under the summer stars in a black, black sky.

You can't help but realize, as you are dancing back and forth, vibrating with music, that this form of intertribal communication has been important for thousands and thousands of years—song overcoming the barriers of language and creating unity, asserting kinship, passed from one community to the next by decades and centuries and millennia of intertribal gatherings. We see it going on all over Native California. The Bird Songs themselves are sung throughout southern California, by people of many different linguistic heritages. Diegueño, Quechan, Mojave, Cahuilla, Cupeño, Luiseño, and Chemehuevi are among those California groups that sing the Bird Songs. In Chumash country, along the Santa Barbara coast, there are records from Mission days of gatherings where tribes came from all over southern California, and even as far away as Tucson and northern Mexico.* Today we can see the use of song in intertribal communication in the powwows of the California urban centers, attended by people from tribes all over the country. The same kind of unification through song has been going on for centuries in the Deerskin Dances and Brush Dances of northwestern California, where Yurok, Karuk, Hupa, and Tolowa people traditionally come together; and in the Bear Dance of the Maidu, Pit River and Northern Paiute tribes in eastern California—all tribes separated by language, but united by song.

Thus, many song types are universally known across large geographic areas by people who speak many different languages. Songs can travel fast from group to group. They can be traded just about as easily as a basket, or a bundle of corn, or a string of dentalium shells. People all over California know the songs of many tribes, and can sing them well. Some songs became widespread so long ago that no one knows which tribe they started with. Others, traded perhaps a hundred years ago or

---

* José Ignacio Rivera, KPFA interview, September 1993

less, are of well-known origin from a specific tribe, often with a fine story attached as to how they got to other communities.

The best story I know about song travel is the one the Havasupais tell about their Horse Songs. In the winters, the Havasupais would camp on the plateaus above their summer canyon home. One time in the early nineteenth century, Navajos raided a Havasupai camp and carried off a baby boy. A Navajo family adopted that boy and raised him as their own. But as a young adult, Hopis came to tell the boy about his origins, and he decided to go home to his people. In the dead of night he took his adopted father's best saddle blanket and saddle, and rode off on his best horse. When he arrived at the Havasupai camp, he dressed and rode like a Navajo, and spoke only Navajo. This was a dangerous moment: if they thought he was a Navajo enemy, the Havasupais might have killed him then and there. But when he saw his people, he just sat on his horse and folded his arms, and bent his head down and wept. So the Havasupais knew him for a long-lost relative and took him down off his horse and welcomed him. He lived with them the rest of his life. One of the gifts he brought for the Havasupais was a set of songs, changed now but still recognizable as being from the Navajo Blessingway. He had not only brought the Navajos' best horse, but also their best songs. The Havasupais have sung these ever since, and they call them the Horse Songs.

Now that English serves as a lingua franca in California, spoken communication between tribes is not so limited. But it is easy to imagine the old days a couple of hundred years ago, when a visit between tribes was like the meeting between the Diegueño and the Kiliwa—a very special time, where feelings are warm but words are few; but the singing can flow and flow.

This is one reason, no doubt, why so many Indian songs have no intelligible words.* Words are barriers to unity; words separate people, sorting them out by language and by opinion. But music unifies. Songs without words are vocal music in its purest form, music that brings people from different tribes together, brings out their fundamental unity, and communicates that important message far better than language ever can: I respect you; I feel kinship with you; I am happy to be here with you.

---

*   For more about these "songs without words, " see Chapter 14.

Then afterwards, he said,
"All right, I'm going now; be sure and stay here."
Then he left, going

    " t^{h}ónononononononon,

    t^{h}ónononu,

    t^{h}ónonononon,

    this Old Man Coyote."

He went somewhere on the other side of the hill.
When he went somewhere near Sacramento, what they heard was Coyote going

    " t^{h}ónononononononono,

    t^{h}ónononononono

somewhere through the field—that's how he went.

           —Callaghan, "Coyote the Imposter" (Lake Miwok), p. 10

3

Coyote Talk

Like song, humor can cross emotional barriers. Using language to make people laugh must be a practice as old as language itself. Native Californians have always had lots of funny stories to tell, and there is a tradition in California and throughout the West of making animals in the old stories talk in characteristically humorous ways.

Old Man Coyote is especially prone to speak in a funny voice. In the Yahi tales that Ishi used to tell, Coyote lisped so that his **s**'s sounded a bit like **sh**, as if teeth were missing. And wherever normal Yahi would have an **l** or an **r**, Coyote used **n** instead, so that, for instance, the phrase **yap'lasa:sit^hi** (it is well done) came out as **yap'nasha:shit^hi*** in Coyote talk. So if Yahi Coyote were to speak in English, he might sound something like this:

> *Nateny I've nosht a not of annowsh. Wenn, then, I'n make shome annowsh now. Okay, thatsh enough wonk! Nooks nike it'sh time fon shomething to eat! Ah, thatsh nishe and wenn done!* (Lately I've lost a lot of arrows. Well, then, I'll make some arrows now. Okay, that's enough work! Looks like it's time for something to eat! Ah, that's nice and well done!)**

Of course, writing can't do justice to Coyote talk, because voice quality is important too. We don't know what kind of voice quality Ishi's Coyote had, but there are plenty of people around who still tell Coyote stories and use funny voices. In Hualapai, every word in Coyote talk has a **th** sound in it, either replacing an **s** sound or else added on at the end. And words also have an extra long **iiiii** sound, said in a high falling voice that sounds like the howl of a coyote.

Hualapai: **miviyama!** (Run!)
Coyote: **miviyamiiiiiiith!**

So an English translation of a Hualapai Coyote might sound like this:

---

*   Changed sounds are underlined. See Appendix for explanation of spelling conventions.

**   The theme for this utterance by Coyote comes from the tale "Coyote Rapes his Sister," from the unpublished Yahi version (Sapir 1917).

Oh, ye-iiiith, thith ith your old friendiiiith, Coyotiiiiith, jutht talkiiiiiithing up a thtormiiiiiith! (Oh, yes, this is your old friend, Coyote, just talking up a storm!)

It's not only coyotes that do funny talk. In Cocopa,* people talk to domesticated animals with special sounds, and portray animals as talking that way too (Langdon 1978). Cocopa animal talk uses a special slurpy **l** sound sort of like **ly** (see Appendix for description of **ly**), but strongly whispered instead of voiced. We'll write it here as **lly**, using the Diegueño practical writing system. At the same time, the speaker twists the lips and talks from the side of the mouth. So a Cocopa woman might say to her cat:

Cocopa: **Makáy mwayá:ts myu?** (Where have you been?)

animal talk: **Makálly mllyá:ts mllyu?**

And she might imagine her cat saying back:

Cocopa: **Nyasáw pmwí:a?** (Have you seen my babies?)

animal talk: **Nyallyáw llypmwí:a?**

The rule is that each word must have one and only one instance of **lly**. If a word has sounds like **s, l, ts** or **y**, the first occurrence of that sound is replaced by **lly**. Otherwise, **lly** is added in front of the word.

A quote from a Cocopa cat translated into English might sound like this (read aloud, and don't forget to sound slurpy and say it out of the side of your mouth):

Llygee! LlyI'm jullyt llyadmiring llyou llymaking tortillyas! Llyoon llyou willy frylly llye llymeat, llyou willy llyget llye tortillyas llyand llyrap llye llymeat llyin llyem llyand llyi llyget llyto llyeat llyome! (Gee! I'm just admiring you making tortillas! Soon you will fry the meat, you will get the tortillas and wrap the meat in them, and I get to eat some!)

Cocopa Mountain Lion speaks with extra r's in his speech:

Markáy mmá:xmyú? (Where are you going?)

Treat this **r** as a low lionish growl, so that in English we might say it like this:

Wherrrre arrrr you gorrrring?

Cocopa Rabbit talks with a lot of **f** sounds, as befits his buck teeth:

---

* Cocopa is spoken just over the California border in Arizona and Baja California, and is closely related to Diegueño.

Ofooh, Fountain Fion, I'm juft gofing to fee my fick grandmofer.

(Oh, Mountain Lion, I'm just going to see my sick grandmother.)

All up and down the West Coast, the animals are portrayed with these special voices. In the Northwest, Deer, Mink, Bear, Fox, and Skunk all have their particular ways of speaking. In Nez Perce, Skunk speaks in a high-pitched, nasal voice, and changes consonants, such as **s** to **ts** (Aoki 1979).

Pleatsed to tsee you, I'm Tskunk!

In the Coeur d'Alène language, Skunk talks with a lot of extra glottal stops (the breaking off of sound for a split second, indicated with apostrophes:

'I' ju'st go't ba'ck fro'm' Wa'shing'to'n.

Deer and Mink in Nootka change **s** and a lot of other sounds into "slurpy l" sounds (Sapir 1958), while in Kwakiutl it is the reverse: l sounds become **s**. In Takelma, a whispered l is placed before any word spoken by Bear. Nez Perce Coyote changes **n** to **l** (just the opposite of Yahi), and, like Yahi, changes **s** to **sh**.

Of course, this sort of animal talk is not limited to Indian languages. Just watch any cartoon and hear all the animal voices in English: Mickey Mouse and Donald Duck talk just like mice and ducks should talk if they spoke English; and don't forget Porky Pig's stutter. There is Tweety Bird's **t** and **d** substitution in "I tought I taw a puddy tat!" and Sylvester the Cat's wet lisp might as well have been borrowed straight from Cocopa.

Having begun this chapter with Old Man Coyote, we will end with him. In Quechan,* Coyote adds a lot of **ly** sounds to his speech (not the whispered kind like Cocopa, but more like the "lli" in "million"). If Coyote decided to combine the speech mannerisms attributed to him from all the different languages we have discussed—and that is the sort of thing that Coyote would be likely to do—then some winter when we are sitting by the fire telling stories, we might hear something like this out of the darkness.

Lyish ilysh Conyotiiiith, tlyanking to lyou-iiiith. I lyam hlyere to thtlyay flyoneveniiiiith, mlyaking mlyithchief lyevenywhene! Iiiiiith! (This is Coyote, talking to you. I am here to stay forever, making mischief everywhere!)

---

* Quechan is another Yuman language spoken along the Colorado River just north of Cocopa.

First direction names taught.—[Mastamho] said again: "Now we are here in this house: all will know and hear it. Now when I mean here," and he pointed his hand to the north, "all say: 'Amaihayame.'" But they did not do so: they kept their hands against their bodies; they wanted another name; they did not like that word. Then he said: "And there is Amai-hakyeme; all say that!" And he pointed south. But again all sat still: they did not want to call it that. He said again: "Well, there is another: there is the way the night goes. I do not know where its end is, but when we follow the darkness that is called Amai-hayime." He said that, but none of the Mohave said a word: they sat with their hands against the body. Then Mastamho said once more: "You see the dark coming. I do not know where it comes from: I did not make it. But where darkness comes from, I call that Amai-hayike." Again they sat still and did not point.

Final direction names taught.—Then Mastamho said once more: "I have named all the directions but you have not answered. Well, there are other names. Listen: I call this (the north) Mathak. Can you say that?" Then all said, "Yes," and stood up, and pointed north, and said, "Mathak." He said again: "This (to the south) I call Kaveik. Can you say it?" Then all said, "Yes," and pointed and called the name and clapped their hands and laughed. He said again: "I told you that the night went in that direction. I gave it a name, but you did not say it. There is another way to call it: Inyohavek. All of you say that!" Then they all said: "Yes, we can say that. We can call it Inyohavek," and all pointed as he directed them. He said again: "Where the dark comes from, you did not call that as I told you to. There is another way to call it: Anyak." Then all said: "Anyak," and pointed east and clapped their hands and laughed. Then Masthamo said: "That is all."

—A.L. Kroeber, *Seven Mohave Myths*, p. 60

4

Upriver, Downriver:
The Vocabulary of Direction

Having introduced California languages through song and story telling, we now go to what might be thought of as a more basic and mundane function of language—that of referring to and describing the world around us.

I finished writing this essay on the day of the vernal equinox, when the sun rises due east and sets due west. The perception of this basic fact about the solar system is shared by everyone in the world: no matter where one is on earth, the sun rises due east on the equinox, and sets due west. And while the precise location of the sun varies on other days, it nonetheless rises and sets in the general vicinity of the east and west all the time. Because this is part of all human experience, words for east and west are extremely common (though not quite universal, as we shall see) in the languages of the world. In some languages the terms for east and west would translate literally as "place where the sun rises" and "place where the sun sets." Note, on the other hand, that in the Mojave tale that introduced this chapter, the creator explained east and west as being where the *dark* comes from and goes!

Most languages also have words for north and south. This may of course be due simply to the logical need to talk about directions other than east and west, and that may be coupled with an innate sense of geometry that leads humans to set up lines at right angles to each other. But also, just as with the words for east and west, there are natural phenomena that lead to the establishment of the terms for north and south. Many animals—birds, for instance—have a sense of direction based on ability to perceive the magnetic field of the earth, which means they perceive north and south directly through this sense. Geophysicists are now trying to determine whether or not humans also have this magnetic sense. And whether we do or not, humans all over the world see birds migrate every year from north to south, and then south to north. Native Californians have a long tradition of astronomy as well, and anyone who often sleeps under the stars knows the North Star (Polaris, the Pole Star), that always stays in the same place while all the constellations wheel around it.

Directions in relation to the land and water

The importance in many California languages of words showing direction of movement is demonstrated by this brief excerpt from a Wintu tale:

> They went to the east side of the house, they went around to the east side, and after that they went up the hill to the north, following him running. They went northward at a running pace over the north flat, wishing to see the man who had gone down the hill northward. And the man was not there but there lay his tracks going forward. And they ran, they went at a running pace, they went rapidly. And at the South-slope-climb, when they came in full view of the north, they looked northward but they did not see him. (Lee 1959, 139)

While the cardinal directions are used with great frequency in this passage, it also contains many words that talk about direction with regard to features of the landscape instead—"up the hill," "down the hill," and "over the flat," for example. For many languages of California, direction words are not based on the sun, but rather on geographical features, and the direction of flow of the watercourses. The use of riverine direction words is mainly the case in northern California, and during a recent trip to Hupa, Yurok and Karuk country, the reason for this was borne home to me clearly. The mountains are innumerable, steep-sided and high, ranging from difficult to downright dangerous to climb. The river terraces are the only places where towns can be built, and the only way to get anywhere is and always has been to travel in or along the river. People used to travel in boats and on foot; now winding roads along the watercourses add cars to the same routes. On our trip, we travelled upriver or downriver. Whether we went east or west or north or south at any given moment was fleeting and irrelevant to our general direction.

A.L. Kroeber explained the riverine direction terminology very well, and I quote him at length here.

The Yurok, and with them their neighbors, know no cardinal directions, but think in terms of the flow of water. Thus **pul** is the radical meaning downstream; **pets**, upstream; **hiko**, across the stream; **won**, up hill, that is, away from the stream on one's own side; **wohpe**, across the ocean, and so on. Such terms are also combined with one another. If a Yurok says "east" he regards this as an English word for upstream, or whatever may be the run of the water where he is. The name Yurok itself—which in its origin is anything but an ethnic designation—means "downstream" in the adjacent Karok language. The degree to which native speech is affected by this manner of thought is remarkable. A house has its door not at its "western" but its "downstream" corner. A man is told to pick up a thing that lies "upstream" from him, not on his "left." The basis of this reckoning is so intensely local, like everything Yurok, that it may become ambiguous or contradictory in the usage of our broader outlook. A Yurok coming from O'men to Rekwoi has two "upstreams" before him: south along the coast, and south-southeast, though with many turns, along the Klamath. When he arrives at Weitspus, the Trinity stretches ahead in the same direction in the same system of valley and ridges; but being a tributary, its direction is "up a side stream," and the direction "upstream" along the Klamath suddenly turns north, or a little east of north, for many miles. Beyond their Karok neighbors the Yurok seem to have a sense that the stream comes from the east. At least they point in that direction when they refer to the end of the world at the head of the Klamath.

This plan of orientation is characteristic of all the northwestern tribes, and is followed in some degree in central California. The Yokuts terms of direction, in the far-away San Joaquin Valley, are at least shifted from the cardinal points in accord with the flow of water, if indeed they do not refer to it. The cognate Maidu words are said to have the same meaning as our own. But it is possible that the Maidu have given a sun-determined meaning to original drainage terms under the ritualizing influence of the Kuksu cult. This may also be what has happened among southern Wintun, Pomo, and Yuki, who constantly use words like "north," while the central Wintun think in terms of waterflow. It has been customary among inquirers to assume that Pomo **yo** means "south" because a group consistently uses it for that direction; which, of course, is no proof. In any event it is likely that exact south, when they knew a south, was determined for most California tribes by the prevailing direction of their streams as much as by the meridian of the sun. The rectangular and parallel disposition of drainage in the greater part of the State must have contributed to this attitude. Only in southern California, where water runs far apart and intermittently, and the ceremonializing symbolism of the southwestern tribes is a near influence, is it certain that we encounter true terms of solar orientation. (Kroeber 1925, 15–16)

Along rivers with innumerable bends and curves, landmarks can be a better reference than cardinal directions. Here, the rock Oregos, at the village of Requa at the mouth of the Klamath River. Courtesy of Phoebe Apperson Hearst Museum of Anthropology.

A redwood dugout canoe, probably Hupa, on the Trinity River. 1902 photo by P.E. Goddard, courtesy of Phoebe Apperson Hearst Museum of Anthropology.

My friend Jean Perry says that she learned a good lesson in the Yurok river-oriented directionals one day when she was staying with Florence Shaughnessy in her lovely home near the mouth of the Klamath River. Jean was trying to cook dinner on a stove that was still unfamiliar to her, and was having a hard time figuring out which way to turn the knobs to reduce the flame. Florence finally clarified it for her by saying, "It's like this: you turn it down by turning the knob 'downriver', and up 'upriver.'"

The use of landmarks instead of cardinal directions makes perfect sense in a country like northern California, where there are rivers and mountains everywhere, where people follow watercourses in their journeys, and where travelling in a straight line is simply impossible. But in fact, speakers of northern California languages still must have had the concepts of the cardinal directions, at least with regard to movement of celestial bodies, because they have a strong tradition of astronomy. Nancy Richardson pointed out to me that, in the following Karuk tale where Coyote kicks dirt in four directions to celebrate arriving home, he kicks dirt in the four *cardinal* directions—but the directions are named for landmarks.

And Coyote jumped up. And he said, "My country!" And he kicked earth out towards the river. And he kicked it out from tishánniik [a village-site at Camp Creek, below Orleans]. He kicked it out from káttiphirak [a village site across-stream from Camp Creek]. He kicked it out from túuyvuk [a village-site at Ullathorne Creek, below Camp Creek]. Coyote was so happy, when he came back to his country. That's why he kicked it out. (Bright 1957, 169)

Kunpiip, "Xâatik 'áppap yúruk 'uvuunúpahitih, káru 'áppap káruk 'uvuunôovutih.
(The gods) said, "Let (the river) flow downstream on one side, and flow upstream on the other side.

Xâatik vaa 'ukupitih."
Let it do that."

Kári xás "chémmi."
Then (they said), "All right."

Vaa 'uum vúra payúruk tá kunvíitrup tuthívruuhrup yúruk.
When they traveled downstream by boat, they floated downstream.

Ithyáru k'na 'úpviitrooveesh, 'uthívruuhrooveesh káru, káruk 'uvuunôovahiti pa'íshshaha.
They would travel back upstream on the other side, they would float upstream also, the water was flowing upstream.

Kári xás pihnêefich 'uppiip, "Pûuhara.
Then Coyote said, "No.

Xáyfaat vaa 'ukupitih.
Let it not do that.

Kôovúra yúruk kámvuunupahitih.
Let it all flow downstream.

Vaa 'uum vúra káan 'ifmaaráppiit kamíktaatroovutih, káru 'uvítroovutih."
Let the new married man push his way upstream there, (when) he is traveling upstream."
—Bright, *The Karok Language*, pp. 200-201

Directional affixes

To the English speaker, one of the most amazing aspects of the grammar
of most California languages is how much can be said in a single word.
Verbs, especially, through processes of affixation, are incredibly rich in
meaning. Directional affixes are part of this complex verb structure in
many languages. For example, in Yana, directionals are obligatory on
verbs of motion. One cannot simply say that someone is "going" without
saying which direction he or she is going in. So in Yahi (Ishi's language,
a variety of Yana), there is a full set of suffixes that go on verbs of
motion, one set for going in a cardinal direction, and another for coming
from a cardinal direction. And these are also different from the independent words for the cardinal directions.

t^héndji "west"
  -pdji "to the west, in the west"
  -haucu "from the west"

Doors of traditional Karuk houses are on the upriver side of the house facing the river.
Yurok doors are at the downstream corner of the house. Photo of Karuk house at
Kat'im'íin courtesy of California State Parks.

tʰé:nauna "east"

    -hau, -au "to the east, in the east"

    -t'kʰi "from the east"

tʰéndjam "north"

    -sdjam, -djam "to the north, in the north"

    -gam "from the north"

Directional suffixes in Karuk

-mu thither
-rupu hence downriverward
-unih down from a considerable height; hence downhillward
-uraa up to a considerable height; hence uphillward
-rôovu hence upriverward
-sip(riv) up to the height of a man or less
-kath hence across a body of water
-kara horizontally away from the center of a body of water
-kara into one's mouth
-rámnih into a container
-vara in through a tubular space
-rúprih in through a solid
-fúruk into an enclosed space
-vrin in opposite directions
-várayva here and there within an enclosed space

-raa hither; hither from downriver; hither from downhill
-faku hither from uphill
-varak hither from upriver
-ish(rih) down from the height of a man or less
-rina hither from across a body of water
-rípaa horizontally toward the center of a body of water
-rúpaa out of one's mouth
-ríshuk out of a container
-kiv out through a tubular space
-rúprav out through a solid
-rúpuk out of an enclosed space
-tunva toward each other
-thuna here and there in an open area

—Bright, *The Karok Language*, p. 95

tʰéntʰpʰa "south"
> **-tʰpʰa** "to the south, in the south"
> **-wacu** "from the south"

Like the Yurok language, Yahi also has many directional affixes that are in reference to landmarks rather than the cardinal directions. But Yahi, unlike Yurok and Karuk, combines the landmark directionals with the cardinal directionals. Here are a few examples out of hundreds that can be found in texts:

bah-du-wíl-gam'
> (run-back-across stream-to north)
> He ran back north across the stream.

bi:-lo-tʰpʰa-'anti'
> (go-up on mountain-south-then)
> Then they went south up on the mountain.

néh-du-ri-hau'
> (walk-back-down hill-east)
> He went back east down hill.

djé:-ye:mai-cʰit'-gam
> (came dancing-in midst-off-from north)
> He came dancing into their midst from the north.

Directional prefixes or directional suffixes take up pages of description in grammars of California languages. In the box on the previous page is a rich set of such affixes from Karuk. As in the other languages of northern California, the directional affixes of Karuk tend to refer to landmarks such as rivers and hills, and to other types of objects that movement occurs in reference to. So for example, **path** means 'throw'; **pathfaku** 'to throw down from uphill', **pathfuruk** 'to throw into the house', etc.

Egocentric directionals

It was interesting to see that he was aware of the differences due to tones, but of course he had no idea of arranging tones in a sequence or scale. And *my* conception of a tone as "low" and another as "high" was extremely puzzling to him. "Why don't you say that one is to the right and the other to the left?" he asked. I had no answer, of course. (de Angulo 1932, 24)

In English, besides our words for cardinal directions and all our preposi-
tions, we have the words "left" and "right," which refer to the two sides
of our own bodies. These are used as direction words as well, so that we
can tell people to look left, or turn right at the third stoplight. Unlike all
the other directionals we have mentioned here, "left" and "right" are
egocentric terms: they are about orientation on the human body rather
than environment. The problem comes when we are talking face to face
with someone—our left is his right and vice versa. The order "Look left!"
confuses conversational participants. My left or yours?

Some languages of Native California don't talk about right and left
hands at all; they talk about east and west hands, or north and south
hands, or upriver and downriver hands. So the hands change names
depending on which way someone is facing. As Dorothy Lee eloquently
states it in *Freedom and Culture*:

> The Wintu use of *left* and *right*, as compared with ours, shows again the
> difference in orientation. When we go for a walk, the hills are to our right,
> the river to our left; when we return, the hills change and the river, while
> we remain the same, since we are the pivot, the focus. Now the hills have
> pivoted to the left of me. This has been English practice for many years,
> since at least the fourteenth century. To the Wintu, the terms left and right
> refer to inextricable aspects of his body, and are very rarely used. I think
> that only once the term left occurs in my texts, referring to a left-handed
> mythical hero; I cannot remember any occurrence of the term for the right.
> When the Wintu goes up the river, the hills are to the west, the river to the
> east; and a mosquito bites him on the west arm. When he returns, the hills
> are still to the west, but, when he scratches his mosquito bite, he scratches
> his east arm. The geography has remained unchanged, and the self has
> had to be reoriented in relation to it.* (Lee 1959, 139)

---

*   My father recently pointed out to me that in baseball parlance, a naming reminiscent of
Lee's description has developed: a left-handed pitcher is called a "southpaw." This is
due to the old practice of putting home plate on the west end of the field, thus
decreeing automatically that a pitcher's left hand will always be to the south. The name
still holds nowadays even though, in some of the modern indoor fields, home plate is
put somewhere other than in the west.

Most Native American languages do have constant names for their hands, but as Lee says, these are not directional names. The Havasupais call the right hand **sal gahána**, the "good hand," thus revealing the tendency for right-hand preference common to all human societies, and the left hand is **sal gathát**, "Coyote hand." But a Havasupai would never tell somebody to turn "Coyote" or "good" at the corner! I bet the long-ago Europeans who first named their hands thousands of years ago didn't say "go right" or "go left" either when they were giving travel directions (after all, "right" means "good," just as in Havasupai). Using these words as directionals probably only came about when people started losing their sense of closeness to the land, so that movement oriented to their own bodies became easier to understand than movement oriented to natural features. Maybe it was the development of city streets laid out as grid lines, often ignoring both the cardinal directions and the land forms, that led to this use of body orientation for directionals.

Earthmaker said:
"If I could but see a little bit of land
I might do something very good with it."

Floating along, then,
they saw something like a bird's nest.
Earthmaker said:
"It really is small.
It would be good if it were a little bigger,
but it is really small.
I wonder how I might stretch it apart a little.
What would be good to do?
In what way can I make it a little bigger?"

As he talked, he transformed it.

—Shipley, *The Maidu Indian Myths and Stories of Hanc'ibyjim*, p. 20.

5

Language and
the Structure of Thought

Language has enormous power: "As he talked, he transformed it." As this line from the excerpt opposite this page indicates, language was an important accompaniment to the creation of the world. Or, to quote from another religious tradition: "In the beginning was the word, and the word was with God, and the word was God" (from the Gospel according to St. John).

Ursula LeGuin, the daughter of California anthropologist A.L. Kroeber and author Theodora Kroeber, is an author whose life and imagination have been deeply influenced by Native Californian language and culture. She based her novel *A Wizard of Earthsea* on the notion of the power of words. Her hero Ged speaks of the nature of power:

> My name, and yours, and the true name of the sun, or a spring of water, or an unborn child, all are syllables of the great word that is very slowly spoken by the shining of the stars. There is no other power. No other name. (LeGuin 1968, 185)

As for the linguistic view, it is not so much that language has power to shape the world, but rather that language has power to shape our *perception* of the world. This is known as the linguistic relativity hypothesis—that language influences our thought, our world view. It is also known sometimes as the Sapir-Whorf hypothesis, since linguists Edward Sapir and Benjamin Lee Whorf were the two developers of the idea. Sapir put it like this:

> Human beings do not live in the objective world alone, nor alone in the world of social activity as ordinarily understood, but are very much at the mercy of the particular language which has become the medium of expression for their society. It is quite an illusion to imagine that one adjusts to reality essentially without the use of language and that language is merely an incidental means of solving specific problems of communication or reflection. The fact of the matter is that the "real

world" is to a large extent unconsciously built up on the language habits of the group. No two languages are ever sufficiently similar to be considered as representing the same social reality. The worlds in which different societies live are distinct worlds, not merely the same world with different labels attached. (Sapir 1929, 209)

One of the most lyrical writers to apply this notion to specific aspects of language was Dorothy Lee, who described how the Wintu language expresses Wintu philosophy:

Among the Wintu Indians of California, the principle of the inviolate integrity of the individual is basic to the very morphology of the language. Many of the verbs which express coercion in our language—such as to take a baby to (the shade), or to change the baby—are formed in such a way that they express a cooperative effort instead. For example, the Wintu would say, "I *went with* the baby," instead of, "I *took* the baby." And they say, "The chief *stood with* the people," which they have to translate into English as, "The chief ruled the people." They never say, and in fact they cannot say, as we do, "I have a sister," or a "son," or "husband." Instead, they say, "I am sistered," or "I live with my sister." To *live with* is the usual way in which they express what we call possession, and they use this term for everything that they respect, so that a man will be said to live with his bow and arrows. In our society, when we try to express respect for individual uniqueness, we have to do it in so many words, and even then we have to grapple with an uncooperative language. This is why we have to resort to terms which actually defeat our ends; terms such as *permissiveness*, or phrases such as *to give freedom to the child*. In Wintu, every interpersonal reference is couched in grammar which rests on the principle of individual integrity. Yet, for this people, the emphasis on personal inviolability does not mean that the individual was an isolate. There was such pervasive empathy among them that this, too, was expressed in the grammatical forms; if a boy was sick, the father used a special form of the verb phrase *to be sick*, and thus said "I-am-sick-in-respect-of-my-son." (Lee 1959, 7)

The differences between English and Wintu world view become apparent even when one simply tries to translate words from one language to another. The phrase **pʰoyoq teːluna:** is given as the Wintu equivalent of "to shave the head," but whereas the English idiom means to use a tool to take off all the hair, in Wintu it literally means "to make the head shine." It can also be used to describe someone with sweat on his forehead. The English phrase focuses on tool use, the Wintu phrase on the visual features of the result.

When using English, we are required to state whether or not there is more than one of the entities expressed by a noun, such as "girl" or "girls." Only a few objects are expressed as "mass nouns," such as rain, snow, wheat and rice, which aren't pluralized. Wintu, on the other hand, does not mark nouns as singular or plural; instead, words have what have been described as *generic* and *particular* forms. The generic word **wimay** means "grizzly bear," in general, without referring to any specific individual bear. To point out an individual bear or small group of bears, one says **wimah**, "a bear, that bear, those particular bears." As Lee describes it in *Freedom and Culture*:

> A hunter went out but saw no deer, **nop** (generic); another killed a deer, **nopum** (particular, object case). A woman carried deer, **nop**, to her mother; a hunter brought home deer, **nopum**. Now the woman's deer was cut in pieces and carried, a formless mass, in her back-basket; but the man carried his two deer slung whole from his shoulder. Some brothers were about to eat venison; they called, "Old man, come and eat venison, **nop**." The old man replied, "You can eat that stinking venison **(nopum)**, yourselves." The brothers saw it just as deer meat; to the old man it was the flesh of a particular deer, one which had been killed near human habitation, fed on human offal. (Lee 1959, 123)

A speaker has free choice of whether to use the generic or particular forms; Lee recorded two versions of the same story, one told by a man, the other by a woman. The man referred to men's weapons and tools using the particular forms; the woman referred to them all in generic form, perhaps thereby showing that she viewed them as less important than the man did.

Sometimes the generic and particular forms get specialized meanings. The root **se** in its generic form refers to the hand, but in the particular form it refers to the fingers. Similarly, **ma** in generic form is "feet," but in the particular it is "toes." The root **tʰuli** in the generic form refers to swimmers, but in the particular it means "otter." Generic **sede** is the coyote, but in the particular it is Coyote, the mythical hero.

So the language reflects and encourages a certain world view on the part of its speakers. Where English, with its distinction between singular and plural, divides the physical universe into individual items, Wintu instead describes unified categories of beings, to be viewed as such unless one is specifically pointing to an individual member of that category. Lee says this is one of many examples of how the Wintu language expresses concern with the whole, as opposed to English, which tends to assert the isolable individuality of all beings. On the other hand, as pointed out in Lee's earlier passage, the Wintu language conveys a sense of humans as individuals, in that they are not to be coerced or owned, while English often asserts relationship as ownership. We talk about "my sister" or "his father" with the same construction as

Some words in their generic and particular forms:

	GENERIC	PARTICULAR
Blue grouse	**niri**	**nirit**
Mother	**ne:h, ne:t**	**ne:n**
Slingshot	**bimchus**	**bimchut**
Grizzly bear	**wimay**	**wimah**

Some special meanings for generic and particular forms:

	GENERIC	PARTICULAR
tu	face	eye
ma	foot/feet	toe
se	hand	finger, hand
k'aha	fingernail	quick of nail
** łal**	shell	mussel
nur	salmon meat	live or whole salmon
nop	venison	live or whole deer
chi:r	fish; fish meat	live suckerfish; a specific spirit
tʰuli	swimmer	otter
wi	men, people	chief ("*the* man")

—Pitkin, *Wintu Grammar*, p. 212

A general sense of "deerness" is conveyed by "Deer Dance Spirit," a painting by the Wintu artist Frank LaPena. Photo courtesy of Carla Hills.

"my house" or "his books." We also talk about body parts in the same way: "*Her* hands are dirty"; "*My* head aches." But in Wintu, the possessive construction is not used with things that are attached to the body; it is used with things you *own*, not things that are part of you. If one used an expression like "my head" in Wintu, it would sound as if the head had been severed! One does not say, "My head aches" but rather, "I head ache" (using the generic form of head rather than the particular). Similarly, when clothing is on the body, it is not to be talked about as a separate thing, but as part of the body. When talking about a girl wearing a dress, one could not say, "Her dress was striped," but would say instead, "She was dress striped." Only when the dress is not on her, such as when it is hanging in the closet, can it then be viewed as a separate object, and can therefore be called "her dress."

In English, we think of verbs as having past, present and future tenses. "Now" is the universal reference against which all events are measured: either they are happening now (present tense), or happened before now (past tense), or will happen in the future. But in a large number of languages around the world, including Wintu, how an event relates to "now" is not automatically expressed; instead, the language may express how events relate in time to each other. In Wintu, a speaker can set up any time as the point of reference, and then use aspect suffixes on the verbs to show whether an event preceded, followed, or was simultaneous with that point of reference.

A whole range of other ideas is also expressed with suffixes on verbs. One of the most interesting is a set of "evidential suffixes" that state how one came by the evidence for some claim. If you saw the event you might say, "The child is playing in the sand," with no suffix. If you perceived it through other senses you might say, "This is sour" or "he is yelling," adding **-nte** to the verb. If your information came from logical deduction: having seen their tracks, you said, "A doe went by with two fawns," you would add **-re**. If it was hearsay: if you said, "They fought long" because someone told you so, you would add **-ke**. Unless you saw something in front of your very eyes, you could not say a sentence like, "It was bread." You would have to use evidentials to say, "It feels-to-me bread," or "I have-heard-it-to-be bread," or "I infer it to be bread." Thus any statement a Wintu speaker makes must bear with it the evidence for the speaker's claim—a greater responsibility than English speakers have!

There are many verbal endings in Wintu that cannot be easily translated into English. Take the suffix **-m**, which generally means that the verb has a generic object. Lee noticed that one interesting use of this suffix was to show "a relationship of great intimacy between self and other." The word **birama:lebo:sken** would translate as "Your children shall hunger," but literally means "Children you shall hunger in respect of." Or, as Lee states above, when a man says, "My child is ill," he would say **koyuma:da ila:m**, literally, "I am ill in respect to my child." This may seem like a strange way to say things, but it might seem more familiar if I point out that in English we sometimes express a similar close relationship between ourselves and our cars, such that if his or her car breaks down, an English speaker might say, "I broke down on the way to work today." Because we ride around in cars a lot and because their movements reflect our own movements and our own wills, they become extensions of ourselves. This may be why English speakers say things like, "I'm not parked very far away from here," which might seem very strange to people who don't come from car cultures. In Wintu it is not cars, but relatives who are identified with.

The concept of linguistic relativity should not be carried too far. We know that people can express any concept in any language. To illustrate, let us look again at the evidential suffixes the Wintu use to indicate how they got the information they are conveying. In English we are not required to provide this information, but we can and very often do express the same thing by using slightly more complex constructions: "I *hear* that they had a fight," or "It *tastes* sour," or "It *looks like* a doe with two fawns passed by here." It is not at all difficult for an English speaker to express the same thing expressed in Wintu evidentials. On the other hand, given that a Wintu speaker *must* state the source of his knowledge whenever he makes a statement, it could be argued that constant usage and exposure to evidentials make him more sensitive to the source of evidence.

The strength of the linguistic relativity hypothesis is much debated among linguists. Our thought cannot be *completely* constrained by our language; after all, we are capable of changing language to match new thoughts, such as names for new ideas in science. California Indian languages have sometimes been cited as counter-evidence to the linguistic relativity hypothesis—Sapir himself pointed out that the Hupa, Yurok and Karuk of northern California have extremely similar cultures but completely unrelated languages with very different grammars:

> The cultural adaptability of the Athabaskan-speaking peoples is in the strangest contrast to the inaccessibility to foreign influences of the languages themselves. The Hupa Indians are very typical of the culture area to which they belong. Culturally identical with them are the neighboring Yurok and Karuk. There is the liveliest intertribal intercourse between the Hupa, Yurok, and Karuk, so much so that all three generally attend an important religious ceremony given by any one of them. It is difficult to say what elements in their combined culture belong in origin to this tribe or that, so much at one are they in communal action, feeling, and thought. But their languages are not merely alien to each other; they belong to three of the major American linguistic groups, each with an immense distribution on the northern continent. Hupa, as we have seen, is

> Athabaskan and, as such, is also distantly related to Haida (Queen
> Charlotte Islands) and Tlingit (southern Alaska); Yurok is one of the two
> isolated Californian languages of the Algonkin stock, the center of gravity
> of which lies in the region of the Great Lakes; Karuk is the northernmost
> member of the Hokan group, which stretches far to the south beyond the
> confines of California and has remoter relatives along the Gulf of Mexico.
> (Sapir 1921, 214)

Such sweeping generalizations about language and culture do not negate
the much more detailed examination that scholars like Dorothy Lee have
made about the relationship between grammar and world view.* Furthermore, as William Bright has pointed out, a closer examination of the
languages and cultures of northwestern California shows some striking
linguistic convergences of Karuk, Hupa and Yurok and also that despite
apparent cultural similarities, there are some definite differences in their
world views that could in fact reflect structural differences in the different languages (Bright and Bright 1965).

We can certainly point to aspects of English grammar that people
believe are influential on thought patterns and feel very strongly about.
There is an example of one in this chapter: "...given that a Wintu speaker
must state the source of his knowedge..." Many people are convinced
that the use of "he" as the generic, impersonal third person pronoun not
only reflects the history of Anglo-American culture as male-dominated,
but even encourages the continuation of this cultural pattern. And the
detractors of "he" point out that just by virtue of being built into the

---

* One criticism made of Lee is that she drew her conclusions about Wintu world view
   only from the language itself, and did not corroborate her conclusions by independent
   studies of Wintu culture (Lucy 1992, 72). Lee herself was the first to admit this:

> The Wintu Indians of northern California have a conception of the self which
> is markedly different from our own. I have attempted to arrive at this
> conception through analysis of linguistic form and structure, as well as a
> consideration of biographical texts and recorded mythical material. My
> study is incomplete, since I have no other record of actual behavior. The
> ethnography of the Wintu as we have it, is an account of a dead and
> remembered culture. (Lee 1959, 131)

("Dead and remembered culture" puts it a little too strongly!)

grammar, it is all the more insidious, a sort of subliminal suggestion. Some writers have argued that "he" really can be used to imply a genderless general referent (this is called the "generic *he*"), but psychological experiments have shown that people never really interpret "he" as generic. It is so important in the eyes of people seeking social equality for the sexes that various attempts have been made to replace generic *he* with other alternatives, such as written *s/he*, or the awkward "he or she," or the grammatically questionable "they" as a singular pronoun. The difficulty of replacing the male-biased "he" with a neutral alternative might make English speakers jealous of Wintu and most other California languages, because they have always had a neutral third person pronoun, one where the referent can be either male or female.

Our minds are not puppets whose actions and beliefs are guided entirely by the strings of our language. We are capable of going beyond our language in thought, and we can in fact consciously change language, especially by adding new vocabulary, to match our thinking. Nevertheless, in a myriad of both obvious and subtle ways, the words and grammatical patterns of our language do influence the way we view the world. Our language does not limit us to certain viewpoints, but it does guide us strongly along particular mental pathways. And from this perspective, languages are far more than words and arbitrary rules of grammar—they are windows to whole systems of beliefs and values. And if the California languages disappear from our land, we lose along with them all their special and wonderful ways of portraying our world.

PART II

Language and History

Quite a while after this a great change came over the world. It happened one night. The people were burning offerings for the dead, when suddenly everybody began to speak a different language; only each man and wife spoke the same language. Earth Initiate came to Kuksu in the night and told him about it, and instructed him what to do. When morning came Kuksu, who was able to speak all the languages, called the people together, taught them how to cook and to hunt, gave them all their laws, and set the time for all their dances and festivals. Then he sent the warriors to the north, the singers to the west, the fluteplayers to the east, and the dancers to the south. He told them that was where they were to live.

—from a Maidu creation story in
Gifford and Block, *Californian Indian Nights*, p. 91

In Part I, we saw ways in which language displays and expresses culture. Language also expresses the *history* of its speakers. I begin this section with an overview of language families in California, and a discussion of what this might have to say about the relationships Californian peoples have to each other and to Native Americans elsewhere. The study of language relationships can give us information about the history of migrations of people, and the history of their cultures. In Chapter 7, "What Language Can Tell Us About History," we show how linguistic detective work—looking at the origin of the names people have for the plants and animals around them—can help us understand where they might have come from before arriving at their present locations. The last two chapters of Part II bring us to modern times, showing the influence of European and Native Californian languages on each other. In Chapter 8, "Native Californian Names on the Land," we look at present-day California place names and discover what they say about our state's Native American heritage. This section ends with Chapter 9, "History Through the Words Brought to California by the Fort Ross Colony," an article by Robert Oswalt on the effect that the 19th century Russian fur trade had on Kashaya Pomo nouns.

After a while each man took a girl. They set out in different directions—one pair to the East, one to the South, one to the North, one to the West; two remained in the center of the earth. Then they began to multiply and raised a great many *real people*. Each group began to talk differently from the others and later each became a separate tribe. This was the beginning of the different Indian languages and tribes of California.

—Woiche, *Annikadel: The History of the Universe as Told by the Achumawi Indians of California*, p. 160

6

Language Families in California

There is a tribe in Baja California called the Paipai, whose language is very similar to three closely related languages hundreds of miles away in Arizona: Yavapai, Hualapai and Havasupai. Predictably, these are sometimes called the "Pai" languages. This similarity would not be remarkable if the tribes all lived next door to each other, but there are in fact a number of very different languages in between the Paipais' home and the Arizona languages. Linguists visiting the Arizona communities over the years have mentioned to the Yavapais and others the existence of this very similar language. This made folks curious, and so there have been several expeditions in recent years by the Yavapais to visit the Paipais. The languages are different, but close enough so that someone speaking Yavapai can understand a fair portion of what someone speaking Paipai says. (The biggest communication problem centers around borrowed words—the Paipais borrow new words from Spanish, the Yavapais from English.) It turns out that the Yavapais have in their oral tradition a historical account saying that a Yavapai band got into a feud with their relatives and departed forever, heading south. Paipais have a similar kind of account as well in their origin tale. This migration may have taken place as recently as two to three hundred years ago.

During these few centuries, the languages have been changing, as languages always do. But the similarity is obvious enough to tell us that they come from the same source; that the ancestors of the speakers of Paipai and the Arizona Pai languages once lived together and spoke the same language.

The history of humankind consists of untold thousands of such migrations. Migration might be motivated by social divisions, such as the feud mentioned in the Yavapai and Paipai oral histories; or it might be motivated by overpopulation, dwindling resources, or just the yearning to go somewhere new. While it is probably an oversimplification to suggest that, at one time, there was only one language in the world, it must nevertheless be the case that at the dawn of human existence there were relatively few speech varieties. As new communities split off and became isolated from each other, speech patterns diverged too. As the centuries and millennia passed, the new communities formed by the original migration would themselves split and differentiate, creating an ever-increasing number of branches on a "family tree" of languages. The six thousand or so languages that are spoken in the world today are all products of this process of language divergence, as were the many thousands of languages that have already disappeared from the face of the earth.

It is not just migration that leads to new varieties of language: *language shift* plays a big role in the history of language divergence too. Through reasons involving such diverse social events as intermarriage and conquest, a group may, after a generation or more of bilingualism, abandon their old language and take on the language of the other group. One example of that process is the Native Californians of today, most of whom no longer speak their languages of ancestry, but have shifted to the use of English. Thus we cannot say that the *speakers* of closely related languages necessarily descended from a single population. But linguists use a metaphor of genetic relationship in their discussion of languages: languages are said to be "genetically related" if they descend from a common ancestral language; groups of related languages are called "language families." And a diagram of language relationships is called a "family tree."

The longer that two languages have been separated from each other, the more different they become. After ten thousand years or so, languages become so different from each other that the relationship

Uto-Aztecan Family Tree

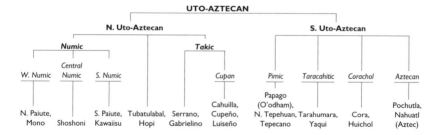

Language names are at the bottom. All other labels are family or sub-family groupings. (Not all of the Uto-Aztecan languages are listed here.)

between them is no longer detectable. Language families, then, consist of languages that have not been separated from each other long enough for their similarities to disappear. We can work on the assumption, though it is an oversimplification, that for each language family, all the languages descend from a single language in a single location that was spoken long ago, before the people of the original community separated.

Given the linguistic diversity of California that we have already described, it is no surprise that there are more different language families here than any other state or region in our country. The Pai languages whose tale began this chapter form a branch of the Yuman family, which includes languages located in Arizona, southern California and Baja California. Some language families encompass places far outside California. For example, Yurok and Wiyot belong to the same family as the Algonquian languages of Canada and the northeastern United States.

Gifford and Block give two other important examples:

> Two of the linguistic families, found in California, are also widely represented elsewhere in North America. One of these is the Athapascan* family, to which belong Hupa, Kato, and several other languages of California. There are also Athapascan groups in Oregon, and a great mass of Athapascan tribes in the Canadian Northwest, and Alaska. The Apache and Navaho of the Southwest are also Athapascans. In spite of this linguistic relationship of the California Athapascans we find that culturally they are like their non-Athapascan neighbors and unlike their linguistic relatives in Alaska and the Southwest. This holds especially in the matter of mythology and folk-tales, although the immediate neighbors of, say, the Hupa, namely the Karok and Yurok, speak languages as different from Hupa as Chinese is from English. Hupa mythology nevertheless closely resembles that of the Yurok and Karok, and is quite different from that of the Navaho and Apache. In other words, the Californian Athapascans have become thoroughly acculturated to the civilization of California, even though still continuing to use their original Athapascan speech.
>
> The second great linguistic family extensively represented in California, as well as elsewhere, is the Shoshonean. In California, the Mono,

---

* Spelled "Athabascan" in this book.

Paiute, Koso, Luiseño, Gabrielino and various other tribes belong to this family. Outside of California such peoples as the Bannock of Wyoming and Idaho, the Shoshoni of Idaho, the Ute of Nevada, Utah, and Colorado, the Hopi of Arizona, and the Comanche of Texas belong to the Shoshonean family. Moreover, the Shoshonean family long ago was shown to be closely related to the Aztekan group of languages in Mexico, so that it is really more correct to speak of the Uto-Aztekan* linguistic family than it is to speak of the Shoshonean and Aztekan families. The term Uto has been used in the compound name to take the place of Shoshonean. (Gifford and Block 1990, 16)

California also has *language isolates*, that is, languages with no known living relatives. Yuki and Wappo, for example, may be language isolates, although some people think they are related to each other. It cannot be the case that these languages were *never* related to other languages; most likely, it means that the related languages disappeared sometime in the past.

We can tell that two languages belong to the same family by finding similarities between them. By way of illustration, a set of Hupa and Navajo words are shown in the box on this page. Ignoring the accent

---

*   Present spelling is "Uto-Aztecan."

Hupa and Navajo words compared

The dash in front means that the word always has some kind of prefix. The prefixes have been left off here for ease of comparison.

HUPA	NAVAJO	ENGLISH TRANSLATION
-de'	-dèè'	horn (of animal)
-ta'	tàà'	father
taaq'	táá'	three
tin	-tììn	road, path
-yang	-yã	eat
-chweek	-chíí'	be red
-xe'	-kèè'	foot
-naa'	-náá'	eye
-sit'	-zìd	liver
-mit'	-bìd	stomach

marks of Navajo (which represent tone), one can see that the words have a striking similarity to each other. There are some differences, of course—otherwise they wouldn't be different languages. Navajo may have a long vowel (such as **aa**) while Hupa has a short vowel (**a**). Navajo regularly has a nasalized vowel (such as **ą**) where the Hupa word has a vowel followed by **n** or **ng**. A Hupa word with **x**, **s**, or **m**, will regularly match up with Navajo **k**, **z**, and **b**, respectively. In some cases where Hupa has a consonant at the end of a word, that consonant has disappeared in the Navajo word. But these are consistent differences that just go to show how the sounds of languages change over time in an orderly fashion. In any case, it is easy to see that Hupa and Navajo are related.

For the language families we have mentioned so far, the relationship between the member languages is very clear. But some relationships that go back to a deeper time level are not so clear. For these deep-time groups I will use the term *stocks*, and reserve the name *family* for the closer, more certain relationships.* Two of these ancient stocks in California are Hokan and Penutian. These two names were invented based on the word for "two." Hokan languages have a word something like **hok** for two; and some Penutian languages have a word like **pen**, while others use a word like **uti**. Some linguists are convinced that these two groupings represent valid relationships, and others are not. Hokan and Penutian actually contain whole language families within them: for example, Hokan includes the Pomoan family (Kashaya, Northern Pomo, Southern Pomo, Southeastern Pomo, etc.) and Yuman (Diegueño, Mojave, Paipai, etc.), along with many other families and languages; and Penutian includes the families of Wintun, Maidun, Miwokan, Costanoan, and others. If Hokan and Penutian are valid groupings, they are many thousands of years old—close to the limit of what can be detected by the comparative method described here.

It is widely, but not universally, believed that there have been at least three major migrations to the Americas across the Bering Strait. The most

---

* The terms "stock" and "family" are used all sorts of different ways in the linguistic literature: some writings use only one or the other to refer to any language grouping; and note that in the quote on the next page Kroeber reverses the usage, making "stock" the smaller grouping and "family" the larger grouping.

The Penutian family has recently been established by a union of five stocks—Wintun, Maidu, Miwok, Costanoan, and Yokuts. Two of these, Miwok and Costanoan, indeed had long been suspected to have affinity, and certain resemblances had also become apparent between Wintun and Maidu and Maidu and Yokuts. A systematic comparison revealed a unitary basis underlying all the languages. Miwok and Costanoan form a subgroup in which some form of the vocable **uti** is employed in the sense of "two." In the three other languages this numeral is **pene, ponoi, panotl.** They may therefore be designated as the "pen" subgroup. From the combination of these two words comes the appellation of the whole family: Pen-uti-an. It is always unfortunate when names must be arbitrarily coined, but native terminology offers no assistance, there is no suitable geographical term available, and an artificial designation of some sort was inevitable.

—Kroeber, *Handbook of the Indians of California*, p. 347

recent people to migrate were the Eskimo-Aleut, about 2,000 years ago; before that were the Na Dené,* perhaps 6,000 years ago; and long previous was a major migration across the Bering Strait land bridge during the last glaciation, perhaps 12,000 to 15,000 years ago. There may also have been people in the Americas long before that, but archaeologists have not found definite proof of this.**

Whether or not the migration of 12,000 to 15,000 years ago was the first, it was definitely major, and it is quite likely that only a few language families made that crossing. My reason for this claim is that in inhospitable climates, people have to use a vast amount of land to find adequate resources for survival, so that a single cultural group and hence a single language or language family is likely to dominate the entire region (Sherzer 1976). On the other hand, as people move on to more hospitable areas, new linguistic families replace them, and it is likely that over the several thousand years that the Bering Strait land bridge was

---

*   Na Dené is the stock that includes the Athabascan family.

**   The land bridge was also open for several periods between 20,000 and 32,000 years ago, and there were humans living in Siberia as long as 35,000 years ago, so the possibility of crossing the bridge at that earlier date seems reasonable.

Etymolology of the name "Penutian"

The word for "two" in Wintun, Maidun, and Yokuts languages generally begins with **p** followed by some vowel followed by **n** (or sometimes **l** or **m**); the word for "two" in Miwok and Costanoan languages begins with **oti** or **uti** or some similar form. The name for the language stock that all these languages belong to is "Penutian," based on these two different words for "two."*

Wintun

Wintu	pale-t
Nomlaki	pale-t
Patwin	pampa-ta

Maidun

Konkow	pene
Maidu	pene
Nisenan	pen

Yokuts

Main Valley	ponoi
Palewyami	pungi
Northern Valley	punoi
Kings River	punoi
Tule-Kaweah	pongoi
Buena Vista	pongoi

Miwok

Sierra	oti-ko
Plains	oyo-ke
Lake	otta
Coast	ossa

Costanoan/ Ohlone

Tamyen	utsi-n, uti-n
Awaswas	uthin
Mutsun	utxi-n
Rumsen	uti-s

---

*   Words based on Dixon and Kroeber, 1919.

intermittently open, several different groups came to the region and passed into the Americas. This would suggest that, at that exceedingly deep time level, most of the languages of the Americas are related to each other and they could be classified into a very few language stocks if our linguistic tools were adequate.

Indeed, Joseph Greenberg (1987) claims to be able to detect relationships among the Native American languages by comparing them to the extent that he can collapse all but Na Dene and Eskimo-Aleut into a single stock which he calls *Amerindian*, but his work has been roundly criticized for problems in methodology. On the other end of the continuum, Campbell and Mithun (1979) argue that languages should not be classified together until very careful scholarship proves them to be related. This led Campbell and Mithun to posit no fewer than 55 families and isolates in North America, pending further research. A completely different approach has been taken recently by Johanna Nichols (1992), who studies comparative grammar rather than vocabulary; by her new methods she has suggested that Native American languages are so different from each other that they must have been diverging for much longer than 15,000 years. This supports the theory that the Americas were populated before then.

It is not possible to assert who is "right" in this debate, and it may never be. No matter what method we use in our attempts to determine relationships, we are limited by the fact that by definition, language change is the slow erasure of the record of those relationships, so that eventually all possible traces will disappear, except for constant basic similarities that are present in *all* languages. This should remind us that we are all, in fact, part of one human family.

Classification of the languages of California

Membership of some languages in some families is uncertain, so every source will show minor differences in classification. Here is one way of classifying the languages of California.

Stock or Family	Family/Branch*	Languages in California
Hokan	—	Washo
	—	Esselen
	—	Chimariko
	—	Karuk
	—	Salinan
	Shastan	Shasta
	Palaihnihan	Achumawi, Atsugewi
	Yanan	Northern Yana, Central Yana, Yahi
	Pomoan	Northern, Northeastern, Eastern, Central, Southeastern, Southern, and Kashaya Pomo
	Yuman	Quechan, Mojave, Diegueño, Cocopa
	Chumashan	Obispeño, Barbareño, Ventureño, etc.
Penutian	Wintun	Wintu, Nomlaki, Patwin
	Maidun	Northeastern Maidu, Konkow, Nisenan
	Miwokan**	Lake Miwok, Coast Miwok, Bay Miwok, Plains Miwok, Northern Sierra Miwok, East Central Sierra Miwok, West Central Sierra Miwok, Southern Sierra Miwok.

---

*   A smaller grouping of languages within a family would be called a "branch." A dash in this column means that the language is not part of any subgroup of the stock or family in the first column.

**   Miwokan and Costanoan together form the Utian branch of Penutian.

Language Families
in Native California

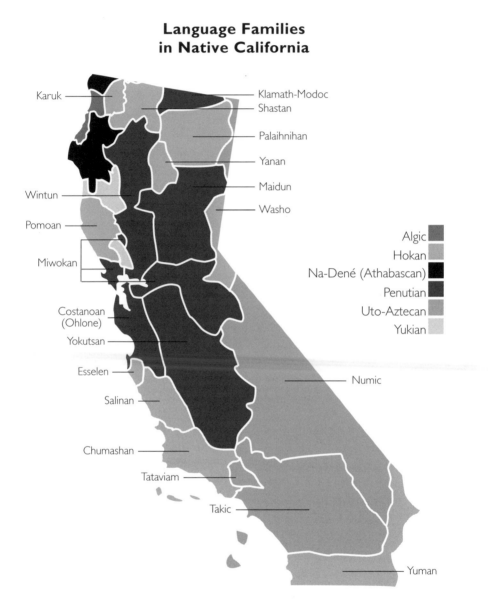

Karuk — Klamath-Modoc
Shastan
Palaihnihan
Yanan
Maidun
Wintun — Washo
Pomoan —
Miwokan —
Costanoan
(Ohlone) —
Yokutsan —
Esselen — Numic
Salinan —
Chumashan —
Tataviam —
Takic
Yuman

Algic
Hokan
Na-Dené (Athabascan)
Penutian
Uto-Aztecan
Yukian

Stock or Family	Family/Branch	Languages in California
Penutian (continued)	Costanoan (Ohlone)	Karkin, Chochenyo, Tamien, Ramaytush, Awaswas, Rumsen, Mutsun, and Chalon.
	Yokutsan	Choynumni, Chukchansi, Dumna, Tachi, Wukchumne, Yowlumni, Gashowu.
	Klamath-Modoc	Modoc
Algic	—	Yurok
	—	Wiyot
	Algonquian	(none in California)
Na Dené	Athabascan	Tolowa, Hupa, Chilula, Whilkut, Mattole, Nongatl, Sinkyone, Lassik, Wailaki, Cahto.
Uto-Aztecan	Numic	Mono, Owens Valley Paiute, Northern Paiute, Shoshoni, Kawaiisu, Chemehuevi
	Takic	Serrano, Cahuilla, Cupeño, Luiseño, Gabrielino, Juaneño, Fernandeño, Kitanemuk.
	Tataviam	
Yukian*	—	Yuki, Wappo.

---

* The family relationship between Yuki and Wappo is not firmly established.

Now the older stood on the east, the younger on the west, both facing the south. It had been night but now it was becoming morning. Then the older said, "The darkness comes from the east and goes west and I will follow it. Now I have another name. My name is Agāga-hatšyara [crow]. I will go to the Kamia. I will never return. I will be crow and will not come to this country." Then he followed the darkness to the southwest.

—Kroeber, *Seven Mohave Myths*, p. 40

7

What Language Can Tell Us About History

Long ago, there was a village of people living in the interior region of northwest California. Encoded in their language was their way of life: they hunted deer and fished for salmon in the rivers, and named these important animals. They named the acorn mush that they made from the black oak, and named the willow and sedge that they used to make their baskets. They named the wild tobacco that they smoked ceremonially. Outside the village, people might see mountain lions and grizzlies, foxes, wild geese, vultures, gopher snakes, and common kingsnakes; at night there were owls, nighthawks and striped skunks. Whatever they knew, they named, in their language that was ancestral to the modern Wintun languages. Their descendents still use names that descend from those long-ago words.

Life was rich and food was plentiful. But, as is always true of human beings, things never were perfect. There may have been a time when people in the village quarrelled over something; or perhaps some people just began to find that they had to go too far away to set up their fishing traps. For whatever reason, some of the people decided to split off and build another village, south a ways. This sort of process could have gone on for centuries, with new villages developing further and further south, until Wintuns were all up and down the Sacramento River and in the western part of the Sacramento Valley. By then the language had begun to differentiate, so that instead of one language, there were several—now known to some as Wintu, Nomlaki, and furthest south, Patwin. As the villages spread southward, the people came into contact with new neighbors and new plants and animals that they had no names for. The southern regions of the valley had different kinds of pine, California juniper, manzanita, buckeye, interior live oak, and blue oak. There were probably even condors there, although it was still far to the north of the final stronghold of the condors of our own lives. Having no names for these species, they had to find words for them somehow. The ancestors of the Patwin had new neighbors in their new location, the Miwoks—and one source of new words was to borrow them from those who already had them.

Villages were often abandoned, or taken over by another group; sometimes intermarriage with people who spoke another language would cause the language of a village to shift. It is possible, then, that the original Wintun community from which all these other communities descended might itself have disappeared.

If all this happened, it happened very long ago. The question is, how can we possibly find out anything about it now? The examination of the mystery of how and where people lived long ago is a kind of detective work, and language is full of clues for interested detectives to use.

The first important clues from the Wintun languages are all the words that they have in common. There are so many words that are similar between Wintu, Nomlaki and Patwin that we can be sure they are closely related. And if these languages are related, it means that the linguistic ancestors of the Wintu, Nomlaki and Patwin peoples long ago

Some Patwin words adopted from Miwok

	PROTO-EASTERN MIWOK	PATWIN
Pine nut	sanak	sanak
Gray pine	sak:y	chusak
Live oak	sa:sa	sa:sa
	PROTO MIWOK	
Manzanita	'ej:e	'e:ye, 'e:ya
Buckeye	'u:nu	'u:no, 'u:nu
Blue (oak)	mul (blue, black)	mu:le (blue oak)
Chief's wife	ma:jVn	mayin
	PROTO-WESTERN MIWOK	
Redwood	lúme	lúmani
	PROTO-SIERRA MIWOK	
Condor	mol:ok	mo:lok

The Miwok words are all reconstructed—that is, a word the way we think it sounded in an ancestral (proto-) language. "V" in a reconstructed word means there was a vowel there, but we don't know what vowel it was.

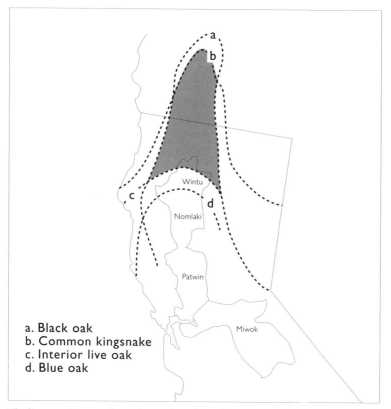

a. Black oak
b. Common kingsnake
c. Interior live oak
d. Blue oak

The lines on the map show the northern boundaries of several plant and animal species. Lines a and b are for species with names reconstructed from Proto-Wintun, and so the ancestral homeland of the Wintun must have been south of those lines. Lines c and d are for species that the Patwin had to borrow words for, suggesting that the original Wintun homeland was north of these lines. The shaded area shows the area most likely to contain the Proto-Wintun homeland.

lived together somewhere and spoke the same language. So the next mystery is, where might it be that they lived?

We can get some clues by looking at the words borrowed by the Patwins from the Miwoks.* We can reason that if the ancestors of the Patwins lived where there were buckeyes, or blue oaks, or condors, then they would already have words for these, and wouldn't need to adopt new words for them from the Miwoks. So if the Patwins do have

---

*   This presentation is based on Whistler 1977.

The Wintu scene along the McCloud River (above) is a markedly different environment than the oak woodlands of the Patwin (right), though both are Wintun groups. Photo above courtesy of California State Parks.

borrowed Miwok words for these plants and animals, it may well mean that the ancestors of the Patwins came from a place where these did not exist. Some of the Patwin words that look like they might be Miwok borrowings are **sa:sa** (interior live oak), **'u:no** (buckeye), **mo:lok** (condor), **mon** (California juniper), **mu:le** (blue oak), **'e:ye** (manzanita), and **chusak** (gray pine). These are thought to be borrowed words for two reasons: (1) they sound very much like words for the same plants and animals in Miwok, and (2) they are not found in other Wintun languages, only Patwin.

So deductive logic leads us to believe that the original Wintun people lived where there were no interior live oak, buckeye, condors, etc. This suggests that the original community might have been out of the range of California's foothill woodland and chaparral communities. They also borrowed a word for redwood, suggesting that they did not live near the coast, where the redwood grows.

A Patwin roundhouse near Colusa. Photo courtesy of Phoebe Apperson Hearst Museum of Anthropology.

We can also tell something about where the Wintun ancestors lived by looking at words that were not borrowed, but are instead in all the Wintun languages, suggesting that they were present in the original Wintun community. There are Proto-Wintun* words for poison oak, which only grows in the west, for black oak acorns and acorn mush, suggesting that they lived somewhere with access to oaks (but not to some of the species found in the Sacramento Valley), and for salmon, indicating that they lived in northern California or north of California, perhaps Oregon. There is also a Proto-Wintun word for the common kingsnake, whose range extends only a little north of the California border. The Wintun ancestors, we can conclude, lived somewhere where all these species overlap. This suggests an area in interior northern California or southern Oregon. The original Wintun

---

* A "proto-language" is the language ancestral to a group of modern languages. Through extrapolation from the modern words, we can make an educated guess about what some of the words in this proto-language were and what they sounded like.

Some words reconstructed from Proto-Wintun

chil bear (probably grizzly)
handVp common kingsnake
hi:n owl (short-eared or great horned)
ha:w fox
hu:s turkey vulture
kuhum basketroot (sedge?)
lol wild tobacco
łup to eat acorn mush with fingers
moł large willow sp.
no:p deer
nur, hur salmon
pate mountain lion
penel California black oak acorn
qho: striped skunk
qo:l-tep nighthawk (lit. "mouth-open")

community, then, was somewhere north of the present northernmost Wintun communities.

And so it is that our languages carry clues to our own histories. We might also wonder how this slow progression of villages was achieved; did the Wintun ancestors fight other people for the land, or was it accomplished peacefully? Archaeological studies suggest some initial conflict.* But while we can never know all the details of history just from a few linguistic clues, there is one word that suggests that the conflict might have been resolved in the long run by people's great efforts and ingenuity. The Patwin word for "chief's wife" is **mayin**, also borrowed from Miwok. This borrowing suggests that there might have been intermarriage between the Patwin and the Miwok at high social levels, a frequent custom throughout California, and indeed the world, that can ensure the peaceful coexistence of communities.

Native American tradition views people as the product, the offspring, of their land. As Matt Vera (Yowlumni Yokuts) writes,

Our bodies were made from the sacred earth, our beautifully colored skin

---

* This is based on burials in the Patwin-Miwok area with arrowheads embedded in them. (David Fredrickson, personal communication.)

given to us by the sacred fire. The breath of life came to us from the sacred sky. In our bodies flowed the unending sacred rivers. By all the sacredness blending together—earth, fire, air and water—our bodies and blood were created. Through these sacred elements, the people lived and were connected to everything. (Vera 1993, 19)

From this point of view, it is senseless to try to find out when people arrived at a certain location long ago; people were created where their land is. Matt's mother, Agnes Vera, once pointed out to me their sacred mountain where the creation took place, and said her family always tries to live within sight of it.

This religious view, of being so deeply connected to a particular place that a people simply sprang up from it, is almost inconceivable to Europeans, whose history is so rife with migrations that many of us feel that moving somewhere else is the way we carry on our family traditions. Thus European and European-American traditions mythologize "the Journey." Whole genres of novels about the history of the peopling of America focus on the migration itself—for European-American migration, the symbols are the *Mayflower* and the wagon train. For Native Americans, Western culture has now created a new myth, popularized in many novels, of migration over the Bering Strait. We are enthralled by the vision of small Siberian communities living at the threshold of the New World, struggling to stay alive during the long harsh winters, poised for the journey that will ultimately lead them to an earthly paradise never before touched by human feet.

This chapter focused on the Journey, using language as the data to allow speculation about answers to the questions that arise from European-American romanticization of human migrations. Many Native American groups have legends about their own migrations. But for others, the moment of arrival has no interest. As Karuk Indian doctor Jeanerette Jacups-Johnny said to me recently, it doesn't matter whether the Karuk arrived at the Klamath River one thousand or two thousand or ten thousand years ago (the last number is the most likely). From the Karuk point of view, they are tied so closely to their land that the land is in them and part of them, and essential to their self-definition. The same is certainly true of the Patwin.

You will call your countries by different names,
and you will also be differently named peoples.
Then, growing and growing—
when many days have passed—
when many winters have passed—
when the day you will be born has passed—
then you will go on living, having children.
As other winters go by, and they get a little bigger,
going on like that,
going on growing,
after enough winters have passed,
you will have many children,
and there will be enough people.
Each and every one of your children will have a name.
In the same way,
this country will also have a name.
Every country will have a name.
If you go somewhere to have a look around,
and you say, as you set out,
"I'm going to such and such a country,"
calling it by name,
then everyone will know where you are going.

—Shipley, *The Maidu Indian Myths and Stories of Hanc'ibyjim*, p. 27

8

Native Californian Names on the Land

Every language bears with it through the course of time the evidence of its social history. In particular, the vocabularies of languages coming into contact with other languages are enriched by borrowing words. An examination of a few pages of a dictionary will show that less than half of the English vocabulary came down through the ages from its Old English ancestor; most English words were borrowed from Latin, Greek, French, Spanish, Hindi, Arabic, Yiddish, Chinese, and a host of other languages— including Native American languages.

It is not in the basic vocabulary that native Californian languages have had any great impact on English. The only well-attested word I know of is "abalone," probably coming from the Rumsen language (Ohlone). Instead, the impact of California Indian languages on English is seen most clearly on the map. There are many dozens of place names in California that come from Indian languages.*

Of course, every place had already been named by the Indians long before the coming of Anglo mapmakers, and some of those place names were simply carried through as the present-day official names. Lake Tahoe's name comes from the Washo appellation meaning "Big Water." Cuyamaca Peak in San Diego is from the Diegueño name for that mountain—**ekwii yemak** (**ekwii** 'cloud', **'emak** 'behind'), meaning "behind the clouds." Point Mugu, Lompoc and Malibu all come from the names of Chumash settlements at those locations. The small coastal town of Gualala and the river that emerges there have a Kashaya Pomo place name, coming from **ʔahqha wala:li**, "Place where water goes down," the common term for the mouth of a river or creek. "Ukiah" is from the Central Pomo term for "south valley" and "south valley people."

Both traditionally and after contact, places were often named for a people that lived there. Mount Shasta is an example, as are Mono Lake,

---

* The most important sources for this essay are Gudde 1969, Kroeber 1916, and Stewart 1967.

Some California Place Names of Indian Origin

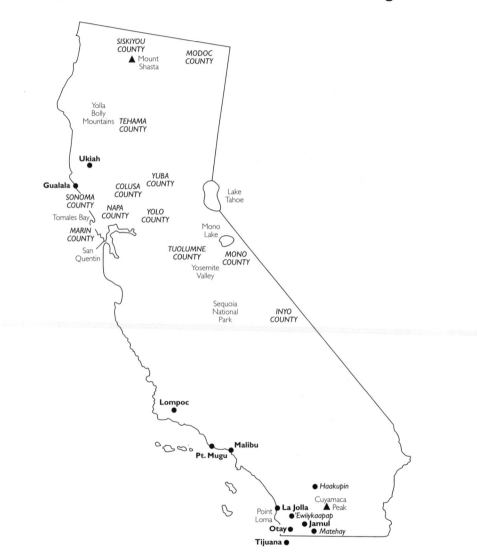

Tomales Bay (Coast Miwok), and Yosemite Valley (Central Sierra Miwok). The latter illustrates another common feature of naming practices: "Yosemite" is not the name that the people who lived there ever used for themselves, but was apparently taken from one of the names given to them by people living outside the valley, although there is some debate as to whether the name designated the people or the grizzly bears who also inhabited the valley:

> The valley has always been known to them, and is to this day, when speaking among themselves, as A-wá-ni. This, it is true, is only the name of one of the ancient villages which it contained; but by prominence it gave its name to the whole valley, and, in accordance with Indian usage almost everywhere, to the inhabitants of the same. The word "Yosemite" is simply a very beautiful and sonorous corruption of the word for "grizzly bear." (Powers 1877, 361)

Frequently, Indian place names are used not for their original designation, but instead for some new political/geographical unit, such as a county. Twelve California counties bear Indian names, often the name of a village that once existed somewhere in the region. There is Siskiyou County (actually a Chinook word), Modoc County, Tehama County (from the name of a Wintun village), Colusa (River Patwin, from the name of a major village at what is now the county seat), Yuba (Maidu), Yolo (a southern Patwin village name), Napa (a Hill Patwin settlement), Sonoma (Wintun), Tuolumne (Central Sierra Miwok, but possibly originally from Northern Yokuts), Mono County, and Inyo County. Marin County is named after one of three California Indian leaders (Marin, Quentin and Pomponio) who led a rebellion against Mexican military forces. San Quentin Prison is named after another of that trio.

There are some places named in Indian languages from outside California. Sequoia (the tree, and thence several California place names) was

---

The Indians had names for every little spot. Many names I have forgotten, but each name meant something about that place. ʔuˑtay (Otay) means a kind of weed that grows there, that is, a lot of that weed grows in that place. xamcaˑ (Jamacha) is the name of a wild gourd and a lot of them grow in that place. xamuɬ (Jamul) was named for a kind of weed that grows there. The xa part of the name means that it grows where there is lots of water. Point Loma was called mat kunʸiɬʸ (black earth) because that is how it looks from the distance.

—Shipek, *Delphina Cuero: Her Autobiography*, p. 24

named for the great Cherokee who was famed for inventing the Cherokee syllabary. The town name "Seneca" comes not from the Roman philosopher, but instead from Algonquian (**assini** 'stone', and **ka** 'people') that was first applied on the east coast, and from there carried to places all over the nation. When the Spaniards arrived in California, they came speaking a form of Spanish deeply influenced by the native languages of Mexico, and some of the place names from that era come from those languages. In Oakland, Temescal Creek (which now flows through buried storm drains) was once the site of many active sweathouses. "Temescal" derives from the Aztec word for sweat house. Words such as "mescal," "mesquite," "coyote" and "chocolate" also derive from Aztec, and so we have Aztec place names in California, such as the Chocolate Mountains, Coyote Hills, Mesquite Valley, and Mescal Island. The Spanish word "milpa," for "planted field," also comes from Aztec, and gives us Milpitas. In San Diego, Batequitos Lagoon comes from **batequi** 'waterhole', from the Cahita language of Sinaloa, Mexico. The -itos (or -itas) ending is Spanish, making the two place names above mean "little fields" and "little waterholes."

Some geographical names in English or Spanish are translations from Indian languages. Lost Arrow, in Yosemite National Park, is said to be a translation of the Miwok name for the same place. White Wolf, also in Yosemite, is named for the chief of a band that was camped there at the time of its naming.

Sometimes Indian place names are misunderstood by later generations as being from some other language. For example, some sources have said that the aforementioned Gualala must come from "Walhalla," the abode of fallen Teutonic warriors! Tijuana and the Tia Juana River are probably of Diegueño origin, but even in Spanish times folk etymology had turned the

---

This channel, between this island and the mainland where these Indians were, is in latitude 28 2/3°,* and we called it Pasaje de Belen, because when the Indian called to his companions for help, he said: *"Belen!"*

—Wagner, California Voyages, 1539-1541, p. 332

* This place was probably what is now know as St. Lucas Cove, in about 27°10'.

[Why did this man call for help?—*LH*]

---

river name into the Spanish for "Aunt Jane." Beautiful La Jolla is often called "the jewel of the sea" by its advertisers, based on the false notion that the name comes from Spanish *la joya*, "the jewel." In fact it probably comes from Diegueño **mat kulaahuuy**, "place of holes/caves," referring to the coastal caves there—far from meaning "the jewel," it is closer to "the hole"! The Spanish place name Carne Humana in Napa County was named by an infamous British doctor, who applied for a land grant in 1841 for a place known earlier by its Indian name "Calajomanas." As a sick joke, he twisted the sound of the word into Carne Humana ("Human Flesh").

One of the most often-used geographical terms of native California origin is the Wintun term **buli** 'hill, mountain', which is used in many place names on the east side of the Trinity Mountains. At least twelve peaks in Shasta, Trinity, Tehama and Lake counties are designated by the name, usually spelled "Bally," "Bully," or "Bolly." Among others, there is Bully Choop ("pointed mountain"), Bully Hill (this one means "Hill Hill"!), Bollybokka, Hayfork Bally, Shasta Bally, Shoemaker Bally, Trinity Bally, Winnibulli, and the Yolla Bolly Mountains (from Wintu "Snow Mountain"). Folk etymology has led to many other renditions of **buli**: Hayfork Bally is sometimes known as "Hayfork Baldy." Little Baldy and Indian Creek Baldy both come from **buli**. Even such local place names as Billy's Peak, Ball Mountain, and Bailey Hill are thought by some to be possibly derived from **buli**. (Gudde 1969, p. 20).

There are hundreds of other native Californian place names on the map. Since the early mapmakers usually wrote nothing down about the sources of the names they chose to record, the etymology of many of the names is uncertain or unknown. Place names such as Chimiles (Napa County) and Tunnabora Peak (Sequoia National Park) must be of Indian origin, but authorities know very little beyond that. Often, people studying the history of place names must seek the knowledge of the local people to discover the true source of a local name.

Also, many Indian place names exist that are *not* on any map. For example, some Diegueños still use the old terms for these and other places around San Diego County: Campo is **Matehay**; Mission Gorge is **'Ewiiykaakap**, and Warner's Hot Springs is **Haakupin**. A new California map could be made bearing thousands of such names that are known only in oral tradition.

A drawing of Fort Ross, near Jenner on the Sonoma Coast, when it was a Russian colony. Courtesy of California State Parks.

9

History Through the Words Brought to California by the Fort Ross Colony

By Robert L. Oswalt

When the native peoples of California were introduced to new cultural objects by the European colonists, they naturally needed names for these things. Sometimes names could be created by extending the use of a native term to include the introduced item: among the coastal Indians, for example, the shell of the mussel was used as a spoon, and the same word was applied to both the shellfish and the implement; when metal spoons were introduced, the native term for "mussel" was often extended to include the new instrument. Or new words could be derived from a native form; a spoon, for example, might be called something like "eating-tool." Words could also be taken from the language of those introducing the new objects. Within California, the source languages mainly have been Spanish and English. Thus many native peoples will simply use the English word "spoon" and others will use an adaptation of the Spanish *cuchara* (e.g., Southern Pomo **kuchala**). The Kashaya, whose homeland is on the north Sonoma County coast, were subjected in the early nineteenth century to the additional influence of Russian, from the Fort Ross colony, and as a consequence acquired *loshka** for "spoon," as well as some thirty other words derived ultimately from the Russian language.

A few of the words taken into Kashaya are in a form closely similar to standard Russian, though sometimes with a meaning shift: **chashka**

---

* The technical systems of writing that depict more exactly the sounds of the languages cited herein have been modified somewhat into a single system that should be more readable to speakers of English (although it ignores vowel length, accent, and aspiration). The vowels are to be pronounced as in Spanish and most of the consonants approximately as in English.

'dishes' (Russian 'cup'); **chaynik** 'teakettle'; **chayu** 'tea' (Russian 'some tea'); **kasha** 'gruel'; **parus** 'canvas' (Russian 'sail'); **pechka** 'brick' (Russian 'oven'); **tali** 'pulley'.

With some borrowings there are slight differences between the Kashaya and Russian pronunciations: **kushka** 'cat' from *koshka*; **mishuk** 'bag' from *meshok*; **putilka** 'broken glass' from *butylka* 'bottle'. These irregularities have several possible causes: the first Kashaya to learn the term may not have heard the original correctly, or the person teaching the term may not have been a speaker of standard Russian. This latter explanation is more likely; that is, many of the words that may have originated in Russian were passed to Kashaya through speakers of other languages, namely those natives of Alaska who were brought by the Russian-American Company to the Ross colony. The aberrations are clues to which Alaskan natives supplied the forms. Most of the Alaskan languages make no distinction between **u** and **o**, and naturally substitute their sound **u** whenever **o** occurs in the Russian source, and similarly substitute their **p** for the Russian **b**. Thus the Tanaina language, spoken by Indians around Cook Inlet in southern Alaska, has the words **kushka** 'cat' and **mishuk** 'bag'. The language of the Alutiiq of southern Alaska (linguistically classified as Pacific Yupik Eskimo), also contains similar forms, but there is a dialectal variation in the pronunciation of the sibilant, some saying **kuskaq** and other **kushkaq** (the **-q** is an Eskimo noun suffix). As for "bottle," the Alutiiq **putilkaq** is closer to the Kashaya than Tanaina **petilka** and **vitulka** (two different dialects). The Kashaya do have **o** and **b** in their language and would have had no difficulty in reproducing the Russian sounds—if they had first learned these words from a Russian.

Related forms for all the words discussed here exist in several of the languages of southern Alaska, and only sometimes is it possible to pick the immediate source of the Kashaya. The clearest example is Kashaya **kuluwet** 'cattle': the Russian is *korova* 'cow'; but the word appears in Alutiiq as **kuluwat** 'cows', formed from **kuluwa-** plus **-t**, a plural suffix which is distinctively Eskimo. Besides the expected replacement of Russian **o** with **u**, the Alaskan languages, as well as Kashaya, will often replace the trilled **r** of Russian with **l**; **v** between vowels becomes **w**; **d** becomes **t**; and **g** becomes **k**.

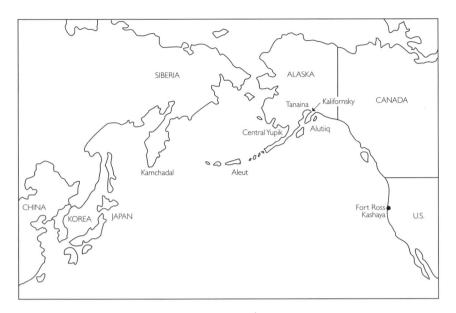

Other words also show the probable influence of Alutiiq: Kashaya **tupulu** 'axe' from Russian *topor*, by way of **tupulu-q**; **'ukuluta** 'fence, garden' from Russian *ogorod'*, by way of **ukuluta-q**.

There are also words in Kashaya which have no origin in Russian but come straight from one of the Alaskan languages: **chamay** 'hello' from Central Yupik **chama-i**; **chawik** 'iron, metal, nail' from Alutiiq **chawik** (with cognates in all the Eskimo languages); **kichak** 'anchor' from **kichaq** (also in many Eskimo languages); **nuhkuk** 'meat jerky' from Alutiiq **neqkaq** 'prepared food'; **shakitaq** 'a species of pelagic bird' from Eastern Aleut **shakitar** 'murre'; **taqma** 'dress (of a woman)' from Alutiiq **taqmak** or perhaps Tanaina **tahmak**; **'ayayo** 'cross (of Christianity)' from **agayu-**, an element in several Eskimo languages in words concerned with religion; **'eqshe** 'fishhook' is related to Tanaina **iqshak** and Alutiiq **iqsak**. That the diverse northern languages contain similar words for cultural items indicates that in Alaska, too, such terms were being passed from language to language, even as they were passed to the Kashaya from the Ross colony.

One of the most widespread terms is that for "paper, book, letter." In Kashaya it is **kalikak**, and either Alutiiq **kalikaq** or Aleut **kalikaq** could be its immediate source. The Tanaina word **kelek** is related but too aberrant in form to be the immediate source of the Kashaya. All these words could ultimately be derived from a Siberian language, where Chukchi, Kamchadal, and Koryak all have variations of the root **kali** in the meaning "carve, write," with derivatives meaning "writing, book, letter, paper." This is not linguistic evidence that Siberian natives were actually at Fort Ross, but there is such evidence from a given personal name: the name Kamchatal has been employed in at least one Kashaya family, carrying on the name of an ancestor. That progenitor of the family must have been known by his origin—Kamchadal.

The borrowing of words has not been entirely one way. When those at Fort Ross returned to their northern home, they took with them their passion for gambling the California way, by the hand game, and along with the game went some of its calls, which are known today to a few of the Tanaina and the Alutiiq.

The Kashaya called all those from the far north "people from under the water" or "Undersea People," perhaps because it seemed to them that, as the ships approached from beyond the horizon, they were rising up out of the water. Their term "Undersea People" includes without distinction the Russians and all the native people from the north that they brought with them. The Russians themselves referred to the Alaskan seahunters as "Aleut" without distinguishing one linguistic community from another. With new and better recording of all the native languages concerned, the evidence from the loan words is that, of the "Undersea People," it was not the Russians but the natives of Alaska that had the strongest social contact with the Kashaya and that those Alaskans were not one "Aleut" people, but were speakers of three distinct languages. Apparently those of most influence on the Kashaya were the Alutiiq, speakers of the Pacific Yupik Eskimo language of southern Alaska, especially those known as Chugach Eskimo. Also present at Fort Ross and of some influence were the Aleuts and the Tanaina Indians from the Cook Inlet. In addition, there was at least one Kamchadal from eastern Siberia.

The social contact diffused more than words: since many of the northern natives married local women and produced children, their genes entered the Kashaya community and Kashaya genes were taken north when the colonists returned to Alaska, some with their families, some leaving descendants behind.

Postscript

A Tanaina man from the Kenai Peninsula in Alaska worked at Fort Ross from about 1812 to 1821, and took the surname Kalifornsky ("the Californian"). Upon his return to Alaska, Nikolai Kalifornsky founded a village and gave it the Russian name *Kalifornskoe selenie*, "the Californian settlement." The village still bears the name "Kalifornsky" (although it was misspelled for many years on official government documents and maps as "Kalifonsky").

In 1979 one of Nikolai's descendants, Peter Kalifornsky, came to give a talk about his ancestral ties to California; he visited Fort Ross, and also went to meet the Kashaya people who had played such an important role in the life of his ancestor. Thus the effects of this meeting between people long ago are still present in languages and in human concerns.

—L.H.

PART III

Words

These words are going to be right and thus everything will be.

from de Angulo and Benson,
"Creation Myths of the Pomo Indian," p. 264

I said: "Jack, a while ago you called to me in English. You said 'let's eat.' Now, how would you say that in Indian?"

"*Laham.*"

I wrote it down in my notebook. Then I asked: "Which part in it means 'eat'?"

Jack looked at me with a very puzzled expression on his face. "I dunno what you mean, Doc, what part you eat..."

"All right... Never mind... How do you say 'I eat'?"

"*Saama.*"

"And how do you say 'You eat'?"

"*Kaama.*"

"And how do you say 'He eats'?"

"*Yaama.*"

I thought to myself: Of course! That's what the grammarians call pronominal prefixes. The *s*..., *k*..., and *y*... stand for the pronouns, I, you, he. I felt very proud of myself. I was getting along fine. "And now, Jack, how do you say 'We eat'?"

"How many of us eat, Doc?"

"What's that got to do with it? If I say 'we' I mean more than one. That's what we call singular and plural."

"I dunno what you call 'em things. I never went to school. But in Pit River talk it makes a lot of difference whether it's one man, or two people, or more than two people. For instance, you and me sit here, and here comes another fellow, and he says: 'You fellows eat already?' Well, we answer in Indian: *Sahaama.* That means: 'Yes, we two eat already.' but if we had been more than two, like for instance you and me and Lena, then we would say: *Sahammiima.* 'Yes, we all eat already.' Just like you say to a fellow if you invite him to eat: *Tamma.* That means: 'You eat!' But if you are talking to two people you say: *Dzammi.* And if it's more than two you say: *Dzamma.* Savvy now, Doc?"

I was jubilant. "Why yes, Jack. It's what they call the dual. That's the way it is in Greek!" Jack had a very kind face, and it was now wreathed in smiles. He evidently felt very proud of the Greeks. He said: "Well, well. What do you think of that now! I always thought them Greeks were nice people."

I was astounded. "What do you know about the Greeks, Jack?"

"They was a couple of them had a restaurant here a while back. I used to listen to their talk but I couldn't get a word of it, although I know some Mexican too. I didn't know they talk like us."

—de Angulo, *Indians in Overalls*, pp. 5-6

W ords—those powerful entities that embody our world. A word in our native language evokes a complex range of memories, images, emotions, associations and values, based on a lifetime of experiences that surround its usage.

Besides the complexities of meaning, in many Native American languages, words contain a complex grammar as well.* A single word in a California Indian language may have to be translated by a whole sentence in English. We saw examples of this in Chapter 5, where a tiny evidential suffix in Wintu would take many words to express in English. Or, to take an example from Ishi's Yahi language, examine the word below (where I separate the meaningful parts by dashes) and the rough translation of each part of it:

pop-sta-k'au-ram

>**pop** 'hit with arrow point'
>**sta** 'straight'
>**k'au** 'cut'
>**ram** 'out of enclosed space'

This single word would translate as something like, "He hit them straight on with his arrows from where he was hiding" (Hinton 1987).

It takes book-length bibliographies to list the large number of books and articles written on the grammar of California languages. But it is not my aim for this to be a book about grammar. In this volume I mention only a few of the virtually infinite delightful aspects of the grammar of Native Californian languages. I present here a few samples of the nature and grammatical structure of words.

Chapter 10 begins this section with a discussion of numbers. Counting is a universal human behavior, but it can be done in many fascinating different ways. I show in this chapter the range of counting systems in California, how the number words are structured

---

* Some might think that a *word* cannot have grammar, since grammar is often thought of as the way words are combined into sentences. But a word itself may be a compound of two roots (like "blackbird") or may have affixes (like "un-know-ing-ly"). This is grammar too.

mathematically, and how these words relate to objects and activities that California cultures use in their counting traditions.

English is reputed to have more words than any language in the world. This is primarily because we have so many specialized vocabularies that are only known by members of particular professions—special jargon for physicians, physicists, economists, naturalists, and so on. The members of each profession have a set of names for the concepts and objects and actions that concern their work. The California Indian languages, too, have such specialized vocabularies—known only to basketmakers or to shamans or to singers or traders or fishermen. Many of these realms never make it to dictionaries of Indian languages, because the speakers who worked on such a dictionary were not involved in these specialized activities. Or perhaps the words were already forgotten, along with the profession itself. Chapter 11 displays some of these specialized words that have survived and been committed to print—words for ideas and objects that most English speakers have never dreamed of.

In Chapter 12 we explore one aspect of the grammar of words—a set of interesting affixes in Kashaya Pomo. In Kashaya, action words involving use of a tool or body part, such as "hit," take a choice of prefixes that describe the nature of the instrument used to hit with. There are twenty or more different words for "hit"; one cannot just say that someone "hit" something—one hits with a round object, or a long object, or a flexible object, or a fist. By combining different "instrumental" prefixes with various verb roots, there are thousands of words that can be formed. This is only one example out of innumerable interacting aspects of grammar; again, it may serve to demonstrate how many different ways there are for people to structure their experience into language.

Words do not just describe or refer to things. They also express something about the speaker and the person addressed. In Yurok culture, people used to say words differently depending on their social class. In Cocopa, people had a whole different way of pronouncing words if they were speaking to a child. In Yana, as I show in Chapter 13, there is a strong difference in the pronunciation of words depending on the sex of the speaker and hearer. While any language exhibits some sexual differences in speaking style, the Yana language of California is especially famous for its sex-based variation.

"Words" have two basic properties: form and meaning. But what if we have a sequence of sounds (the "form") that has no recognizable meaning associated with it? We would probably say that such a sequence is not a real word. To end the section on words, we talk about such sequences of syllables, which occur in many Native Californian songs. These sequences are sometimes called "nonsense syllables"; yet in subtle ways, meaning is always present, even in these. Thus Chapter 14 talks about the very edge of the concept of "word."

In the morning Mastamho went outside. He wanted a place to put the people out-doors. He said: "Tonight some of you will become Mohave, some Chemehuevi, some Walapai, some Yavapai, some Yuma, some Kamia; and some of you will become birds. I will tell you about that tonight, but not during the day."

First, second, third counts taught.—When the sun set, all went into the house, and Mastamho stood up. He said: "You are all alive now. I will tell you what you will eat. I will tell you about corn and beans and melons and other food. But first I will teach you how to count. I will show you how to use your fingers. When you want to say: 'Four days,' do like this." And he held up four fingers. "When you want to tell of as many as all these fingers, show them all. Now listen, all be quiet and listen to me counting. Then perhaps you will like it. If you do not like it, you can listen to another way. **Sintš, tšekuvantš, tšekamuntš, tšekapantš, tšekaθara, umota, kutšyeta, koatša, kwisan, noe.** Can you say that? How do you like that counting?" Now those who were to be Mohave did not say a word. They could not count that way.

So Mastamho said again: "Count like this: **sinye, mivanye, mimunye, mipanye, miranye, miyuš, mikaš, nyavahakum, nyavamokum, nyatšupai, nyavali, nyavalak.** Can you say that? Do you like that counting?" But they were silent. There were too many words in that: more than ten.

So Mastamho counted for them again: **"Hatesa, hakiva, hakoma, tšimkapa, θapara, tinye, sekive, kum, ayave, apare.** Now I have counted ten. Perhaps you will like that." Again they did not speak a word.

Final count taught.—Then he said: "Well, I will make it four times: I will count once more; that will be all. Then I will teach you other things: for you do not yet know east and west and north and south: I will teach you that. Now I will count. **Seto, havika, hamoka, tšimpapa, θarapa, sinta, vika, muka, paye, arrapa.** Do you like that? Can you say that?" Then they all said it after him. They could count and liked it; they knew how to do it and clapped their hands and laughed.

—Kroeber, *Seven Mohave Myths*, p. 59

10

California Counting

Numbers are very important and powerful concepts. Each language has its own peculiar way of constructing its number system. In the native languages of California, we can find a rich variety of interesting ways to count.

Words for numbers are always expressed in part by mathematical operations, mainly addition, multiplication and subtraction. In English, we have what is called a decimal counting system, where the higher numbers are based on multiples of 10. Some California languages also have decimal counting systems, but others are quinary, meaning they are based on the number 5; and some are even quaternary systems, based on the number 4. Some Californians may even once have had number systems based on 6 (Beeler 1961). Wintu and some of the Pomo languages are partly vigesimal (based on 20). Actually, very few languages can be easily classified as completely one or another of these. Cahto is quite close to a quinary system, since the words for 5 and 10 include the root for "hand," and the numbers 6-9 are based on 1-4. But unlike a pure quinary system, 4 is expressed as a multiple of 2.

1	łaxa'	6	**yiban łaxa'** (*yiban* is 'on the other side'; *łaxa'* is 'one')
2	naka'	7	**yiban naka'** ('on other side, two')
3	tak'	8	**yiban tak'** ('on other side, three')
4	naka'-naka' ('two-two')	9	**yiban naka'-naka'** ('on other side, four')
5	la'sane (*la'* is 'hand')	10	**la'ł ba'an**

Notice that the higher numbers imply addition: for 7, "on the other side, two" means that we start with 5, and add 2 to it.

Many counting words in California use the word for hand. Perhaps "on the other side" originally referred to the use of the other hand to continue the count after 5. All cultures use some visual way of counting, whether it be the use of written numbers or the use of hands, sticks or other objects. In California languages many number words seem to be descriptions of these visual modes of counting.

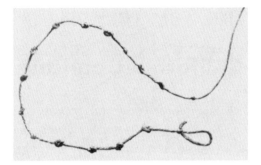

A Miwok message string, used to count the number of days before a scheduled event. Photo courtesy of Phoebe Apperson Hearst Museum of Anthropology.

The Lake Miwok counting system has some similarities to Cahto although the words themselves are completely different. Like Cahto, Lake Miwok uses "two twos" for 4, and the words for 5 and 10 contain the word for hand. But 6 and 7 are primary number words; that is, they have no known etymology from another word or combination of words.

1 **kénne**	6 **páttsadak**
2 **'ótta**	7 **semláawi**
3 **teléeka**	8 **'óthaya** (from "two" and *-haya*, an old word for "four"; so this means "four twos")
4 **'otótta** ('two twos')	9 **kénnenhelak** ('one lacking'; that is, one lacking from ten)
5 **kedékku** ('one hand')	10 **'ukúukotsi** (meaning "two hands," using *'ukúu* 'hand' and *-kotsi*, a suffix that means "two.")

Here the word for 9 is an example of using subtraction. The word for 8 is especially interesting because it means "two fours," using an old word for 4; this is still the word for 4 in other Miwok languages, but survives only in the word for 8 in Lake Miwok. This is a clue that perhaps Miwok languages once had a quaternary number system. Now it is partly quinary, and after 10 it becomes decimal: the word for 20 in Lake Miwok is **'ótta tumay** 'two sticks', 30 is **teléeka tumay** 'three sticks', etc. This use of a word for "stick" is very common in northern California. Wappo also uses the word for stick for multiples of 10; most of the Pomo languages use a word for stick to refer to multiples of 20 instead. Northwestern

Konkow uses the word for arrow. Hupa uses the word **bikin** 'stick' for the number 100. Probably sticks were used traditionally for counting larger numbers.

But getting back to hands, the Luiseño language used to take the words for hands and feet to a logical extreme in counting. At the turn of the century a man named Felix Calac told about counting in Luiseño. The numbers 1 to 5 were: 1 **supúl**; 2 **wéh**; 3 **páahi**; 4 **wasá'**; 5 **maháar**. The numbers from 6 on to infinity used the words for 1 to 5 plus the following vocabulary: **no-ma, no-maik** 'my hand, to my hand'; **no-e', no'ek**, 'my foot, to my foot'; **wacháyakut, wacháywunik** 'my finger or toe, to my finger or toe'; **awó', awái, awáik** 'another, to another'; **choun** 'all'; **wewun** 'both'; **tapaxot** 'finished'; **chapál, chapálaxot** 'passing, crossed over'; **pe'** 'and'; **pa'ák** 'upon'; **yu'pun** 'again'. The phrases for the numbers themselves were never published, but examples of the translations of the phrases were, and for the most part one can construct the phrases in Luiseño oneself. They go like this:

6	five one upon, or passing-over to-my-hand to-one to-finger
10	my-hand finished both
11	besides other my-hand one finger
15	all my-hand finished and one my-foot
16	besides my-foot one toe
20	four-times five, or another finished my-foot the-side
21	besides other my-foot one finger
25	all my-hand my-foot finished and another five
30	five times five, five upon
40	twice my-hand my-foot finished
71	five-times five another five-times five, and four-times five, one upon
80	four-times all my-hand my-foot finished
100	five-times all my-hand my-foot finished
200	again five-times all my-hand my-foot finished

(Kroeber and Grace 1960)

Wintu adds another component to the body-part image by calling 20 **k'etewint^hu:h** 'one person'; 40 is **pa:lwint^hu:h** 'two people'; and so on.

Wiyot doesn't use either body part or stick metaphors, but just descriptive phrases. Wiyot numbers are verbs; when counting, instead of

The numerals to four are common to the Athapascan languages, most of which have cognate words for five also. From five to nine the Hupa numerals are not easily analyzed. Ten (**minLûñ**) means *enough for it*. The numerals above ten are made by expressing addition for the numbers lying between the decimal terms and by multiplication for those terms. The meaning of **Laᶜitdikkin,*** one hundred, is not evident. No higher numbers exist, but the hundreds may be enumerated to a thousand or more.

A special termination is used when enumerating people. This seems to be an old suffix, **-nī** or **-ne**, meaning *people*. Compare **Laᶜ** and **Lūwûn nax** and **nanin, tak̲** and **tak̲ûn, diñk** and **diñkin,** and **tcwōlaᶜ** and **tcwōlane**, the numerals from one to five, for things and people respectively.

—Boas, *Handbook of American Indian Languages*, p. 149

"one, two, three" a fair translation of Wiyot would be "It is one, they are two, they are three."

   1 **kútsad** 'it is 1'
   2 **dítad** 'they are 2'
   3 **díkhad** 'they are 3'
   4 **diyóhwad** 'they are 4'
   5 **hehsoghálad** '5 so many they are'
   6 **takłalukhálad** '6 so many they are'
   7 **hohlaw hálad** '7 so many they are'
   8 **híwitaw hálad** '8 so many they are'
   9 **basharúk hálad** '9 so many they are'
  10 **dalúk hálad** '10 so many they are'
  11 **dalúk hálad bé kucad** '10 so many they are, over it is 1'
  12 **dalúk hálad bé ditad** '10 so many they are, over it is 2'
  20 **dit bo hálad** '2-beyond so many they are'
  21 **dit bo hálad bé kucad** '2-beyond so many they are, over it is 1'
  50 **wehsog halabéyalad** '5 again beyond so many they are'
 100 **kutséswoni** '1 full'
 200 **ditabéswoni** '2 full'
1000 **kutserawagátorił, píshwak** 'the counting runs out entirely once'

(Teeter 1964)

---

* The raised epsilon (ᶜ) is an old way of writing glottal stop; capital L is "voiceless l" (see Appendix).

Because we have hands and feet, with five fingers or toes on each, we have seen that it is typical for a counting system to be based on the number 5 or 10 or 20. Thus it is very interesting to find that in California there are several languages that base their counting system on 4 instead. For example, in the Ventureño Chumash numbers below, notice that the numbers 5 to 7 come from 1 to 3; 12 is 3 x 4; and 7 and 28 have the same name, with 28 presumably meaning 7 x 4.

 1 **pakeet**
 2 **eshkóm**
 3 **maség**
 4 **skumú**
 5 **itipakés** ('one more [than 4]')
 6 **yetishkóm** ('two more [than 4]')
 7 **itimaség** ('three more [than 4]')
 8 **malahua**
 9 **etspá**
10 **kashkóm**
11 **telú**
12 **maség skumú** (3 x 4)
13 **maség skumú kampakeet** ([3 x 4] + 1)
14 **eshkóm laliét** (2 less than 16)
15 **pakeet sihué chigípsh** (1 less than 16)
16 **chigípsh**
17 **chigípsh kampakeet** (16 + 1)
18 **eshkóm sihué skumuhúy** (2 less than 20)
19 **pakeet sihué skumuhúy** (1 less than 20)
20 **skumuhúy** (based on word for 4)
21 **skumuhúy kampakeet** (20 + 1)
22 **eshkóm sihué etsmajmaség** (2 less than 24)
23 **pakeet sihué etsmajmaség** (1 less than 24)
24 **etsmajmaség** (contains word for 3)
25 **etsmajmaség kampakeet** (24 + 1)
26 **eshkóm sihué itimaség** (2 less than 28)
27 **pakeet sihué itimaség** (1 less than 28)
28 **itimaség** (7 [meaning 7 x 4])
29 **itimaség kampakeet** ([7 x 4] + 1)

30 **eshkóm sihué eshkóm chigípsh** (2 less than 2 x 16)
31 **pakeet sihué eshkóm chigípsh** (1 less than 2 x 16)
32 **eshkóm chigípsh** (2 x 16)　　　　　　　(based on Beeler 1964)

My first thought when puzzling about these quaternary systems was that perhaps their existence is related to the fact that the "pattern" number is 4 in many California languages. For example, in the tale at the beginning of this chapter, four sets of numbers were presented before the Creator finally got it right. But then a friend pointed out a passage in Kroeber's *Handbook of the Indians of California*, and it became obvious that there might be a much more practical reason for number systems based on 4 or 8: sure, the hand has five fingers, but there are four spaces between the fingers!

> The Yuki system of counting—and it alone among all the Yukian languages—is not decimal or quinary, but octonary. Only the Salinan and Chumash, far to the south, follow an analogous quaternary method. It is remarkable that the Yuki counted on their fingers as regularly as any other people in the State. The explanation is that they did not count the fingers but the spaces between them, in each of which, when the manipulation was possible, two twigs were laid. Naturally enough their "hundred" was 64.

> The younger men, who have associated with the Americans, seem not to realize that their fathers thought by eights instead of tens, and are so confused in consequence that they give the most contradictory accounts of even the lowest native numerals. The old generation, on the other hand, is as innocent of our method. One of these survivors, when asked if he knew how many fingers he had, answered without hesitation, **huchamopesul**, ten. Asked how many fingers and toes he had, he replied that he did not know. If the query had been how many spaces there were between his fingers and toes, which would trip up many a civilized person required to answer without calculation or actual count, he would no doubt have known instantly. Two pairs of hands were then spread before him as the accepted equivalent of his own fingers and toes, and he began a laborious count, pushing the digits together into groups of fours. The result he announced was **molmihuipoi**, nineteen. Unaccustomed to handling fingers, he had overlooked a thumb. When the same man was allowed to

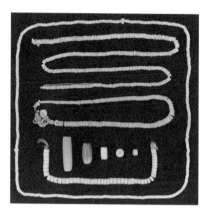

Pomo beads. Photo by Scott Patterson, courtesy of the Grace Hudson Museum.

The Pomo are great counters. Their arithmetical faculties must have been highly developed. They counted their long strings of beads. Methods of measuring such as most California tribes use were probably also in vogue, but must have been less usual, since they have not been described. In early days of contact with Caucasian civilization the unit of exchange was 400 clam-shell beads for $2.50. After the introduction of the pump drill the beads were manufactured more readily, and the value of the same unit quantity fell to $1. A tale relates that the first bear shaman gave 40,000 beads in pretended sympathy for the victim whose death he had caused. The use of these enormous figures is not incredible. A unit of 100 fours being once established, a reckoning to 100 such units presented no great difficulty to one who was interested. The significant thing is that the Pomo were interested. They evidently liked to deal with numbers, which had come to have a meaning to them and whose mere size did not terrify them. That they were a wealthy people would accordingly go without saying, even if we did not know that they were the principal purveyors of the standard disk currency to north-central California. It can also be inferred that this advance did not proceed without a corresponding development in other fields of the intellect or a reflection in many of their institutions.

There is nothing to show that the Pomo multiplied or divided in our customary sense of these operations. But constant dealing with units and higher units—fours, tens, hundreds, or four hundreds—must have resulted in a frequent familiarity with the result of many combinations of fairly large figures and some facility in dealing with new ones.

—Kroeber, *Handbook of the Indians of California*, pp. 256-257 place pairs of little sticks between his own fingers, as was habitual to him, he reckoned rapidly and correctly.

The Yuki managed their count with only three real numeral words: **paⁿwi**, one; **opi**, two; **molmi**, three. Every other word denoting the numbers up into the hundreds is a description of the process of counting. Thus, a translation of their numerals from four to twenty runs as follows: two-forks, middle-in, even-chilki, even-in, one-flat, beyond-one-hang, beyond-two-body, three-body, two-forks-body, middle-in-body, even-chilki-body, even-in-body, middle-none, one-middle-project, two-middle-project, three-middle-project, two-forks-middle-project. Sixty-four is two-fork-pile-at. There are sometimes several ways of denoting a number. Thus eight is one-flat, or hand-two-only. (Kroeber 1925, 176-177)

One of the most striking systems for counting is found in the Yurok language. Yurok has many different words for each number, depending on what is being counted. For example, the word for 3 when counting people would be **nahkseył**, as in **nahkseył pegerk**, 'three men'. But when counting rocks, the word for 3 is **nahksoh**, as in **nahksoh ha'aːg**, 'three rocks'.

Below are listed fifteen different ways of counting to 3 in Yurok, depending on what is being counted. (The higher numbers are different too.) As if this weren't complicated enough, note that there are even several alternatives for some numbers.

	ONE	TWO	THREE
Human beings	koːra', ko'r ni'ił ni'iyen ni'iːn	ni'iveł	nahkseył
Animals and birds	kerhter'y kerhter'er'y kerhter'ery	ner'er'er'y ner'er'erył	nerhkser'er'y nerhkser'erył
Round things, rocks, dollars	kohtoh	no'oh	nahksoh
Tools	kerhterpi'	ner'erpi'	nerhkserpi'
Plants other than trees	kohtek'ʷo'n	na'ak'ʷo'n	nahksek'ʷo'n
Trees, sticks	kohte'r	na'a'r	nahkse'r
Body parts, streams, utensils, clothes	koːra', ko'r	na'a'n	nahkse'n

	ONE	TWO	THREE
Worms, snakes, ropes	kohtek'	na'ak'	nahksek'
Flat things	kohtok's	no'ok's	nahksok's
Houses	kohte'li	na'a'li	nahkse'li
Boats	kohtey	na'ey	nahksey
Times (adverbs)	kohci (once)	na'mi, na'ami (twice)	nahksemi (3 times)
Days	kohcemoyɫ (one day)	na'amoyɫ (two days)	nahksemoyɫ (three days)
Arm's lengths (depth measurement)	kohcermerysh (one arm's length)	na'amerysh (two lengths)	nahksemerysh (three lengths)
Length measurement for dentalium shells	kohtepir (one finger joint)	na'apir (two finger joints)	nahksepir (three joints)

(Robins 1958)

Each number system seems strange and exotic if you are seeing it for the first time. But as in the Mojave creation tale, each people has a way of counting that seems just right to them.

This Tolowa man is measuring dentalia by holding the strand against calibration marks tattooed on his arm. Photo courtesy of the Smithsonian Institution.

Dentalia are known to have been fished by the Indians of Vancouver Island, and were perhaps taken by some tribes farther south; but it is certain that every piece in Yurok possession had traveled many miles, probably hundreds, and passed through a series of mutually unknown nations.

The Yurok grade their shells very exactly according to length, on which alone the value depends. They are kept in strings that reach from the end of an average man's thumb to the point of his shoulder. Successive shells have the butt end in opposite direction so as not to slip into one another. The pieces on one string are as nearly as possible of one size. So far as they vary, they are arranged in order of their length. But shells of sufficiently different size to be designated by distinct names are never strung together, since this would make value reckoning as difficult as if we broke coins into pieces. The length of "strings" was not far from 27-1/2 inches, but of course never exactly the same, since a string contained only an integral number of shells and these, like all organisms, varied. The cord itself measured a yard or more. This allowed the shells to be slid along it and separated for individual measurement without the necessity of unstringing. The sizes and names of the shells are as follows:

LENGTH OF SHELL (INCHES)	YUROK NAME OF SHELL	HUPA NAME OF SHELL	YUROK NAME OF STRING	HUPA NAME OF STRING	SHELLS TO STRING OF 27-1/2 IN.
2-1/2	Kergerpitl	Dingket	Kohtepis	Moanatla	11
2-5/16	Tego'o	Kiketukut-hoi	Na'apis	Moananah	12
2-1/8	Wega	Chwolahit	Nahksepitl	Moanatak	13
2	Hewiyem	Hostanhit	Ta'anepitl	Moanadingk	14
1-7/8	Merostan		Tsepupitl		15

The Yurok further distinguish **tsewosteu**, which is a little shorter than **merostan**, though still money. Possibly **tsewosteu** was the name of the 15-to-the-string shells, and **merostan**—sometimes called "young man's money"—denoted a size of which 14-1/2 measured a string. The Yurok further specify the length, both of pieces and of strings, by adding a number of qualifying terms, especially **oweyemek** and **wohpekemek**, which denote various degrees of shortness from standard.

—Kroeber, *Handbook of the Indians of California*, p. 23

11

Specialized Vocabulary
in the Languages of Native California

For any occupation or activity that the speakers of a language undertake, a specialized vocabulary develops around it. These technical terms may be known only to those people who participate in that activity. Physicians' vocabulary, computer jargon, and baseball terms are just a few of the specialized lexicons that exist in English. In California languages, there are sets of technical terms surrounding shamanism, hunting, and plant nomenclature, to name just a few examples. Scattered throughout this chapter are selections from some of the specialized domains in California languages, such as the vocabulary for strings of dentalia shells that began this chapter.

Among the most impressive sets of terms are those in the area of basketry, where a language may have hundreds of words and phrases that identify and describe the materials, technology, shape, function, and design of baskets.

A detailed study of basket-making terminology is found in a monograph by S.A. Barrett (1908). This book contains a large set of words for and descriptions of the materials used for basketry, types of baskets, and weaving techniques. But most interesting are the 231 design elements shown, with each one having one or even several names attached to it. The bulk of this essay is devoted to showing examples of some of these designs and the beautiful terms that identify them. Notice that the terminology links these designs closely to nature: references abound to butterflies, grasshoppers, striped water snakes, deer, quail, killdeer, sunfish, ants, acorns, and wild potatoes, as well as items in traditional culture such as arrowheads and tattoos.

By just giving sample names, I am leaving out a good deal about the categorizations of designs. Some generic terms are used to group some of the designs together. For example, terms like "butterfly" or "arrowhead" may be used to refer to many of the triangular designs, even though they can also be referred to by the more specific terms. This list will simply give an idea of the richness of this vocabulary.

Words are given in three different languages: Northern, Central and Eastern Pomo (these will be abbreviated as NP, CP and EP, respectively). Often the languages have very different words for the same design, and each language may also have more than one term, such as for the first triangular element:

NP **ditáska** 'spotted'; **ditás chidíyemul** 'spot [+ unknown word]'; **daṭípka** 'sharp points'

CP **kachá-dalau** 'arrowhead half'; **kachá-mtil chiltau** 'arrowhead-slender stuck-on'

EP **kagá** 'arrowhead'; **kacáishai kudja** 'butterfly small'

I will generally just reproduce one term for each design, rather than all the available terms in all the languages.* Now let the terms speak for themselves.

Triangular elements

CP **kachá-dalau** 'arrowhead half'

CP **kawína-ucha** 'turtle-neck'

NP **kasháishai** 'butterfly'

CP **tsiyótsiyo-balau** 'zigzag-half'

CP **kachá-dalau chtot** 'arrowhead-half band'

CP **úi-balau-ai** 'eye-half'

NP **kawína-chidik** 'turtle-back'

EP **kawásha daṭoi** 'pine-tree design'

---

* Robert Oswalt has kindly corrected some of Barrett's transcription errors. The transcriptions have also been rewritten here into the standard writing system of this book.

EP **túntun winalihempke** 'ants crossing'

 CP **kól-kachá** 'inward arrowhead'

 NP **daṭói kaṭa** 'design empty'

 EP **xasháishai winalihempke kaluṭuduk koldaiyauhmak** 'butterfly crossing striped-watersnake meeting-together'

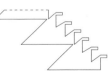 EP **xasháishai hna chagáxe** 'butterfly with quail-plumes'

EP **xasháishai tsawal-misak** 'butterfly sunfish-rib'

NP **daṭói diṭíp** 'design sharp'

EP **xagá-daṭip** 'arrowhead-sharp-pointed'

NP **daṭói kaṭa xoltu kachak daien** 'design empty on-both-sides arrow-heads collected'

 CP **shakaga-keya kachá** 'quail-plume arrowhead'

EP **kaluṭuduk hna xaga-daset** 'striped-watersnake with arrowheads-barbed'

NP **daṭói maa mina-datékama** 'design acorn crossing'

Rectangular Elements

NP **biché-o** 'deer-teeth'

CP **baiyákau kamtiltili-ui-kuwi** 'finishing design killdeer's-eyebrow'

NP **biṭámṭa daṭói** 'mosquito design'

EP **kalúṭuduk na xam bú-dile** 'striped-watersnake among potato-forehead'

CP **pshé-meo shtot** 'deer-back band'

NP **bishémao** 'deer-back'

CP **pshé-meo shtéltele** 'deer-back hitched-together'

CP **pshé-meo chi takanma chiltau** 'deer-back design far-apart stuck-on'

EP **bú-dile winalihempke** 'potato-forehead crossing'

EP **túntun jiyojiyo** 'ants zigzag'

Rhomboidal elements

NP **daṭípka** 'sharp points'

CP **kaái-kama** 'crow-foot'

EP **łal-a-pa** 'goose-excrement'

NP **dachékka** (name of a game where a wooden skewer is thrust through a string of fish vertebrae)

EP **có bax kama** 'east this mark' (i.e. design from the east)

NP **daṭíp dile kachák kale shiden** 'sharp-point in-the-middle arrowhead white lead'

Linear elements

EP **kalúṭuduk hna biche-yao** 'striped-watersnake with deer-teeth'

EP **winali-hempke** 'crossing'

NP **misákalak** 'striped-watersnake' (white line on black background: CP **sléma** 'string')

Southern Sierra Miwok Acorn Vocabulary

Acorn	myj·y-
Acorn bread	hutaj-·a-; hytyl-·a-; ʔyl·e-
Acorn cache	cak·a-
Acorn cracker	pasak·i-la-
Acorn cup	not·a-
Acorn flour, coarse	wasaj-·a-
Acorn meal	kaw·an-
Acorn mush, medium texture	ʔeca-·ma-; ʔec·a-
Acorn mush, thick	hyhak·aly-; maṣak·aly-; ʔyl·e-
Acorn mush, thin	nyp·a-; nyp·a·ṭi-
Acorn mush, to make	mola·p-
Acorn soup	hoju·m-aH-; hojum-·a-ṭi-; siwak·i-la-
Acorn top	tyŋha-
Acorns, pounded	maṣak·aly-
Acorns, shelled	watuk-·a-

—Broadbent, *The Southern Sierra Miwok Language*, p. 299

NP **da̧t̪ápka** 'a large area'

CP **tsawálmsak** 'sunfish rib'

NP **da̧t̪ói biyobiyoka** 'design little pieces'

NP **dikát̪ka da̧t̪ói** 'pushed over design'

Zigzag elements

NP **tsiyótsiyo** 'zigzag'

NP **da̧t̪ói kata dile tsiyotsiyoka** 'design empty in-the-middle zigzag'

CP **shakó-piya** 'grasshopper elbow'

EP **bishéto xam túntun gadil** 'deer stand-in among ants passing along'

NP **háske da̧t̪ói** 'tattoo design'

Diamond-shaped elements

NP **pdú-shna** 'acorn-cup'

CP **kachá kapokpoko** 'arrowhead spotted'

EP **xagá gaushaiyauhmak** 'arrowheads interlocking'

The Vocabulary of Basket Types

Some words for basket types in Northern, Central and Eastern Pomo:

ENGLISH	NORTHERN	CENTRAL	EASTERN
Basket (generic)	piká	ónma	shádi
Burden basket	bijí	pchi	bugú
Openwork burden, peeled rods	tsói	ikál	tsói
Openwork burden, unpeeled rods	hái-dukal	chamáu	tsói
Truncated conical basket	uyíl-ţo	shtúpchi	ţirí-bugu
Hemispherical basket	baţíboom	shţu	
Openwork sifter	shakán-tin	sál-stin	caláp
Culinary openwork sifter	shakán	sal	
Plate-form	dalá	nasú	dalá
Small plate-form	dalákan	ţóu	ţéu
Plate-form sifter		súkan	
Cylindrical basket	ţoó-pika	ţákan	
Small cylindrical basket	dem	sheét	
Spherical basket	piká-chadol	sheéţ-chibuchibu	gumúţu
Boat-shaped basket	shiló	kaláshuna	xaláshuna
Cylindrical fish trap	kákoi	báiya-hako	xáxoi
Conical fish trap	bukál	háko	buxál
Truncated cone fish trap		shá-mche	shá-mije
Half-cylinder fish trap		tsadát	tsadár
Quail trap	shakága-hakoi	shakága-hakoi	shagáx-hakoi
Handled seed beater	baţú	baţú	baţó
Openwork storage basket	pasé	iţíţ	ditír
Small openwork storage basket		tsói	bitsúl
Mortar basket	mijé	mtshe	mijé
Cradle	siká		xái-kaţoli
Feathered basket	ţá-pika, ípika	ţá-sţol	ţá-siţol, yiií-shaţ

Karuk Shamanistic Terms

em, supernatural power, such as a shaman possesses.

em-yav, "good shaman."

patunukot, sucking shaman.

maharav, clairvoyance

anav, a sacred formula

anava-kiavan, one who knows formulas, either to cure sickness with herbs or for any other purpose.

ara-tanwa, "person die," a pain, i.e., disease object

apuruwan, an "Indian devil," i.e., a person secretly in possession of a magical object that produces death; also apparently the object itself.

yumara, ghost, spirit of a dead human being.

ikhareya, ancient spirit, i.e. member of the race of beings that preceded mankind. Yurok **woge,** Hupa **kihunai.**

yash-arara, "real person," a human being; also, a true man, one of wealth and authority, a "chief."

kemish, any monster; also poison; also wickedly fearless.

ipshanmaskarav, poison.

pikship, "shadow," soul.

imya, breath, life.

ikhareya-kupa, ordained by the former spirit race, sacredly established.

pikuah, myths.

ih, to dance; **ih-an,** dancer.

ih-uk, girl's adolescence dance.

hapish, to make the "brush" or curing dance.

wuwuhina, any great dance, either the Jumping or the Deerskin dance; **wuwuhansh,** those who make or provide for such a dance.

ishkaship, "leap up," the Jumping dance.

isivsanen pikiavish, "making the world," the "new year's" ceremonies at Katimin, Amaikiara, etc.

isivsanen pikiavan, "world maker," the old man who recites the formula for this rite.

fata-wen-an, another name for him at Amaikiara.

sharuk-iruhishrihan, "down hill he eats salmon," or **sharuk-amavan,** "down hill he leaves salmon," assistant in the Amaikiara ceremony.

ahup-pikiavan, "wood maker," the woman assistant who cuts firewood; there are two at Katimin.

imushan, the male assistant at Katimin.

—Kroeber, Handbook of the Indians of California, pp. 106-107

Quail plume elements

 EP **shakága-ke** 'quail plume'

 CP **msákale shtot ṭul shakága-keya** 'striped-watersnake band side quail-plumes'

 CP **shakága-keya unaɫiu** 'quail plumes crossing'

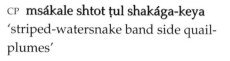 CP **kachák kaṭuk** 'arrowhead elbow'

NP **bitámta** 'mosquito'

A wonderful example of Pomo weaving. Photo courtesy of American Museum of Natural History.

12

"Slapping with the Mouth" and Other Interesting Words

Instrumental Prefixes in Kashaya

Linguist Edward Sapir saw the complexity of word level grammar as a basic difference between European and American Indian languages. He classified some European languages (especially English) as "analytic," meaning that each item in a sentence is "analyzed" out into a separate word. Other European languages (such as French and Spanish) are "synthetic," meaning that some concepts are typically expressed as affixes—that is, a number of concepts may be "synthesized," or combined, into a single word. But American Indian languages, he noted, are largely "polysynthetic"—each word consists of many parts, and many different concepts are combined into a single grammatically complex word.

Kashaya Pomo, one of seven Pomo languages that together form a family within the Hokan stock, is one of the languages that Sapir would classify as polysynthetic. One year, Kashaya speaker, singer and storyteller Milton ("Bun") Lucas came to the University of California at Berkeley to teach a group of us something about the Kashaya language. For two semesters, he met with the class twice a week, spinning his own special magic in the form of great stories, songs, and jokes, answering our questions about the language with constant patience and good humor, and teaching us far more than we ever knew how to ask.

One day someone asked him the word for "hit," and he responded, "What *kind* of hit?" He revealed that there are in fact numerous Kashaya words that translate as "hit." There's **pʰanem'** 'hit with fist', **moʔk'ow**, 'hit with rock (by throwing)', **caʔk'ow** 'hit with shoulder', **coʔk'ow** 'hit with head', **danem'** 'hit with palm', **diʔk'ow** 'hit by force of gravity', **pʰiʔc'aw**, 'hit with strap', **pʰiʔk'ow** 'hit with bat', and so on. As a friend noted recently, "You know how Eskimo is famed for having so many words for "snow," and how that's supposed to show that snow is really important to those people? Well, Kashaya ought to be famous as a language full of words for hitting!"

As an aside, recent studies have pointed out that Eskimo doesn't really have all that many different words for snow after all (Pullum 1991). And in any case, Kashaya doesn't have all these words because hitting is an important part of the Kashaya way of life. It turns out that most Kashaya verbs are formed with what have been called "instrumental prefixes:" each verb must bear a prefix saying what kind of object you use to take the action it describes. Take a verb stem like ṱʼašciw, which seems to mean something like "smash." This stem can never occur alone, but must always bear one of the instrumental prefixes. So Kashayas have words like these:

baṱʼašciw	smash with mouth (i.e., kiss really hard!)
duṱʼašciw	smash with finger
maṱʼašciw	smash with foot
piṱʼašciw	smash with long, thin object

In each case the stem **ṱʼašciw** is combined with a different prefix to form a word. Sometimes, of course, a stem will translate into English as an entirely different verb, depending on the prefix added to it. The stem **nem'**, for example, with the prefix **pʰa** 'with the end of a long object', comes out as **pʰanem'** 'punch with fist' (the long object is an arm, in this case); but with the prefix **ha** 'with a swinging motion' it comes out as **hanem'** 'kick'.

It turns out there are close to twenty of these prefixes. Years ago, the instrumental prefixes were ably described by Robert Oswalt in his dissertation on Kashaya grammar (1960). Most of the prefixes are listed below, with simplified versions of his translations; the words exemplifying the prefixes were written by Bun Lucas and Gene Buckley, with some added examples kindly provided by Robert Oswalt.

ba	with the lips, snout, beak; by speech or hearing;
	baʔcʼam' eat noisily (i.e., 'slap with the mouth');
	this can also mean to shock someone with words.

Milton "Bun" Lucas, Kashaya Pomo speaker, singer, storyteller and language teacher. Photo by Christina Kessler Noble.

bi   by encircling (with arms, or lips, or by sewing)
      biʔs'iw be pleated, folded
      biʔt'aw to taste acorn mush

ca   with the rear end, with a massive or bulky object
      cahqʰay' slide on rear end

čʰi   by holding the handle of something
      čʰiq'aːṭi' shave

cu   with front end, with flowing or blowing
      cuhpʰuw blow on; winnow

da with the hand, palm
  daq'a' scratch

di by gravity; by falling
  dis'aw fall and break

du with the finger
  du?t'aw feel with fingers

ha with a swinging motion
  hac'o' throw a knife or axe and have it penetrate something

hi with the body
  hihkow sit down (plural form)

ma with the sole of the foot
  mas'aw break with foot

mi with small projection near end of long object: toes, nose, etc.
  mide:du move ball along with toes, like in soccer

mu with a moving object detached from person doing action
  munem' bump something with front end of car

pˠa with the end of a long object
  pˠac'o' to harpoon

pˠi, pi with the side of a long object; with the eyes
  pit'aw beat with side of stick; tenderize
  pˠi?t'upˠi?t'uw to squint eyes

pˠu by blowing
  pˠus'aw for the wind to snap or break something

qa with teeth
  qanew to bite (i.e., 'to grab with the teeth')
  qat'aw to taste something that is chewed

si by water, by licking, sucking
  si?t'aw to taste liquid; to leach
  sis'aw to kiss

ša with a long object moving lengthwise
  šaht'iw jump up and down

šu by pulling
  šu?t'em' pull out from hidden place

Putting together roots and prefixes and deriving meaning from the resulting word can be a very creative thing. Here are some words from

Bun Lucas that have interesting and unusual meanings:

ca?t'em' sit on by accident
dahsaw stop fight by holding people back with hands
hahwen' rock something back and forth with foot
haṭ'ili' lie on back with legs stuck up in the air
pʰa?t'em' poke around aimlessly with a stick
pʰi?diway' see something secret
pʰi?q'obo' hit golf ball in a sand trap; hit a soft, spongy ball
šahkišahkiw jump in place with bare legs, in shorts

Every language in the world has its own power, and humor, and beauty, and genius. Many California languages are like Kashaya Pomo in that they have a system of instrumental prefixes. Yana is one such language,* and Diegueño is another. Other languages might lack this particular interesting characteristic but have other astounding features instead.

Language has sometimes been linked metaphorically to biology, with the argument that just as the loss of biological diversity threatens human welfare, so does the loss of linguistic diversity. Whether or not this metaphorical leap makes sense, I have always been of the persuasion that the presence of many different languages enlivens the world. There are so many delightful, playful ways that different languages structure themselves. All in all, it seems to me that a world without Kashaya instrumental prefixes would be a little bit sadder to live in.

---

* Sapir analyzed these as roots rather than prefixes, but I have argued that there is little real difference between the Yana instrumental "roots" and the Pomo prefixes. (Hinton 1987).

Wandering still further afield, we may glance at the Yana method of expression. Literally translated, the equivalent Yana sentence [the farmer kills the duckling] would read something like "kill-s he farmer he to duck-ling," in which "he" and "to" are rather awkward English renderings of a general third personal pronoun (*he, she, it,* or *they*) and an objective particle which indicates that the following noun is connected with the verb otherwise than as subject. The suffixed element in "kill-s" corresponds to the English suffix with the important exceptions that it makes no reference to the number of the subject and that the statement is known to be true, that it is vouched for by the speaker. Number is only indirectly expressed in the sentence in so far as there is no specific verb suffix indicating plurality of the subject nor specific plural elements in the two nouns. Had the statement been made on another's authority, a totally different "tense-modal" suffix would have had to be used. The pronouns of reference ("he") imply nothing by themselves as to number, gender, or case. Gender, indeed, is completely absent in Yana as a relational category.

—Sapir, *Language*, p. 91

13

Men's and Women's Talk

Social structure and social differences are reflected in language. Certainly the most universal category of social differentiation is based on gender. Pronouns in many languages, such as "he" and "she" in English, indicate the gender of the person they refer to. On the other hand, some languages do not differentiate gender in their pronominal systems. As Sapir notes above, Yana is one of them. But in *all* languages the sex of the *speaker* is expressed in one way or another in speech. One very obvious difference in the way the two sexes use language is in the pitch of the speaking voice. This difference is based on physiological differences in the larynxes of men and women. But people may also modulate their voices, either unconsciously or consciously, to be higher or lower. It is rumored that the difference in pitch between men and women is often greater than would be predicted by size differences in the larynx alone. Some of the difference in pitch may be due to the social need to symbolize sex differences.

Beyond pitch differences, there are many other ways around the world in which men and women differ in how they speak, and all these are purely learned differences rather than physiological. In English, women are reputed to use more in the way of weak expletives (such as darn, gosh, and phooey), while men use more strong ones (unprintable) (Lakoff 1975). Both sexes actually use both kinds, and certainly there are lots of men and women who don't fit the pattern. The difference is just statistical in nature; that is, one observes the difference by simply counting how many of each type are heard from a large sample of the two sexes. In some languages, on the other hand, the language differences between the sexes are more extreme. In the Lesser Antilles, men and women actually used to speak different languages altogether! This was due to a violent event of history: several centuries before the arrival of European explorers, Carib-speaking men from the mainland of South America conquered the islands, and then took the Arawak-speaking women to wife. From then on through the generations, the children grew up speaking Arawak, but then the men would take the boys aside as adolescents, and teach them Carib. Thus Island Carib, as this language is called, became a sort of male secret language, used only by men speaking to men.

In modern times, Native American languages also show differences between the sexes due to historical events. For example, among the Havasupais in Arizona in the 1970s, the language was changing rapidly under influence from English, but the women tended to speak more conservatively than the men, using older speech forms and fewer English loan words. This may reflect the fact that men left home more often, to get work, and thus spoke more English, while women tended to stay home, retaining greater ties to their older relatives (who spoke the older way) and speaking more Havasupai (Hinton 1980b).

There are also Native American languages where sex differentiation in speaking is due not to events of history, but instead to internally-developed tradition—and perhaps the most famous of these languages is here in California. One of the first things that anthropologists such as Dixon, Kroeber, and Sapir noticed about the Yana language was that there were quite obvious differences between the speaking patterns of men and women. Dixon, Kroeber, and Sapir went to study Yana at the turn of the century under the tutelage of Sam Batwi, Betty Brown, and other Yanas (see especially Sapir 1963). Later on, the same linguists studied Yahi, which is closely related to the other Yana languages, with the famous Ishi. But in Ishi's language, no differences between male and female forms of speech showed up.

Despite the fact that there is no gender expressed in Yana pronouns, Sapir identifies a few verbs which apply only to one sex or the other. The verb stem **ni** means 'a male goes', but **ʔa** means 'a female goes'; **buri** 'a male dances', **cari** 'a female dances'.* There is also a suffix **-ya** 'female' which may be attached to nouns: **k'uwi-ya** 'medicine woman'. The suffix **-si** may be attached sometimes to nouns referring to men: **baicu-si** 'male

---

* In Yana, the letter **c** varies in sound between "ch", "ts" and "dj". Letters with an apostrophe before or after them (such as **t'** or **'n**) stand for glottalized consonants. For **'n**, **'w**, etc., it sounds as if a glottal stop precedes the sound. For **p'**, etc., it sounds as if a glottal stop occurs almost at the same time or immediately after the sound.

hunter', as compared to **baicu-ya** 'female hunter'. Some verbs also have suffixes identifying the subject as female: **lulmai-ʔa** 'to be blind (said of a male)', **lulmai-yai-ʔa** 'to be blind (said of a female)'.

But it is not for these gender-related verbs and suffixes that Yana is so well-known—it is for the actual differences in the speech of men and women. These differences are most audible at the ends of sentences. Words have a final vowel or syllable that appears only at the ends of sentences, but only in men's speech. In women's speech, these finals are either whispered or left off altogether. Thus a word like "deer" would be **pana** at the end of a sentence in male speech, but **pa** (or **pah**) in female speech. Men's forms **ʔauna** 'fire', **ʔau-'nica** 'my fire', correspond to the women's forms **ʔauh** and **ʔau-'nic**. At the end of a sentence, the male form of the following phrase might be: **é·c'alsi'numà** 'You will dig for damna roots', but women would say **é·c'alsi'nu**ᵐᵃ (the superscript letters mean they are whispered) or **é·c'alsi'num**. The same word before the end of the sentence would simply lack the final vowel for both sexes: **é·c'alsi'num áikiceʔe** 'You will dig for damna roots over there'; but in women's speech, the last word ('over there') would be **áikice**.

The box shows some examples of how sentence-final words differ between male and female speech.

	MEN'S SPEECH	WOMEN'S SPEECH
Deer	pana	pa, or **pah**
Person	yana	ya, or **yah**
Dance! (command form)	puriʔiʔ	puriʔ
Try it!	haní·na'waip'aʔaʔ	haní·na'waip'aʔ
We will try it	hacílsi-'numa	hacílsi-'num
Day after tomorrow	t'úixalai-kʼìʔà	t'úixalai-kʼìʔ
Arrow	sawa	saw
Man	hi·si	hi·s
Woman	mari'mi	mari'ᵐⁱ
Heron	mimk'a	mimk'ᵃ
Coyote	mec'i	mec'ⁱ
Ear	ma'lku	ma'lkᵘ

Sam Batwi (left) and Ishi, 1911. Photo by A.L. Kroeber, courtesy of Phoebe Apperson Hearst Museum of Anthropology.

Actually, it is not so simple as to say that Yana men spoke one way and women another. The male speech was used only by men talking to men. Female speech was used by women talking to either men or women, and by men talking to women. Furthermore, both men and women knew both forms of speech, and could use both when called for. In storytelling, when the narrator would quote a character in the story, he or she would switch back and forth between male and female speech depending on the sex of the character being quoted. (That is how we know that Ishi didn't make a distinction between male and female speech: he did not switch speech styles when quoting women in stories.)

In his recent dissertation for the University of California at Berkeley (Luthin 1991), Herb Luthin revisited male and female speech in Yana texts narrated by Sam Batwi and Betty Brown (Sapir 1910), and found that there were further complexities in the usage of the two styles. He found, for example, that even though men addressing women are supposed to use women's speech, in fact they use men's speech when talking to their mothers-in-law. Furthermore, men's speech is used when someone makes a formal public speech, regardless of the composition of the audience. This public speaking is a formal style known as **ka·c'an?i,** and is used in the texts when, for example, a leader addresses his people, even if he is talking to an all-female audience.

So Herb Luthin suggests that what first appeared to be a male-female speech distinction is not really a gender-based distinction at all, but rather one based on the degree of formality of the speaking occasion. Thus we might infer that men in Yana society were relatively formal and reserved with each other, and with certain female relatives, such as their mothers-in-law. Women speaking with each other, and in general men and women speaking together, tended to be more informal. Herb suggested a new terminology: instead of calling these styles "male speech" and "female speech," he introduced the terms *reserved speech* and *common speech.* (Dropping word-final elements in Yana common speech is reminiscent of some distinctions between formal and informal speech in English, such as the dropping of "g" for the -ing ending in informal styles.)

What all this goes to show, really, is that speech communicates a great deal more than just the topic of discussion. It communicates a lot about the sort of situation one is involved in at the time, who one is, and what the relationship is between speakers. Speech expresses one's social identity. It is no wonder, then, that people feel an emotional attachment to their own languages.

He asked: "Can you girls and boys give me a song?"
They answered "Yes" and one girl Goose sang:

> Wi'-noo-nee
> Wi'-noo-nee
> Lah'-lah-lah
> Lah'-lah-lah
> Lah'-lah-lah

Jā'mul exclaimed, "That's good, but there are no words, only sounds."

—Woiche, *Annikadel: the History of the Universe*
as told by the Achumawi Indians of California, p. 12

14

Songs
Without Words

Many of the songs that are heard and sung by Native Californians contain sequences of syllables that do not appear to be real words. This is also true elsewhere in Native North America. To non-Indians, this may seem strange, perhaps because of the definition of the English word "song," which refers to music that one generally assumes will contain words. But even in the English-language song traditions, there are some song types that consist of nonsense syllables, such as skat-singing in the jazz world, and shape-note hymns in some Southern churches. Syllables that are not real words are sometimes called "nonsense syllables" or "meaningless syllables." But these names are problematical: "nonsense" implies something silly and unimportant, and songs without real words are far from being either "nonsensical" or "meaningless." So I prefer to borrow a term from musicology and call these syllables vocables, a word that doesn't carry those negative connotations. As Ernest Siva, Cahuilla/ Serrano singer and musicologist, has pointed out, many syllables that might be thought of as vocables by an outsider are not really thought of in that way by singers. They are instead thought of as being real words with unknown meaning. As we shall see, seeming vocables may be from an ancient form of the language, or from another language, or from the language of animals or spirits.

Most song traditions in California have both songs with real words and songs consisting mainly of vocables. Songs that are rich in vocables are the ones that are heard most often in public. Vocables are often found in the dance songs, for example, where any message conveyed by words is secondary to the rhythm and music; songs with fewer words are often considered to be better for dancing to. Just to give a feel for what vocables are like, here is the text of a Wintu round dance song. (All the Wintu songs I will be talking about here were sung by Grace MacKibben, and recorded and transcribed by Alice Shepherd.)

we no ho ho we no (this line repeated 15 times)
ho we no we no ho ho we no
ho we no

The Wintu handgame songs are another genre where most songs consist of vocables. One handgame song contains this line of vocables sung over and over:

no wani no wani no wani no

Another handgame song contains this line:

hanani owi nohohena

In the traditional gambling songs of California the team who is hiding the bones will usually sing in vocables until the other team makes a wrong guess. At that point the singers increase their volume triumphantly and they might then shift to singing real words, often poking fun at the other team.

A Diegueño stick game at Mesa Grande. 1907 photo by Edward H. Davis, courtesy of the National Museum of the American Indian.

Cahuilla Bird Singers Robert Levi, Alvino Siva and Ernest Siva, 1987. Photo by Paul Apodaca.

Vocables in songs have many reasons for being. In some cases, vocables actually derive from real words, but the meanings have been lost for one of the following reasons.

The songs may have come from a different language. In the Bird Songs of southern California, which are sung by several different tribes, many of the words have meaning in one language but not another. Ernest Siva says that in Bird Songs sung by the Cahuilla, there are some words which come from Serrano: an example is the word **nato** "the time has come" (referring to the time when people separated and went their different ways all over the world; and another is **mih?**, meaning "to go" in Serrano, but not Cahuilla.

Some songs whose words appear to have no meaning are said to be in spirit language or animal language, which humans don't know. Among the Atsugewi, if a spirit liked a person, it sang to him, and then the person could sing the song under appropriate circumstances. It has been written that the

names and words of Atsugewi shamanistic songs were understood only by
the guardian spirits to which they were addressed.

In some songs, the words are real words, but either changed so that
people no longer recognize them, or else lost in spoken language so that
people no longer know them. To take an example from the Havasupais
of Arizona, one song begins with these syllables:

nya ge ge ŋe the

Havasupais who didn't know the song would not be able to recognize
these words, but the singers of this song know that it is the word for "my
younger brother," **nya gina**. The sung phrase has been changed enor-
mously from the spoken version. The phrases that get changed this way
are usually at the beginning of a song, and sung several times before
going on to the rest of the text; and that is the very place where vocables
most typically occur too. It is easy to see how a mutated phrase could
become reinterpreted as a sequence of vocables (Hinton 1980a).

In some cases, there are syllables which are true vocables from
anyone's point of view. For example, in some song traditions, vocables

*Northwest California men gambling, probably at the Blue Lake Wiyot/Yurok Reserva-
tion. Photo courtesy of Humboldt State University.*

are inserted as a way of making words conform to the rhythm of the song. Again, a couple of lines from a Havasupai song can illustrate this. The first column shows the words as they would be spoken: each phrase consists of three syllables. However, they have to be fit into a rhythmic pattern that demands six syllables. The solution to this problem is to fill out the phrase with vocables, as shown in the second column (vocables are underlined).

SPOKEN WORDS	SUNG WORDS	ENGLISH
nyaj evah	<u>ve</u>nya<u>jo</u> e va <u>ha</u>	I will feel it.
giyu ʔim	ge yo <u>ye</u> ʔi<u>me</u> <u>wa</u>	That is what I desire.

Sometimes vocables are there just for aesthetic reasons—because they make the song sound more beautiful; there are certain sounds that are generally thought to go with music better than others. In English and other European languages, singers are taught that the "**a**" sound (as in the word "f**a**ther") is the best vowel, because the mouth is the most open and the musical sound is strongest and best balanced, and the next best vowels are "**e**" (as in "p**e**n") and "**o**" (as in "ph**o**ne"). And in the Western tradition of lyric poetry, poets preferred the soft, continuous, "singable" consonants such as **y**, **w**, **h**, and **n**. These kinds of preferences might be almost universal, because in Native American singing, these same vowels and consonants are the most common in vocables.

Even though vocables are not real words, vocables still have *meaning*. Sometimes vocables are meaningful because they imply some kind of emotion. In English, the best-known vocables are "tra-la-la"; they are meaningful in that they convey a sense of happiness. In one Havasupai song, there is a line of vocables like this:

heyaŋa yaŋa yaŋa

These sounds also convey a sense of happiness. In another Havasupai song, the vocable refrain **ha ŋa** conveys a sense of sadness and mourning. This refrain actually changes to rhyme with the last vowel of the real words in the verse—it may also be **ho ŋo**, **he ŋe**, etc.

In Wintu, the Cry songs have vocables that express mourning: **aní, aní, aní**.

Another way in which vocables have meaning is in their signalling of song type. In Wintu, many types of songs always begin with a particular sequence of vocables. The love songs usually begin with the vocables "hi ni ni ni," as in this example:

hi ni ni ni ni ni ni	hi ni ni ni ni ni ni
hi ni ni ni ni ni ni	hi ni ni ni ni ni ni
ʔaniːye: ʔanaqtoːt	Oh my father
henuh war henuh war	What will you do?
ʔelcoːdi poʔilawih	Elco:di the Younger
hiseːr wayharaːntheːm	danced and I'm going North.
heyano heyano	heyano heyano
ʔanaqtoːt	Oh my father.

Wintu love songs are often called "nini" because of these vocables. In the song above, composed by a woman who fell in love with a man at a dance, we see a second set of vocables, **heyano heyano**, that are a typical refrain of the Hisi Dance. The woman thus identifies and recalls the dance where she met her lover, by using its vocables.

A frustrating practice of some anthropologists and musicologists who have written about California music has been their tendency to dismiss vocables as useless to their concerns, and not even write them down when they transcribe the text of a song. Frances Densmore, who wrote dozens of otherwise very useful volumes about Native American music in the 1930s, just transcribed the musical notes, leaving out the text if it consisted of vocables. See, for example, *Yuman and Yaqui Music* (Densmore 1932). When Dorothy Lee collected Wintu music in the same era, she wrote down the text translation but not the vocables. But you can see from the above examples that important information is lost if the vocables are not transcribed. Vocables are in fact quite rich in meaning, even though they can't be translated, and don't "mean" in quite the same way that words "mean."

A final point about meaning is that it is really the song itself that holds meaning, not just the words. A song that consists solely of vocables can still be full of meaning. Here, a Havasupai snake bite curing song consists completely of vocables:

yoŋaŋa 'e yoŋa
yoŋaŋa 'e yoŋa
yoŋa yoŋa
yoŋa yoŋa
hayuya hayuya
'eyanaŋa
yoŋaŋa he yoŋa yoŋa
hayuya
'eyanaŋa

But here is how its meaning is described by its singer, Dan Hanna: "This song means that when the snake bite comes here, the pain goes in every muscle of your body. But we are singing this song for you and it reaches those muscle places and we know already that the pain will be gone when we finish."

Finally, vocables can also be misused on purpose to evoke humor. No one illustrates this better than Old Man Coyote himself. In a song from a Wintu story, Coyote sings a song beginning with these syllables:

soweni soweni soweni sowen

This is actually another illustration of how something from another language can be interpreted as vocables. Alice (Schlichter) Shepherd pointed out to me that **soweni** is a word borrowed from Yuki, referring to the unmarked bone in the handgame. The use of this word must have been a joke, because Coyote should be guessing where the marked bone is, not the unmarked bone!

In another story, Coyote is pretending to be a shaman. Wintu shamanistic songs also typically begin with a series of characteristic vocables, but Coyote begins his doctor song with the same handgame syllables as before:

soweni soweni soweni sowen

These syllables are of course completely inappropriate for a doctoring song. That Coyote always messes things up!

PART IV

Language and Dominion

Naming is an act of power. In Genesis, Adam's first recorded act of domination is naming, assigning the symbol, the act of a I-am-he-who-tells-you-what-or-who-you-are. It is the ultimate gesture of paternalism. The infant child is named. Similarly the first response to the other, to the outsider, is to assign a name. The one who assigns is the insider, the decider, the winner.

In early California there was little question who were the winners, who were the namers and who were the named.

—Judge Gary Strankman on the occasion of the naming of
Ishi Court at UC Berkeley, 1993

All talk about Native Americans takes place against the backdrop of a spoken or unspoken understanding that over the last 500 years, one of the great injustices of human history has unfolded, as Europeans have systematically killed, tormented and dispossessed the American Indians of their land and cultures. Even now that the worst is over, intensive pressures of many sorts continue to burden Native American cultures, land tenure, and languages. It is not the purpose of this book to dwell heavily on this nightmare; instead, most of the last portion of this volume presents the ways in which Native Californians withstand these pressures against their cultures. Further on, we look specifically at how Native Californians are working to maintain and assert their identity through language.

Nevertheless, in a book about language, I would be remiss not to point out the role language plays in prejudice and repression. Language is the basis of law, which either legislates repression or acts to mitigate it. And language expresses and transmits attitudes toward others, whether respectful or prejudicial.

I begin this section with a discussion of how the California Indians got the names they are popularly known by. These are the names that the explorers, authors, and mapmakers gave them, which usually do not coincide with the names they gave themselves, an example of how Europeans have usurped the power to define Native Americans. Next I include a short essay about the name "digger pine," and how that tree came to be named with an opprobrious term for California Indians. Chapter 17 focuses on moving autobiographical accounts by two California Indian women who experienced, early in this century, the repression of their native languages through the policies of government-run schools. It was these policies more than anything else that caused the alarming decline of Native American languages in our time. To end the section on a more positive note, I present the Native American Languages Act, which shows the *new* language policy of the United States government, 180 degrees removed from the policy of forced linguistic assimilation that dominated in the first half of this century.

Mispronounced tribal names.—Mastamho said: "Some of you are outside, east of the house: I want you to be the Hamapaivek. Some of you are outdoors west of the house: I call you Hamivevek. You people in the house, just west of the door, I call you Hamitšanvek. You just inside the door, near these last, I call Hamiaivek. You people near the fire here, not against the wall, I call you Hamahavek." He called them by these names, but all the people did not answer. They did not say: "Yes, we will be called that." All of them said nothing.

Walapai and Yavapai tribes named.—Then Mastamho said again: "This time I will call you who are on the east Havalyipai." Then those people called that name easily, and all those indoors said: "Now they are the Walapai." Then he said again: "Those will be the Yavapai also. I want them (the Walapai and the Yavapai) to live near each other in the mountains." Those are the ones that at first he had called Hamapaivek.

Chemehuevi named.—Then he said again: "Those outdoors on the west, whom at first I called Hamivevek, I now call Tšimuveve. All say that!" Then all said: "Chemehuevi."

Yuma and Kamia named.—He said again: "Those just inside the door on the west of it I called Hamitšanvek. Now I call you Kwitš(i)ana (Yuma)." He said again: "You near them, whom at first I called Hamiaivek, I now call Kamia. You will live near each other."

Mohave named.—Then he said: "I have made you all to be tribes, Walapai, Yavapai, Chemehuevi, Yuma, and Kamia: you are all different. I also spoke the name Hamahavek. Now I call them Hamakhave. All will call you that, you Mohave, and will know you by that name."

—Kroeber, *Seven Mohave Myths*, p. 60

15

On the Origins of
California Tribal Names

The frontispiece of this book, a map of Native California, depicts language groupings and original territories where the languages were spoken. Yet very few of the territories on the map match up with what Indians used to think of as the significant social divisions between peoples, and very few of the names on the map have any relation to what the groups called themselves.

Then how in the world did the California Indians get the names they are now known by?

The early literature is full of so many different designations for people that it boggles the mind. For example, in the California volume of the *Handbook of North American Indians,* the following are given as a partial list of names by which the Yurok have been known: Al-agnas, Al-i-kwa, Alioquis, Aliquois, Aliquor, Allequa, Alth, Cuthacs, Down-stream People, Eurocs, Eurok, Eurooks, Eurucks, Hiktin-taretahihl, Kanuck, Kenuck, Kenuk, Kiruhikwak, Klamath, Klamath River, Kyinnáa, Lower Indians, Lower Klamath, Palegawonáp, Palik-Ai-li-qua, Poh-lik, Poliklan, Pulíklan, Tlamath, Tolick Si-liqua, Tútlmús, Ulrucks, Wait'spek, Weits-pek, Weitspekan, Wish-pooke, Witsch-piks, Youruk, Yurock, and Yurús-árar! (Heizer 1978).

The Yuroks' traditional name for themselves is "Puliklah," which translates as "they walk the shoreside." The name "Yurok" was introduced into the literary fray in the 1870s, as a linguistic label; it is from the Karuk (usually "Karok" in the literature) word meaning "downriver." "Karuk" itself means "upriver"; and although the word is from their own language, it was originally a geographic designation, not what the Karuks used to call themselves. As Kroeber notes:

The term "Karok," properly **karuk,** means merely "up-stream" in the language of the Karok. It is an adverb, not a designation of a group of people. The Karok have no ethnic name for themselves, contenting themselves, in general Californian custom, by calling themselves "people," **arara**. They will sometimes speak of themselves as Karuk-w-arara in distinction from the Yuruk-w-arara, the "downstreamers" or "Yurok"; but this denomination seems wholly relative. In thinking of the Shasta above them on the Klamath, they would probably name themselves Yuruk-w-arara. (Kroeber 1925, 98-99)

Nowadays, the people who used to call themselves **arara** prefer the term "Karuk" with a flapped r.

Most people of California, like the Karuk, used to call themselves "the people." Some of the present-day tribal names come from that self-designation. Chimariko, Maidu, Nisenan, Patwin, Wintu, and Yana all come from the word "people" in those languages. Similarly, Washo comes from the word **washiw**, meaning something like "people from here."

In some cases, one group's name for "people" got extended to a larger linguistic grouping. "Miwok" comes from the word for "people" in Sierra Miwok only, but was extended to other groups speaking related languages as well. "Yokuts" is a name that is applied to over forty politically separate groups speaking related languages; it is the Valley Yokuts word for "people." The Foothill Yokuts word for "people" is Tachi. (Sometimes the Tachi are called the "Tachi Yokuts people"—translate that one into English!) The various Yokuts peoples rarely use that word for themselves, preferring instead their own labels of Yowlumni, Chukchansi, and so on.

One reason why official names don't match with what people call themselves is that explorers first learned about many groups from other tribes, who had their own terms for them. The Karuk, asked about their next-door neighbors, mentioned the Yurok, thus providing the official name. The explorers went on to ask the Yuroks about the tribes living near them, and the Yuroks used their terms, Hupa and Tolowa, which thus became the official names of those tribes—but the Hupas call themselves **natinixwe**, and the Tolowa call themselves **xəsh**—both terms being words for "people." The Yuroks were also the namers of the Chilula, which means "people of the Bald Hills."

Other groups got to do some naming too. The Wailaki were so named by the Wintu. "Wailaki" is from a word meaning "north language," but the Wintu applied it to all the groups, including even other Wintu who lived in that direction. The Wintu named the Yuki—with the Wintu word for "enemy," thus suggesting something about Wintu-Yuki relations. (To the Wintu, "Yuki" was not really their name for that tribe,

---

Kashaya is derived from the native term /k'ahšá·ya/, which probably contains /k'ahšá·ya/ 'agile, nimble.' The people are known to the Southern Pomo as /k'ahša·ya/, containing /k'ahša/ 'light (weight)'; to the Central Pomo of Point Arena as /káša·ya/ 'expert gamblers,' containing /ka/ 'gambling' and /ša·/ 'expert'; to the Northern Pomo as /kašá·ya/, with no meaning recognized for the first two syllables. The final syllable in the above four Pomo languages means 'people, group, race.' The Kashaya are known to the Wappo as /k'áša·ya/, with no analyzable significance (personal communication from J.O. Sawyer). The name is spelled "Kashia" in governmental records and on the sign of the reservation school, and "Kacia" by Stewart….

The older English terms Erio, for the Kashaya at the mouth of the Russian River, and Erusi, for those at Fort Ross, are probably from the Spanish El Rio and El Ruso. Venaambakaiia, employed in Powers' vocabularies (1877) is doubtless the phrase /wina·má·bakʰe ya?/ 'person who belongs on the land,' a term for the native as opposed to /?ahqʰa yów ?bakʰe ya?/ 'person from under the sea, undersea person,' a term for those at Fort Ross from across the seas—Russians, Aleuts, Eskimos, and mixed bloods.

In a letter from Kuskov to Baranov dated October 7, 1813,… a group of Indians to the north of Fort Ross are called the "Wallalakh." This corresponds closely to the Kashaya name for an early Indian settlement at the mouth of the Gualala River, the site of the modern town of Gualala: /qʰawála·li/ and its clipped alternant /walá·li/ 'water coming down place, Rivermouth.' /qʰa/ 'water' + /wa/ 'comes' + /la·/ 'down' + /li/ 'place.' The evidence of the very early occurrence of Wallalakh is important for the etymology of Gualala, for it far antedates any use of Valhalla, believed by many to be the prototype of the modern name. Gualala is pronounced [wəlálə]; the spelling with a "G" is a mistaken Hispanicization of an earlier English form Walalla…. Kuskov seems to have been using a term acquired from the Alaskan hunters at Fort Ross, as the **-kh** of Wallalakh...

—Oswalt, *Kashaya Texts*, p. 8

In native parlance, Achomawi is the name only of that part of the group living in the basin of Fall River. For what ethnologists call the Achomawi, the Atsugewi generic term Pomarii, which denotes all the people speaking the same language—the Hamawi, Atuami, Ilmawi, and others, as well as the Achomawi proper—would therefore have been a more appropriate designation. But Achomawi is so well rooted that a new term would cause confusion. The universal local denomination "Pit Rivers" is appropriate even if it is inelegant and without native flavor.

—Kroeber, *Handbook of the Indians of California*, pp. 307-308

but rather a descriptive term for any group with whom the Wintu had hostile relations. It was the Americans who redefined it as a tribal name.)

A great many names originally referred only to one village, and later got extended to a larger grouping. "Achumawi" is a native term for "river people." Originally, it was used to refer only to the Fall River group, but later historians and anthropologists extended it to include all who speak closely related dialects of the same language. To illustrate the complexity and potential for confusion found in tribal names in California, Shirley Silver provides the following discussion of "Pit River":

The term "Pit River" can be used to refer to all eleven bands that live in the Pit River area as the river flows westward from the northeastern corner of Modoc County down into Lassen County and on to the Montgomery Creek area.

Two of the eleven bands are known in the anthropological/linguistic literature by the cover term "Atsugewi," which is derived from the Indian language name for the area in which one of the bands lived. That band is known in English as the Hat Creek people: the other band, the Dixie Valley people. Politically, the Hat Creeks and Dixie Valleys are often locally referred to as "Pit Rivers," a term used to also designate the other nine bands along the Pit River. These nine bands are grouped under the cover term "Achumawi" in the anthropological/linguistic literature. This term is based upon the word for "river" in the language shared by the nine bands. However, from the perspective of most of the members of these bands the term "Achumawi" refers only to those Indians whose traditional territory was located around what is now the town of Fall River Mills.

The nine bands fall into two major dialect groups which more or less correlate with distinctive differences in physical environment and traditional cultural orientation. The upriver bands include: The Goose Lake people (Hewisedawi), the Alturas people (Kosalektawi), the Likely people (Hammawi) and the Canby people (Astariwawi). The terms in parentheses are anglicizations used in the anthropological literature. The downriver bands include: The Big Valley people (Atwansini), the Fall River Mills people (Ajumawi), the Goose Valley people (Ilmawi), the Montgomery Creek people (Madesi) and the Big Bend people (Itsatawi).

In addition to these major band determinations, there are also designations which refer to minor subgroups at the boundaries between the major groups (e.g., the people from Stonecoal Valley or the Ash Valley people.) And of course, the terms "upriver" and "downriver" can be used relative to the immediate location of the speaker—so a person from Goose Valley, for example, might refer to someone from Adin, which is in Big Valley, as "upriver."

The moral of this story is, of course, that today's local usage by Indian people more closely represents the "indigenous" perspective than does the terminology used by scholars—also, this usage reflects the pre- and early contact situation more accurately than the scholarly terminology.

It is sometimes to the benefit of a group to use the anthropological/ linguistic designations—for example, when dealing with the U.S. government re land claims. And sometimes, the localized usages are more advantageous—for example, because of the demands of internal group politics. To my mind, the problem is with the scholars—because we insist on static, discrete labelling. (Shirley Silver, personal communication, 1993)

The Wiyot used to be divided into three separate political groups, which were known as **patəwát, wikí,** and **wíyat.** The latter was the native name of the Eel River delta, and applied only to the people who lived there. It was later extended by anthropologists to the entire linguistic group. "Nomlaki" is a River Nomlaki name meaning "west language," referring to the Hill Nomlaki on Thomes Creek. The name "Chumash" was arbitrarily chosen by record-makers from among the names that a dozen or so politically separate groups had for themselves. "Chumash" was a Coastal Chumash word for Santa Cruz Island and its inhabitants.

> The only general names applied to people by the Miwok were terms
> formed upon the names of the cardinal points. Examples of such names
> are: ta'mūlekō, northerners, from ta'man or tama'lin, north; hī'sōtoko,
> easterners, from hī'sūm, east; tcū'metoko, southerners, from tcū'metc,
> south; and olowītoko, westerners, from olo'win, west.
>
> —Barrett, *The Geography and Dialects of the Miwok Indians*, p. 341

Some other groups whose names come from single village sites
include the Cahto (a Northern Pomo name for an important village,
meaning "Lake"; the Cahto themselves are speakers of an Athabascan
language, completely unrelated to the Pomo); and the Esselen, where a
major village name was extended to the whole linguistic group by the
Spanish. Pomo was the name of a village on the east fork of the Russian
River, meaning "At Red Earth Hole"; but Kroeber notes that most place
names in Pomo languages ended with the word **-pomo** or **-poma**, which
must mean "town"; he cites the names Buldam-pomo, Dapishul-pomo,
Sedam-pomo, Shanel-pomo, and even, for Red Earth Hole, Pomo-pomo
(Kroeber 1925, 227-228).

A number of names were given by the Spanish. "Costanoan" is the
linguistic term for the Ohlone languages, from a Spanish term meaning
"coast people." "Salinan" was so named because of that group's location
on the Salinas River ("salinas" means "salt mines"). The Gabrielinos,
Luiseños and Diegueños all got their names from the Spanish missions
that governed their territories. The Serranos have their name from the
Spanish term for "mountaineer" or "highlander." The Cupeños were
named from a native place name, **kúpa** (now called Warner's Ranch), to
which the Spanish ending -eño was added. Further north, "Wappo" is
believed to be from the Spanish word *guapo*, "harsh, severe; daring,
brave; handsome, showy." In the *Handbook of the Indians of California*,
Kroeber says this was a "sobriquet which they earned in Mission times
by their stubborn resistance to the military adjuncts of the Franciscan
establishments." (Kroeber 1925, 217). The Wappo used to call themselves
ʔonaʔcátis, "the people who speak plainly and truthfully."

A few tribes have always been known by their own names for
themselves, such as the Mojave. In recent years, some California tribes

have made an effort to make official their own names for themselves. The terms "Ipai" and "Tipai" (meaning "people") and "Kumeyaay" are self-designations that replace the Spanish cover term "Diegueño." The term "Yuma," which was first recorded in Spanish, was probably a borrowing from Pima-Papago for the Quechan. The name "Quechan" was the tribe's own name for themselves, meaning "those who descended," referring to the creation tale. The tribal council has now officially adopted the term Quechan, and encourages its usage by others. Similar action has been taken by the Tongva and Ajachmem, who have been known in the literature as the Gabrielinos and Juaneños.

Names, as George Stewart wrote (1967), are "symbols of empire." He was talking about land names, but in the same manner, he who names a people demonstrates the dominion of his society over their definition and perhaps their future. Naming is an act of power. Not all namers are like Mastamho, who, in the tale heading up this essay, shows a different sort of leadership than that of empire builders—Mastamho led by consensus, and the ones being named had to agree before their names became official. By retaking their own names, California Indians are asserting power over their own identities, redefining themselves in their own terms.

At dawn,
Lizard took his quiver and his storage baskets.
Now he went west,
Went west across the water,
Went west up the mountain.
He put his quiver down on the ground.
He climbed up to get pinenuts.
He climbed back down.
And then he piled pine-nut cones all around the fire.
Now he worked at pounding.
He pounded the pinecones for nuts,
    That's what he did.
He picked up his storage basket,
Picked up still another basket,
And now he gathered up the nuts.
He took them up in his hands.
A great sound descended.

—Hinton, *Ishi's Tale of Lizard*, p. 22

16

A Pinenut By Any Other Name...

Juliet was wrong about roses. A rose by any other name does not always smell as sweet. A name confers meanings on the named that are not inherent, but derive from the minds of its namers. The horribly-named "Digger pine" (*Pinus sabiniana*) is a case in point. *Sabiniana* is a lanky pine, usually taller than most of the vegetation that shares its habitat, distinguished from other pines by a tendency to branch, and to lean out at odd angles from hillsides. It grows in dry foothill regions of central California. This species and the pinyon (whose territory does not overlap with *sabiniana*) are the most important food-giving conifers. They bear the largest, most accessible, and most flavorful nuts of any pine (although some people prefer the sugar pine). In its region, *sabiniana* used to be second only to the acorn in culinary importance. Besides the nuts themselves, the soft core of the green pine cones could be eaten, and the young buds, interior bark and resin also provided food. It was probably the pine nuts of *sabiniana* that Lizard collected in the tale excerpted opposite this page. And it may have been *sabiniana*, along with the heroism of Native Californians, that saved the life of one William Eddy, a member of the ill-fated Donner Party, in 1846. A group snowshoed out of the starving camp at Lake Donner in December, getting lost for weeks in the rugged canyons of the western Sierra, and losing many of their party to starvation and cold along the way. When they could find it, they ate grass; there was nothing else. After nearly three weeks, the survivors stumbled into an Indian village in the foothill region. The people of the village came to the aid of the emaciated wanderers and immediately gave them food, but Eddy was on the point of death, and could not even keep down the acorn bread that was provided him. For several more days, the party was led from village to village, with Eddy being carried or supported all the way by his hosts. Finally on the morning of January 17 someone was able to find the cure:

The chief of the village managed with great difficulty to gather a large

handful of pinenuts, which he gave to Eddy. These seemed to supply
some deficiency in his body, so that on eating them he felt wonderfully
refreshed. His courage and energy revived, and he became the leader
instead of the laggard. He was again able to proceed without help.
(Stewart 1936, 125)

The *Oxford English Dictionary* cites this 1837 passage from Washington
Irving's *Captain Bonneville II* as the earliest published reference to
"Digger Indians":

Sometimes the Diggers aspire to nobler game, and succeed in
entrapping the antelope.

The "Digger pine" is so named, of course, because it was the "Digger
Indians" that utilized the nuts. It would seem appropriate that this
wonderful tree, bearing some of the richest nutrition in the plant world,
should be named in honor of the people who pioneered its use. Unfortu-
nately, the name does no honor, but instead denigrates the Native
Californians. The term "Digger" is rooted deep in the soil of racial
prejudice. Early references to Native Americans by this term are all
either blatantly or subtly derogatory. Here is an 1848 passage from
Blackwood's magazine:

They came upon a band of miserable Indians, who, from the fact of
their subsisting chiefly on roots, are called the diggers.

Around the same time, the term was also showing up in the diaries of
early wagon train migrants on their way to California. A diarist for the
Stevens Party in 1844, no doubt using a term that had already been
around for a number of years, applied the name "Digger" to Native
Americans encountered on the trail in what is now Nevada. The travel-
ers had no curiosity about the richness and diversity of the myriad
cultures they beheld, and held all Great Basin and California tribes in
contempt: "They were not really warriors at all; they fought in self-
defense, and had no interest in counting coup or taking scalps. They had
neither guns nor horses" (Stewart 1962, 93). Such an indictment!

It is strange that the migrants disrespected the Indians for digging for

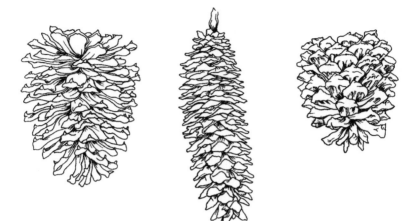

From left: cones of ponderosa pine (Pinus ponderosa), *sugar pine* (Pinus lambertiana) *and gray pine* (Pinus sabiniana).

roots, since the migrants themselves dug for roots regularly along the trail. And, it was the maligned roots, provided through the generosity of another unnamed Native Californian, that fed still another of the starving members of the Donner Party.

> Then one day he was amazed to see a solitary Indian walking along from the direction of the lake, carrying a heavy pack. He seemed not to feel the slightest curiosity [no doubt because he had been aware of the party's presence from the moment they arrived in the mountains—LH], but as he caught sight of the white man merely gave a sign for him to keep distance. Then he took from the pack half a dozen fibrous roots, laid them on the snow, and went on his way. When he had gone as mysteriously as he had come, Breen went up and took the roots. They were shaped like onions, and tasted to him somewhat like a sweet potato. (Stewart [1936] 1960, 178)

To Native Californians, the term "Digger" ranks alongside the worst of racial epithets. And even though many contemporary people are unaware that the name is derogatory, there is evidence that it was originally given to the pine with full consciousness of its hateful connotations. David Douglas, the famous Scottish naturalist for whom the

Douglas fir was named, admired *Pinus sabiniana* greatly, and wrote in the early 19th century that it was a fine species for cultivation, but he mentioned that the settlers hated the pine. In 1953, Donald Culross Peattie expanded on this in his book, *A Natural History of Western Trees:*

> The tree was despised by the white settlers. Their thinking apparently ran something like this: the Digger Indian, a contemptuous name by which the pioneers inaccurately lumped all California tribes together, used the tree as food. What is good for an Indian is beneath notice for a white man. Ergo, the tree merited about the same respect as the Indians, who were dispossessed, when not enslaved, beaten, or killed. (Peattie 1953, 94)

The tree and its nut still lack public respect, while the nut of a better-named relative, the pinyon pine, has become a popular part of present-day California cuisine. Perhaps its shaming name is part of the reason for this disrespect.

Native Americans are openly questioning racist terms now, and this is having an important impact on public opinion. In response to the Native American outcry about racial epithets used to name sports teams, the Portland newspaper *The Oregonian* has recently stated that it will no

---

A few Native Californian names for *Pinus sabiniana*

Achumawi	**tujhalo**
Chimariko	**hatcho**
Karuk	**axyúsip**
Klamath	**gapga**
Maidu	**towáni**
Mono	**tunah**
Patwin	**tuwa**
	sanak (*sabiniana* pinenut)
South Sierra Miwok	**sakky**
Wappo	**náyo**
Wintu	**xisi** (unripe *sabiniana* pinenut)
	chati (ripe *sabiniana* pinenut)
Yana	**c'ala'i**

longer print offensive names such as "The Washington Redskins." It is time and far past time that the equally offensive term "Digger" be removed from common botanical nomenclature. This must of course be accomplished by a grass roots movement; common names are not regulated by any administrative or scientific authority; the best we can do is refuse to use a given term in print and in voice, and always use another instead.

What should *sabiniana* be called, then? Several candidates have arisen. Some people have suggested a variation on the scientific name, to call it the "Sabine pine." The name "Sabine" has a number of possible meanings. When I first heard the name *sabiniana* I thought (not knowing Latin) that it might be related to the Spanish verb *saber* "to know," and that perhaps it would give us reason to call the tree the "wise pine." But the Latin ancestor of *saber* is *sapio*, which originally meant "to taste or have flavor." That meaning would be appropriate to this flavorful pinenut—the "tasty pine" would be a truthful if not very poetic name— but *sabiniana* does not come from that verb at all. A look in the dictionary reminds us that the Sabines were a tribe in ancient Italy who were overrun and incorporated by the Romans—which would make "Sabine pine" a painfully ironic name in light of California history. As it turns out, however, the name *sabiniana* doesn't refer to the Sabines either. David Douglas named the tree himself in 1830, and he named it for Joseph Sabine, who was the secretary of the London Horticultural Society. Douglas's own admiration for *sabiniana* is described by Peattie, who preceded the paragraph below with a description of the tree's poor reputation:

> So it may seem surprising that David Douglas, the first discoverer of this tree, should have described it as "a noble new species" and "one of the most beautiful objects in nature," and that in sending it to Joseph Sabine, secretary of the London Horticultural Society, in whose honor he named it, he should have ventured to express the hope that in English gardens the Digger Pine would "exist and flourish when we shall cease to be, when we shall be gone forever." (Peattie 1950, 93)

The needles on *sabiniana* are distinctively grayish, making it stand out from the other greener plant life around it. Once while I was driving in *sabiniana* country and thinking about the naming problem, I decided that from that time on I would call it the "gray pine." It turns out that this is such an obvious name that many people have independently come up with the same idea. This name, "grayleaf pine," and "bull pine" are listed in Peattie's book as alternative common names for *sabiniana*. Someone mentioned to me another common name, "ghost pine." While Peattie does not mention this common name, he does refer to ghosts in his description of the tree, which he says is so sparse of needles that it has been described as "the tree that you can see right through." He goes on to say:

> It springs now on hillsides which still bear the scars of the mad rush for gold and encroaches upon the old graveyards of the Argonauts. If indeed you "can see through" this tree, it is ghosts that you see. (Peattie 1953, 93)

Yet another possibility would be to call the tree by a name originally given to it in any of the Native Californian languages (see page 168). A name like "Towani pine" or "Nayo pine" would sound especially lovely.

But whatever choice any of us make, let it be anything but the old name, given as a name of hate in a dark period of our history. Juliet was wrong about roses. They would not smell as sweet to us if they were named with a racial epithet.

Afterword

The new version of the most important California botanical reference, *The Jepson Manual: Higher Plants of California*, has just been published (Hickman 1993). Originally published in 1925, this has long been the standard source for native plants, and now contains references to 8,000 varieties of plants indigenous to California—twice the number identified in the original manual. This tome will set the standard for future plant terminology for the state. The editors of the new edition recommend these two common names: "gray pine" and "foothill pine," adding, "the common name digger pine is pejorative in origin, so best avoided."

Several plant names that contain the derogatory word "squaw" have also been left out of the new version, replaced by non-pejorative common names. The manual no longer shows the common name "squaw bush" for *Rhus trilobata*, listing only its other common name, "skunk brush." Also expunged was "squaw mat" for *Ceanothus prostratus*, in favor of "Mahala mat." Some of the "squaw" words still remain, however: no longer listed in the index but still in the text is "squaw waterweed" (*Baccharis sergiloides*), also known as "desert Baccharis." And "squawroot" (*Apiaceae perideridia*) remains in both the index and the text, along with its other common name, "yampah." (The word "squaw," by the way, comes from a perfectly nice Algonquian word for "woman"; it only became derogatory after being borrowed into English.)

In government-run schools, young women were trained to weave lace instead of baskets, and to speak English over their own languages. 1904 photo of Luiseño students by Edward H. Davis, courtesy of the National Museum of the American Indian.

17

Languages Under Attack

During the first part of this century, Indian schools saw as part of their charge not just the teaching of English to their students, but also the forced eradication of their native languages, backed up by severe corporal punishment. It was not just Native Americans who suffered from this policy: this was part of an overall policy against "foreign languages" that the United States government adopted during World War I, and its reverberations are still with us today. The psychological devastation of children whose first language was not English had a fearsome impact on their lives and on the languages of their heritage.

There are in fact good reasons for people to give up a language in favor of another, and this choice is made all the time, all around the world. In our country, immigrants and indigenous minorities alike make conscious decisions to teach their children only English, hoping to give them a head start on social and economic assimilation to the American mainstream. Parents who decide not to teach the family language to their children do so out of love, to keep their children from suffering. Nor do parents who try to teach their children their language of heritage always succeed in doing so. In this environment where English is so dominant in daily life, teaching another language in the home is challenged by many factors—television, playmates, older siblings who have developed English-speaking habits. Children often reject their family language at school age, if not before, when they realize that it separates them from their classmates. It often takes only a single incident of being teased to make a child refuse to speak anything but English from then on.

There is no doubt that English fluency is an essential part of life in America. But that doesn't mean that people cannot know other languages as well. Bilingualism, we now know, is not only a very normal skill in most of the world, but seems to be beneficial to the intellectual development of an individual. If we can succeed in making our children bilingual, they have many more choices open to them in life. And people who have not learned their language of heritage often come to feel a

Elsie Allen, 1981. Photo by Scott M. Patterson.

great sense of loss as adults, believing that their ability to express their cultural identity has been denied them.

The point here is not that people ought to speak their language of heritage, but rather that they ought to have a choice. The schools and government policies of the first half of this century denied them that choice and robbed a generation of the right to feel pride in their language and culture.

Following are excerpts from the personal memories of two Pomo women about their school days in northern California. Native American children were forced into very hard choices by the language policies of the schools. As the narratives show, one woman chose to reject her language and, so that they would not suffer in school as she had, she never taught it to her children. The other woman rejected school instead, quitting out of a sense of loyalty to her language. Virtually all Native American children of that generation had to make the same painful choices.

The excerpts are from tapes made in 1987 for an oral history documentary of Pomoan people, "These Things That Cannot be Replaced," by Vic Bedoian and Roberta Llewellyn. The tapes aired on KPFA radio in November/December 1988. They were transcribed by Vera Mae Fredrickson, who also wrote the introduction below (Fredrickson 1989).

Introduction

Indian children were not permitted to attend public schools in California until several court cases established their rights in the 1920s. Previous to that, the elementary school age children either attended the "separate but equal" schools established on the rancherias or the government boarding schools such as the one at Covelo in Round Valley. For further education, government-run Indian boarding schools were located at Riverside, California; Chemawa, Oregon; Phoenix, Arizona; or Haskell, Kansas. The expense of maintaining the Indian grammar schools, and the eventual refusal of the children to attend such schools which had a reputation for poor facilities and teaching, finally closed down the separate but empty schools.

Elsie Allen

Elsie Allen was born in 1899 in Santa Rosa. She went to school in Hopland and to the Indian boarding school at Covelo in Round Valley, which was closed in 1957. She was well known for her basketweaving and as the author of *Pomo Basketmaking* (Naturegraph, 1971). She passed away in 1990.

"They built a Catholic church and they opened up a building for the children to go to classes—religious classes. It bothered me; those children were still all small. Here I'm big. I used to lay awake at night and think to myself, 'Why did God make me so dumb, why am I so dumb?' That's the way I felt. I have to be so big to start learning this religion. Why couldn't I know that when I was small? That always bothered me.

"When I went to school at that time [to the boarding school at Covelo] there were three girls there from Hopland. I already knew some of their language, it's a different dialect from mine. I couldn't talk the English language in the school at Covelo so I hollered at them when we lined up. Then one of the girls that was in my line reported me. They took me and strapped the heck out of me with a big leather strap. I didn't know what I got strapped for. Three days later those girls told me it was for talking the Indian language on the grounds which I'm not supposed to do.

"I was eleven years old [when I went to Covelo], and every night I cried and then I'd lay awake and think and think and think. I'd think to myself, 'If I ever get married and have children I'll *never* teach my children the language or all the Indian things that I know. I'll *never* teach them that, I don't want my children to be treated like they treated me.' That's the way I raised my children. Everybody couldn't understand that, they always asked me about it in later years. My husband has a different language. He can't understand me but I learned his language much faster. I can talk it too but I never taught my children. That's why they don't know. [My daughter] can understand it, but she can't speak the language.

"In later years I found lots of ways they could have taught me in school but they didn't. They just put me in a corner and gave me a card with a lot of holes in it and a needle and yarn. They didn't say, 'This is a needle.' I would if I was teaching, if the child didn't know. Nobody said that. Well, I guess they thought I was dumb or deaf or something. They treated me just like I was deaf and dumb. I was eleven years old, I wasn't a little kid, a baby. It should be easy to teach a person like that, but they didn't.

"How I got to school in Covelo was every year the agent of the government school came around in the fall of the year and gathered the children to take them to the school. My mother signed a paper for me to go up there. In the morning (after a two-day trip to Covelo by wagon, flat-bed railroad car, stage coach, and gravel wagon with six other children from the Hopland/Ukiah area), I just kind of stood around and watched the other girls, what they were doing and where to go. I didn't know what to say. I think I only knew two words of English, 'yes' and 'no.' I never got to ask my mother why she sent me like that when I didn't know the English language.

"I was scared, I had no one to talk to [no one spoke my dialect]. That was sure hard. I felt that if I said something or fought against how we

Girls at school in the Hoopa Valley. 1907 photo by A.L. Kroeber, courtesy of Phoebe Apperson Hearst Museum of Anthropology.

were treated, they might kill me. I cried every night. I couldn't talk to anybody or ask anybody anything because I didn't know how to. I was so dumb, that's the way I felt. They knew that I couldn't understand so nobody talked to me. I was the only one that had my language.

"I was just a year at Covelo. In June we started coming home. I was supposed to go back but when my mother saw the kind of clothes I came back with, she got mad and never wanted me to go off to school after that. After that when I wanted to go to school, she said I wasn't treated right. She claimed I was just skin and bones and with ugly clothes— boys' shoes, I was wearing.

"When I was thirteen they opened a school on the Hopland Rancheria. I got a job as a janitor. The teacher was kind of goofy, there was something wrong with her mind. My stepfather was a trustee. He talked to the people in town and they changed her. Another teacher

Frances Jack, 1982. Photo by Scott Patterson.

came and she said, 'You can sweep the floor and be the janitor, but you can go to school too.' That's how I happened to go to school a little bit. I went to about the third grade, just on account of that new teacher."

Frances Jack

Frances Jack, born in 1912, was very active in the schools, in community activities and in the tribal status issues of the Hopland Band of Pomo Indians. She passed away in 1993.

"I must have been about six years old when I started to go to school. My father and my aunt's father, they got together and decided they were going to take a portion of my aunt's lot and my father's lot and give it so they can build a school, so that I can have a short distance to go to school. It was a pretty good-sized building, and it was always full. That was first to eighth, all in one room with one teacher.

"I liked it at first; then later on I didn't care for it. It had to do with one teacher. I talked my mother and father's language, and when I went to school the first thing they told me was, 'No, no, no.' Maybe it was the government that said to stop the kids from talking their language in school. So she told me that anytime anyone speaks their language, their Indian language in the schoolyard, they were going to be punished. And the kids—I guess maybe she gave them something to tattle—she told me, 'You spoke Indian language in back of the school; I heard about it and now you have to go into that little room.' There I would be strapped. Well, I just couldn't help it; I talked my language. Others did too, but so that nobody heard them. One kid would always hang around, so that he could tell on us. Maybe he got candy or something.

"Anyway the last thing that woman did to me is the thing that made me rebel. I was still six years old. Because I got punishment more than the other kids, she was going to use me as an example. She brought me out there in front of all the class—eighth graders and like that, big kids—and she lifted my skirt and strapped me. She made some marks on my back. I never told my mother, and then one time she was helping me dress and she saw that. She asked me what happened. I didn't want to tell her, but I had to. Then she said, 'Well, that's what you're going to school for, to learn what the teacher tells you to do. Why can't you learn to do it that way?' I already had it in my mind that I wasn't going to quit talking my language. I told her that. I said, 'Why is our language bad? Is it bad what you and my father talk? Or other people talk? Is it bad? Why do you people talk it then?'

"So I said I don't want to quit talking my language. So in school I said the same thing. But nobody heard me talk the Indian language in school from that time on. But in my mind [I thought] whenever I get a chance to get out of that school, then nobody's going to stop me. And that's the way it was. I didn't finish school here; a fifth grade dropout. I didn't want to go to school any more."

18

The Native American Languages Act

Who says we can't have an impact on our society? A small group of Native American educators and linguists got together a few years ago to try to influence public policy on Native American languages, with the result that an exciting bill was passed by both houses of Congress and signed into law by President Bush. Basically, the law states that it is the policy of the United States to preserve, protect, and promote the rights and freedom of Native Americans to use, practice, and develop Native American languages. The law recognizes the right of Native Americans to use their traditional languages as a medium of instruction in the schools, recognizes the rights of Indian tribes to give official status to their Native American languages for conducting their own business, and encourages all educational institutions to allow the same academic credit for proficiency in Native American languages as for proficiency in foreign languages.

Is this the same government that used to run schools where children were beaten for speaking their language? It is hard to say what sort of impact a law like this will have, for it is largely symbolic, but at least, for the very first time, the government has officially recognized the right of Native American languages to exist.

To understand the social attitudes and events that led to this law, we must look at United States language policy in historical perspective, back to the turn of the century. Native California and the rest of our country emerged from a long period of warfare and attempted genocide against American Indians by Euro-Americans into a more peaceable era, but one where Native Americans experienced social and legal oppression by the government. It was determined that Indians should be assimilated as quickly as possible into mainstream American society, which meant they must be socialized to give up their traditional ways of life, including their languages.

Indian language policy of the early twentieth century was also shaped by philosophical tenets that developed in the United States from two events that had nothing to do with the Indians: the giant wave of recent immigration from Europe, and World War I. Americans felt threatened by the influx of foreigners, and the war increased their sense of hatred toward newcomers. Theodore Roosevelt gave a speech in 1917, during World War I, which expressed the cultural and language attitudes of the times:

> We Americans are the children of the crucible. It has been our boast that out of the crucible, the melting pot of life in this free land, all the men and women of all the nations who come hither emerge as Americans and as nothing else....
>
> The crucible must melt all who are cast in it; it must turn them out in one American mold; and this must be the mold shaped 140 years ago by the men who under Washington founded this as a free nation, separate from all others....
>
> We must have but one flag. *We must also have but one language* [emphasis added]. That must be the language of the Declaration of Independence, of Washington's farewell address, of Lincoln's Gettysburg speech and second inaugural.... (*Annals of America* 1968, 14:129)

During this era, which supplanted a time of relative linguistic freedom and tolerance in the United States, many new laws were passed against the use of languages other than English in schools and elsewhere. There was even one law on the books in the Midwest that made it illegal to use a foreign language over the telephone. To make matters worse, during the twenties the I.Q. test was developed, and a battery of faulty, poorly designed research projects seemed to show that speaking two languages was correlated with low intelligence. (Whether bilingualism was the cause or the result of low I.Q. was a matter of debate in those days!)

This, then, was the mood of the times when the Bureau of Indian Affairs schools established their policy of punishing Indian children who spoke their language. Generations of Native Americans were made to suffer corporal abuse whenever they dared use a word of the language of their heritage.

But in the late fifties and the sixties, a new attitude toward language began to develop in the United States. The Civil Rights Movement led to increased protection under the law for all races, and this relatively benign atmosphere, combined with the aftermath of the Vietnam War, resulted also in liberalized immigration laws. In the meantime, new psychological research refuted the earlier findings about the negative effect of bilingualism on I.Q., and in fact discovered the opposite—that bilingualism actually has a beneficial cognitive effect. Then in 1974 came a key Supreme Court decision, *Lau* v. *Nichols*, which said that children have the right to an education in their native language if they do not know English. The new idea that people have the right to speak their language of heritage spelled the end of the old BIA school policies.

But the liberal attitudes that gained ground in the sixties and seventies were countered by a conservative backlash in the eighties. S.I. Hayakawa led the "Official English" movement, and established the U.S. English committee, with the motto "One Flag, One Language." Due to Hayakawa's influence, English became the official language of California during those years. Probably few if any of the backers of English as the official language thought about Native American languages at all; they were more concerned with the influx of immigrants and, especially, the growing number of native speakers of Spanish in the United States. Nevertheless, Native Americans stood a big chance of losing their language rights to this conservative political movement, and one clearly visible result of the backlash was that bilingual education funds were being cut, and many Native American language programs that were funded by Title VII (Bilingual Education) were terminated.

A number of Native Americans and other people concerned with Native American language rights began to fear that if Hayakawa and his friends succeeded in making English the official language of the United States, Indian languages might be doomed. Action seemed necessary to define Native American languages as having special status in our country, in order to protect them from this backlash.

Here is how it happened. In June 1988, a group of people met at a conference in Tempe, Arizona, and wrote the first version of the resolution. Present were Kathryn S. Begaye (Navajo), Paul Platero (Navajo), Lucille J. Watahomigie (Hualapai), Ofelia Zepeda (Tohono O'odham), Elizabeth Brandt, Sandra Johnson, William Leap, Teresa McCarty, Casey A. Nagy, William Wilson, and Akira Yamamoto. After they wrote it, they sent copies of the resolution to the Senate Committee on Indian Affairs, chaired by Senator Daniel Inouye. Senator Inouye introduced the resolution to Congress in September 1988, and it was referred to his committee for revisions. In April 1990 the bill was incorporated into a larger act, H.R. 5040: the Tribally Controlled Community College Assistance Act. On October 11, 1990 it was passed by the Senate; and the very next day, the House. President Bush signed it into law on October 30, 1990.

Here are the most important excerpts from the Native American Languages Act, which was included in Public Law 101-477:

Findings

Sec. 102. The Congress finds that—

(1) the status of the cultures and languages of Native Americans is unique and the United States has the responsibility to act together with Native Americans to ensure the survival of these unique cultures and languages;

(2) special status is accorded Native Americans in the United States, a status that recognizes distinct cultural and political rights, including the right to continue separate identities;

(3) the traditional languages of Native Americans are an integral part of their cultures and identities and form the basic medium for the transmission, and thus survival, of Native American cultures, literatures, histories, religions, political institutions, and values;

(4) there is a widespread practice of treating Native American languages as if they were anachronisms;

(5) there is a lack of clear, comprehensive, and consistent Federal policy on treatment of Native American languages which has often resulted in acts of suppression and extermination of Native American languages and cultures;

(6) there is convincing evidence that student achievement and performance, community and school pride, and educational opportunity is clearly and directly tied to respect for, and support of, the first language of the child or student;

(7) it is clearly in the interests of the United States, individual States, and territories to encourage the full academic and human potential achievements of all students and citizens and to take steps to realize these ends;

(8) acts of suppression and extermination directed against Native American languages and cultures are in conflict with the United States policy of self-determination for Native Americans;

(9) languages are the means of communication for the full range of human experiences and are critical to the survival of cultural and political integrity of any people; and

(10) language provides a direct and powerful means of promoting international communication by people who share languages.

Declaration of Policy

Sec. 104. It is the policy of the United States to—

(1) preserve, protect, and promote the rights and freedom of Native Americans to use, practice, and develop Native American languages;

(2) allow exceptions to teacher certification requirements for Federal programs, and programs funded in whole or in part by the Federal Government, for instruction in Native American languages when such teacher certification requirements hinder the employment of qualified teachers who teach in Native American languages, and to encourage State and territorial governments to make similar exceptions;

(3) encourage and support the use of Native American languages as a medium of instruction in order to encourage and support—

(A) Native American language survival,

(B) educational opportunity,

(C) increased student success and performance,

(D) increased student awareness and knowledge of their culture and history, and

(E) increased student and community pride;

(4) encourage State and local education programs to work with Native American parents, educators, Indian tribes, and other Native American governing bodies in the implementation of programs to put this policy into effect;

(5) recognize the right of Indian tribes and other Native American governing bodies to use the Native American languages as a medium of instruction in all schools funded by the Secretary of the Interior;

(6) fully recognize the inherent right of Indian tribes and other Native American governing bodies, States, territories, and possessions of the United States to take action on, and give official status to, their Native American languages for the purpose of conducting their own business;

(7) support the granting of comparable proficiency achieved through

course work in a Native American language the same academic credit as comparable proficiency achieved through course work in a foreign language, with recognition of such Native American language proficiency by institutions of higher education as fulfilling foreign language entrance or degree requirements; and

(8) encourage all institutions of elementary, secondary and higher education, where appropriate, to include Native American languages in the curriculum in the same manner as foreign languages and to grant proficiency in Native American languages the same full academic credit as proficiency in foreign languages.

No restrictions

Sec. 105. The right of Native Americans to express themselves through the use of Native American languages shall not be restricted in any public proceeding, including publicly supported education programs.

Evaluations

Sec. 106.

(a) The president shall direct the heads of the various Federal departments, agencies, and instrumentalities to—

(1) evaluate their policies and procedures in consultation with Indian tribes and other Native American governing bodies as well as traditional leaders and educators in order to determine and implement changes needed to bring the policies and procedures into compliance with the provisions of this title;

(2) give the greatest effect possible in making such evaluations, absent a clear specific Federal statutory requirement to the contrary, to the policies and procedures which will give the broadest effect to the provisions of this title; and

(3) evaluate the laws which they administer and make recommendations to the President on amendments needed to bring such laws into compliance with the provisions of this title.

(b) By no later than the date that is one year after the date of enactment of this title, the President shall submit to the Congress a report containing recommendations for amendments to Federal laws that are needed to bring such laws into compliance with the provisions of this title.

Use of English

Sec. 107. Nothing in this title shall be construed as precluding the use of Federal funds to teach English to Native Americans.

The Native American Languages Act of 1990 did not include funding provisions. However, a new bill, the "Native American Languages Act of 1992" (S. 2044), was passed by both houses and signed into law by President Bush in November 1992. It amends the Native American Programs Act of 1974 with a new section that establishes a grant program to assure the survival and continuing vitality of Native American languages. The specific purposes for which grants will be awarded include:

(1) the establishment and support of community language programs to bring older and younger Native Americans together to facilitate and encourage the transfer of language skills from one generation to another;

(2) the establishment of programs to train Native Americans to teach native languages to others or to enable them to serve as interpreters or translators;

(3) the development, printing and dissemination of materials to be used for the teaching and enhancement of Native American languages;

(4) the establishment or support of programs to train Native Americans to produce or participate in television or radio programs to be broadcast in their native languages;

(5) the compilation, transcription, and analysis of oral testimony to record and preserve Native American languages;

(6) the purchase of equipment (including audio and video recording equipment, computers, and software) required for the conducting of language programs.

Funding allocated by Congress to pay for this grant program is expected to be available soon. This will be very helpful in the quest of Native Californians to keep their languages alive.

PART V

Keeping the Languages Alive

At some point I realized that I had to look at things and understand things through the language—because the language defines the way we relate to things. And for myself being raised away from that, it was, and has been until the very recent past, difficult for me to understand why the people that were raised on the reservation were not getting that knowledge. So you have to look back at the past and figure out how it is that we have been separated as tribal peoples from our languages. It has a lot to do with the policies that have been set upon us by the federal government, that have tried to separate the people from the ideas that make up their world view. And as time goes by, little bits of that world view just kind of disappear, just kind of fall off and are lost. And as those things are lost, we can see problems of alcoholism and family dysfunction, problems that I think a lot of tribes have experienced. The strength of the value system that we pass on through the language is not there any more.

Then about five years ago I found myself becoming involved, working with a group of elders to try to restore that knowledge and that point of view that is ours—and we start off with the language.

And as I become more aware of the ideas that language represents, and the values and the value system that language offers, I also become more aware of the conflicts between that point of view and the way the modern world works. I teach language classes, and when I look at the students in there, I have to think about what it is that we're giving them. We're trying to give them a language that will identify and allow them to think in certain values and certain lifeways that are important to our people. At the same time we have to take into account how they will fit into the modern world. A lot of change has taken place. But ultimately I believe that our language and that value system have more to offer, have more to offer than all the enticements of the modern world.

...When I go into the classroom, sometimes I look at the kids that I'm teaching, and I see the potential, and I see the desire that they have, and it's like I'm holding this very fragile, precious thing in my hand.

—Parris Butler (Mojave), Chair of the Advocates
for Indigenous California Language Survival,
at a training workshop for the Master-Apprentice
Language Learning Program, June 1993.

A recent article sounded the alarm, not just for California Indian languages, but for endangered languages all over the world. The authors point out that while language extinction has been a fact of life throughout human history, it has taken on a different scale and character in recent centuries:

> From what I have been able to learn, based on the model of early-modern and contemporary hunting and gathering and mobile agricultural peoples, the process of language loss throughout most of human history, i.e. the period prior to the development of large states and empires, has been attended by a period of grammatical merger in situations of multilingualism, in geographically confined areas, and among quite small communities.... By contrast, language loss in the modern period is of a different character, in its extent and in its implications. It is part of a much larger process of *loss of cultural and intellectual diversity* in which politically dominant languages and cultures simply overwhelm indigenous local languages and cultures, placing them in a condition which can only be described as embattled. (Hale et al. 1992, 1)

And yet, it would be nothing short of paternalistic to try to make the decision for people that their language should survive. To quote an example from Africa in Peter Ladefoged's response to Hale et al.:

> Last summer I was working on Dahalo, a rapidly dying Cushitic language, spoken by a few hundred people in a rural district of Kenya. I asked one of our consultants whether his teen-aged sons spoke Dahalo. "No," he said. "They can still hear it, but they cannot speak it. They speak only Swahili." He was smiling when he said it, and did not seem to regret it. He was proud that his sons had been to school, and knew things that he did not. Who am I to say that he was wrong? (Ladefoged 1992, 811)

What if the communities feel it is time to leave their languages behind? Why should they retain traditions that seem so divorced from mainstream modern society? Is there really any place for California Indian languages and cultures today in people's lives?

These are questions that every individual or community must answer for itself. Certainly if the California Indian languages survive in any way other than in university archives, it will only be because Indian communities want them to survive. And in fact, many Indian communities want very much to maintain or restore their languages and cultures. As Parris Butler so eloquently states above, language embodies and expresses culture, and values, and social identity. Language loss is much more than the loss of an arbitrary set of vocabulary items; it symbolizes and embodies the loss of a whole world view.

It is now the goal of many Native Californian individuals and communities to embrace a multi-cultural identity—to be at home in both general American culture and in the Native American culture of their heritage; and to be at home speaking two languages. Understanding and reconciling two different cultures is a challenging task. There are many good reasons why people choose to undertake it.

Yet as we have seen from the beginning of this book, there are few native speakers left of any California Indian languages. The trend toward an acceptance of bilingualism—newly tolerated now by the government—may be coming too late for the California languages.

There are many people working to save the languages of California, through documentation or through learning and teaching. The final section of this book describes some of the efforts people are making to this end. First we look at documentation. Anthropologists and linguists have worked to preserve as much as possible of California Indian languages since the 19th century. We begin the section with a short biography and analysis of the impact of the most colorful and dedicated linguist of all—John Peabody Harrington, who labored earlier in this century to preserve on paper and audio recordings the languages of the West, and most especially California.

The most valuable tool for preserving languages has been writing. With that in mind I next present a history of the writing of California languages, beginning with pre-Columbian forms of rock writing and ending with modern practical writing systems used by different tribes.

Preserving records of language is of course not at all the same as having a population of speakers. Native Californians concerned about language loss see the development of new generations of speakers as the goal. In California, there are no young native speakers; the only way to keep the languages alive now is through the development of programs to teach the languages in the schools, or in the community. In Chapter 21 I introduce the readers to some of the Native Californian language activists at work today—people working in their communities or on their own to teach their languages or to learn them themselves. This new interest in revitalizing languages is part of a general renaissance of Native Californian culture, of singing, basket-making and other traditional skills, ceremonialism, and spirituality.

Finally, Chapter 22 talks about an exciting new language program that is taking place as I write, where committed young Native Californian adults are learning their languages through an intensive program with elder native speakers. It is through the efforts of the dedicated people discussed in Chapters 21 and 22 that the languages of California have their best chance of survival.

*John P. Harrington. Photo courtesy of Santa Barbara Museum of
Natural History.*

19

Ashes, Ashes

John Peabody Harrington—
Then and Now

Angry god, perfectionist, paranoid worrier, culture hero, obsessed genius, thorn-in-the-side, doggerel poet, ruthless slavedriver, inattentive father, valued friend, skinflint, ascetic, academic outcast, great phonetician, indefatigable field worker, outrageous, laughable and endearing eccentric—these are all views of J.P. Harrington, one of the most important linguists in California history.

Harrington was a Californian from birth, educated at Stanford University (B.A. 1905) and the universities of California, Leipzig and Berlin, and later in life given an honorary degree from the University of Southern California. An undergraduate summer session at the University of California at Berkeley taught by A.L. Kroeber and Pliny E. Goddard launched Harrington into a life of total and passionate devotion to the cause of saving dying languages by recording the last speakers. For most of his career, he worked for the Smithsonian Institution's Bureau of American Ethnology and did field work with their support until he retired in 1954. Even then he continued working on Chumash until just a few months before his death. He worked on languages all over the hemisphere, but his most extensive work was on the languages and cultures of California.

During his lifetime, Harrington collected close to a million pages of notes on more than 90 different languages, as well as numerous recordings and artifacts. Everyone agrees that he was a great phonetician, able to hear and write down the sounds he heard with great accuracy; and everyone agrees that the high quality and sheer volume of his field notes are a tremendous gift to posterity. These field notes are the only record of the nature of many languages that are now no longer spoken by a living being.

Harrington also drafted other people to his cause. One person who worked for him for some years was his teenage neighbor, Jack Marr.

Now retired as the general manager of an international engineering firm, Marr says that Harrington was a "family project," for his mother and brother also assisted Harrington many times and in many ways.

Young Jack sometimes accompanied Harrington, but more often was sent alone, to 48 different tribes in California, New Mexico, Arizona, Washington, and Alaska. At Harrington's behest, Jack got into his old car and went off for months at a time, using hand-drawn maps to search out people in the remotest areas, carrying a 150-pound "portable" aluminum disc recording machine over mountains and across rope bridges. To him it was an adventure, one that allowed him to meet people and have experiences and learn things he never would have even thought about otherwise. But he does admit that he probably enjoys thinking and talking about his work for Harrington now more than he ever enjoyed it at the time, given the frequent lack of food and warmth.

When Jack and Harrington's nephew Arthur were in college, Harrington would show up from time to time and talk them into heading off on another field trip.

> We were both going to college at the time, and Harrington would stop by and grab us and send us off, and I don't know how he did this! He really was a con artist at this. He'd grab us out of college, we'd be off for two weeks somewhere in some remote place, and then we'd have to work like the devil to recover our grades when we got back to school! It's a wonder we even got educated, except by Harrington's method. (Jack Marr, at the California Indian Conference, October 1992)

But Jack added later that he thanks God that Harrington used him that way, because of the great good that was accomplished by it. He also attributes much of his success in his own career to the excellent education in vocabulary and writing that Harrington gave him.

Jack recorded many texts on Harrington's giant recording machine, often reading a text in English and having the native speaker say it back in the native language. To date, only about a third of the 950 discs at the Smithsonian have been transferred from the old aluminum discs. Linguists Victor Golla and Geoff Gamble are now searching for grant support to transfer the rest of the discs.

It is through Harrington's letters to young Jack that we can appreciate the depth of his passion for his work:*

> ...You've been a good friend if I ever had one, you just rushed at the work. You know how I look at this work, you and I are nothing, we'll both of us soon be dust. If you can grab these dying languages before the old timers completely die off, you will be doing one of the **few** things valuable to the people of the **remote** future. You know that. The time will come and **soon** when there won't be an Indian language left in California, all the languages developed for thousands of years will be **ashes**, the house is **afire**, it is **burning**. That's why I said to go through the blinding rain, roads or no roads, that's why I thanked God when you tried to cross the Mattole River, haven't I gone back even two weeks later to find them **dead** and the language **forever dead**?... (1941)

And another:

> [There is an old saying]: He robbed the cradle. Do you know what occurs to me, Jack? What you are doing with old Kokel [Coquille Thompson, of Siletz Reservation, who was over 90 at the time, and a speaker of Coquille Athabascan] is something for the ages; you are robbing the cemetery. (1941)

At times, Harrington's letters seem almost cruel and unfeeling for individuals, so focused is his devotion to the cause of saving the languages. George Clipp, the last fluent speaker of Lower Chinook, whom Jack was sent to work with, had a stroke not long before he arrived, rendering him unable to speak. Jack wrote about this to Harrington, who wrote back:

> I have just gotten over crying, that is, partly over; this is the worst thing that ever happened to me. I would much rather have lost five thousand dollars or have been sent up for ten years... Is there **no** hope? Who is the doctor that attends him? Tell the doctor your whole story and ask him if **anything** can be done. Frachtenberg found an old lady who was sick abed and got in with her doctor and that doctor gave the old lady some asperine [sic] or

---

*   Copies of these letters were kindly provided to me by Jack Marr.

hypodermics in some way that **pepped her up** so she felt like a spring chicken again and talked and talked for days. You know a paralysed person often **gets over** the first stroke, it is the third stroke that carries them off. And between strokes they get well and sit up and talk. Some powerful pep might come as a Godsend and make him so he could talk…

Mr. Clipp did recover enough to go home, and Harrington wrote Jack to do anything in his power to force him to dictate:

Now you do just as I say… with the machine set up, let Emma [Mr. Clipp's niece] do all the talking, and tell her in advance never to argue with John [sic] Clipp, you get five dollars greenbacks ready and actually thrust them into his hands, let him keep them even if he still refuses, then Emma will just tell him to take pity on you having come so far for nothing and that **money talks**… just to take the five bucks as a **present**, and to come across even with just a few words and then rest up and then with a few more. **Just keep at the pure Chinook with him till he keeps dictating more and more, any old thing**, for he will die and what you don't get now he will die with. It is a damn lie that a lot of people have been there to try to get him to work, nobody has been there except Ray twice and… Jacobs once, and they wanted to write down on paper, which would be hard on Clipp. Have Emma tell him that what you want is something **entirely** different, just for him to talk into the mike, tell him we'll give him five dollars an hour, it'll pay all his doctor bills and his funeral and will leave his widow with a handsome jackpot. **Don't take no**. Hound the life out of him, go back again and again and again.… He'll come across, and you'll have the rarest thing on earth. And stay with it, if he turns Emma down twenty-five times, still stay with it, prove that you have the qualities of a **go-getter**, of a lawyer that will not be defeated, but who **conquers** over the most nasty obstacles that ever stood in the path of man. Don't take no… just talk your head off and stick with it. Don't take no, don't think of taking no, he has admitted he knows it and he's going to come across, just size up the whole situation and if you can't negotiate it any other way, just you and Emma pester the life out of him till he finds it easier to dictate than to not dictate and he'll do it just as the easiest way out… Now here's to you, Jack, show that you can handle the very devil of a tough proposition with **victory**. (1941)

Harrington could not be bothered with many of what he considered the small things in life—clothes, housing, even food were considered unimportant trifles. He was very much against smoking and drinking, and walked as much as possible, rather than driving. He would work 16 to 18 hours a day when circumstances allowed it. Although he was penurious and fearful of not having enough money to do his work, he nevertheless had money in bank accounts all over the country. Jack remembers that every time they went to a major city, Harrington would visit a bank where he had an account to get some cash. Apparently, he just ignored the existence of these accounts when he stopped travelling. After his death, a number of them were found, some with several thousand dollars in them.

His fanaticism was portrayed in the biographical book *Encounter with an Angry God* by Carobeth Laird, who was once married to him, and who bore their daughter, Awona. Harrington saw even his family mainly as field assistants. Right after his daughter's birth, he wrote to a colleague telling him of her arrival, and then added:

> Then I want to make the Esselen trip, in the auto, my wife going along. She knows how to drive and works hard and no roughing it is too hard for her. (Walsh 1976)

This willingness to commit the lives of all around him to his cause was a poor recipe for a marriage, and Carobeth Laird eventually left Harrington. At age 60, he began to toy around with the idea of marrying again in order to have a son who could carry on his mission. "He wanted a blonde, preferably German, very tall, as much as 6 feet, an intelligent woman who knew how to type. I believe that the final qualification was the most important." (Walsh 1976). Needless to say, Harrington never did remarry.

The people he worked with and those who worked for him sometimes railed at his fanaticism and laughed at his eccentricities, and yet they could share his vision, and saw that his goals were in large part selfless, so they accepted the tasks he put them to. He was better liked and better respected by the Indians than by academics. Academics noted that he was too obsessed with recording languages to ever publish much or make contributions to linguistic theory. As A.L. Kroeber put it in a

When he walked into the rather dim classroom on that first morning of
the summer session, my heart, already strained past endurance, seemed
about to stop. I silently and romantically exclaimed that he looked "like
an angry god." I had not hoped so soon to encounter one of those
mythical creatures, a scholar, a scientist, who was also young and
beautiful. He *was* young, although eleven years older than I. I would be
twenty in a month and he had turned thirty-one. He was tall and thin,
with an abrupt, awkward way of moving. But it was his magnificent head
and face that stirred my imagination. He had dark hair and deep blue
eyes. His splendid forehead was wrinkled into a scowl and his rather
beautiful mouth twisted petulantly. The simple fact was that he hated
teaching, particularly he hated having been inveigled or coerced into
teaching in this summer school, for very little money and at the sacrifice
of time that he might have spent coaxing half-forgotten words from an
ancient informant, someone who might well die even as he wasted time
on this inane collection of normal school aspirants and silly women who
wanted something to fill their empty days and emptier minds.

Even then he was in the grip of his grand obsession, his compulsion to
record all that could be recovered of the remnants of the cultures, and
most especially of the languages, of the Indians of Southern California.
Only here and there a single old man or old woman, worn out, discour-
aged, bewildered, clinging precariously to life, survived as the last
repository of the speech and lore of what had been, before the days of the
Spanish missions, a flourishing tribe. Universities, rich in endowments,
sent expeditions to far-off places. Those ethnologists who worked
intermittently in the California field were more interested in overall
surveys than in compiling painstaking, detailed records. It must have
seemed to this off-beat, obscure young genius that he alone perceived the
value and the transience of material that might yet be obtained.

All this I would soon learn. What I would be much slower finding out
was that he was as painfully self-conscious and as unsure of himself as I. He
needed a wise, firm and sympathetic guide, not a youthful slave and
disciple. By the time I realized this, it was too late; I was no longer interested
in the salvage of the man, only in the dissolution of the relationship. Now
that he is ten years dead and I am old, I begin to understand that in my
place a different sort of woman might—just possibly might—have helped
him to fulfill himself both as a scientist and as a human being.

—Laird, *Encounter with an Angry God*, pp. 22-23

letter to Edward Sapir, "Harrington is too wholly under the sway of an obsession ever to do more than collect…" (Golla 1984, 362).

Even Harrington's greatest talent, that of writing accurate phonetic detail, was considered to be too extreme by Kroeber, as he revealed in this letter, where he was talking about a project of Sapir's to develop a standardized phonetic alphabet:

> I should not be surprised for instance if you would have a good deal of trouble from Harrington. He is as keen and well informed on the subject as anyone in the country, but perhaps because he is a young man has shown a riotous inclination to indulge in the expressions of fine shades of sounds in the symbols used for them. (Golla 1984, 76).

Still, despite the criticism, one also reads between the lines of his letters the respect Kroeber had for Harrington's genius. Harrington once said to Jack Marr that he spoke nine different international languages, and eighteen different Native American languages, all fluently. Ernestine McGovran, whose mother Mary Yee was the last Chumash speaker and probably Harrington's closest friend in his later years, confirms part of this claim:

> … I have to go along with Jack Marr about Harrington being able to speak eighteen Indian languages; I can tell you right now he spoke Barbareño Chumash as fluently as my great-grandmother, and great-great-grand-mother, and wrote it fluently. And they [Harrington and Mary Yee] corresponded in Chumash. (Ernestine McGovran, at the California Indian Conference, October 1992)

A footnote on languages from Jack Marr:

> I have to tell you that there was one language, though. When Harrington was out in the back yard—and we had a duplex; he lived on one side and we lived on the other—my brothers and I used to torment him by getting out there and talking in Pig Latin, which was one language he did *not* understand! And I can see him now, cocking his head and looking at us with an inquisitive look. And we even talked about him. Hopefully he never knew what we were saying! (Jack Marr, at the California Indian Conference, October 1992.)

Harrington was full of fear, worry and jealousy. Despite his deep concern about getting the languages recorded, he wanted no one else to work with the speakers. He was also continually running away from summonses by the Smithsonian to come back and write up his work. For these reasons, he swore Jack Marr and his brother and mother to total secrecy about where they went and to whom they talked. Instructions from his letters reveal his passion for secrecy:

> Then drive to Mrs. C—'s. *Tell her nothing. Have no conversation with her whatever.* Then drive south… (Letter to Jack Marr, 1941)

> Be very careful about publicity. You know they can call by long distance telephone from these remote places to the newspaper office and the clipping bureau in San Francisco gets the clippings in time. Tell them that you are from Los Angeles. (Letter to Jack Marr, 1941)

> If any telegrams come to me from Monterey region, please accept them in my name just as if I were at Santa Ana, open them, and then forward what they say as a new telegram to me, sent by you to me, send the wording by a new telegram addressed to John P. Harrington, Smithsonian Inst., Washington D.C., **collect**. Do this so the people will think I am at Santa Ana, which is my official address. Please tell P——not to give my address to anybody. (Letter to Mrs. Seeley, 1937)

Harrington did everything in his power to keep other linguists from working on California languages. He once offered Bill Bright $50 to *not* work on Karuk! (Bill refused the money.) Ernestine McGovran discusses his jealousy:

> … Yes he did guard everything, and yes he was jealous, and I can see it now, because I'm becoming like that. That was his baby, the Barbareño. Yes he fought with other linguists and other interns when they came around [my mother]. Deby Beeler, who is my good friend, her husband [Madison Beeler] worked with my mother, and they worked with my mother kind of like suitors, because my mother would ship one out the back door when the other came in the front. (Ernestine McGovran, at the California Indian Conference, October 1992.)

But Ernestine, too, goes on to talk about how important Harrington was

The sample of Harrington's Salinan notes above at left illustrates some characteristics of his style: large writing (many pages have only one or two words); the use of more than one language, often in verbatim quotes from multilingual speakers; detailed transcription and commentary on the phonetics of words; and lots of extra tantalizing bits of cultural, biographical and historical information. Above right, a page from Mary Yee's notebook, with a caricature of Harrington in the corner.

to her family. Mary Yee worked with Harrington frequently during the childhood of her daughter. Ernestine thought he was boring, and Mary Yee told her that when *she* was a child and Harrington worked with *her* mother, Mary thought he was boring too! Ernestine gives this personal account of the relationship between Harrington and her family:

> Harrington worked with my great-grandmother [and grandmother and mother], so I'm fourth generation. I didn't get to work with him, but I did get to get in his way. His relationship with my family was as intimate as he was able to get. He had a close relationship with my family, and my mother nursed him right up until the end, until he couldn't get out of bed any more. So—someone made the statement that she got paid when she was working with him. But he got more than his money back, believe me, in nursing care and love.
>
> I don't work with his notes, but I can look at them and they are very

familiar to me; but I prefer to work with my mother's, because it's more of a personal entity, and everything about him is in there anyhow, because as he was writing, she was writing. All their little anecdotes and arguments and her doodling—she was an artist too, in her way—so I have the whole ball of wax right there in my hands.

He would bring things, he would send gifts, he would give my mother gifts towards the end. And so it was kind of nice to see him. I always knew I might get a couple of dollars or something to get lost. And it worked! I was able to go out and hang out at the malt shop just to stay out of their way.

My mother would always call him a cuckoo and draw a caricature of him [in her journal], because they would fight over various words, and they sometimes didn't agree. But they respected one another. (Ernestine McGovran at the California Indian Conference, October 1992.)

While Harrington sent many a box of notes back to the Smithsonian from his field work, there were many more boxes that he would store in the attics of friends or relatives and forget about. After his death in 1961, boxes of "Harringtoniana" began arriving at the Smithsonian in droves. There is *still* material coming in. The discovery of a set of about 175 baskets collected by Harrington was recently reported at San Diego State University by Margaret Langdon. When Harrington's old home in Santa Ana was sold, materials found there were given to a professor at Pepperdine University, who kept them for ten years, and then gave them to Frank Latta in Santa Cruz, who later gave them to the Santa Barbara Museum of Natural History. More materials arrived in Santa Barbara in 1983, willed by Awona Harrington. Just a few years ago, Catherine Callaghan shipped to the Smithsonian a long-missing important set of Harrington notes on Chochenyo, an Ohlone language of the San Francisco Bay Area, which she found at the University of California at Berkeley in the Survey of California and Other Indian Languages.

Catherine Callaghan was the first person to try to organize the Harrington notes at the Smithsonian. When she arrived in 1962 for a few months' worth of work on his materials, she quickly realized that the organization would take lifetimes rather than months. The materials filled portions of three warehouses, and more kept arriving—from

California, from Albuquerque—as she worked. The boxes contained notes, but also a rich store of photos, baskets, pressed plants, and even a desiccated half-eaten sandwich or two. Callaghan writes:

> I found a blasting cap in the first warehouse. When I discovered a bag of unidentified white powder in the second warehouse, I took it carefully downstairs for official identification. I do not remember what it turned out to be. But employees told me that Harrington had once rented an additional compartment in which he stored prune juice, which fermented and blew up one day, fortunately before I arrived. The low point was the discovery of a box of birds that had been stored 30 years without benefit of taxidermy. The name of each bird in some Indian language plus species identification was affixed to the claws. I realized what a life of compulsive research could do to a person, and I resolved to mend my own ways. (Callaghan, ms.)

Catherine Callaghan's months at the Smithsonian stretched to five, and all she could hope to do in that time was to label the general contents of a portion of the boxes.

In 1976, the Smithsonian Institution received a grant from the National Historic Papers and Records Commission for work on the Harrington notes. Smithsonian archivist Elaine Mills was installed as the project editor. She has worked on the Harrington materials for many years, and her quite heroic endeavors have led to making most of the linguistic materials now available to the general public through microfilms. They are not cheap—somewhere around $24,500 will buy the complete set; but luckily they can be bought in smaller chunks.* The University of California at Riverside has a complete set. And a number of archives and libraries around the state have portions of the microfilms.

There are dozens of scholars now working on the notes, writing dissertations and papers about the languages portrayed in them, including even Old California Spanish, which Harrington also transcribed. There is now a network of Harrington scholars, united through a

---

* Microfilms of Harrington linguistic materials can be purchased at Kraus International Publications, One Water Street, White Plains, NY 10601, ATTN: Tony Mitura (telephone: 800-223-8323).

Artwork by Linda Yamane (above, left) based on a Rumsen Ohlone bear story found in Harrington's notes. Above right, Tongva/Ajachmem artist L. Frank Manriquez working on a soapstone bowl as described in Harrington's notes.

newsletter. There was a Harrington conference in Santa Barbara organized by Victor Golla in June 1992, and a second is planned at the Smithsonian Institution in 1993. Other projects are beginning: Kathryn Klar is in the planning stages of a biography of Harrington; and Ernestine McGovran is working on her mother's notebooks and correspondence with Harrington. There are many lifetimes of work ahead for people studying the materials collected by this driven and inspired man.

While scholarship has benefitted greatly from the organization and microfilming of Harrington's notes, there is a deeper and more personal value that the notes have to Native Californians. Linda Yamane (Ohlone) reminds us that the people Harrington worked with are the beloved ancestors of living Native Californians: "There's a real personal, more of a heart connection, for some people whose families these people are."

At the 1992 California Indian Conference, Linda discussed her feelings about her discovery of microfilms of Harrington's Rumsen notes:

> That was the beginning of the answer to a lot of dreams. The beginning of
> a lot of frustration, the beginning of so much excitement, at the same time
> all mixed up with the overwhelming feeling that I would never be able to

get through all of this and that there was a lifetime of work ahead of me, but [there were] all kinds of incredibly exciting things that I just thought were lost, [after I thought] I never would get to know this much about our language, which is what started me off on it to begin with.

But what I didn't know was that I was going to find all this other rich stuff—like little tiny, maybe just a few words, one sentence, and it seems so simple, but such a big, important traditional piece of information for me. For example, accidentally running across this little story, and in fact it was my friend's great-grandmother who someone was referring to, the tradition of putting ashes on the face when someone died. Well, that's one thing, to know about putting the ashes [on], but what we found (and this was great that my friend and I were sitting together when we read this) was that his great-grandmother burned *acorn*, and it was the ashes of the acorn that she put on her face, at the death of her son… Things like that can sound very simple and you wouldn't write a book about that one thing, but you can imagine, knowing that little detail means so much to me. It's not just some old ashes out of a fire pit, but someone deliberately burned acorn and used the ashes of that very important food.

There are stories, or so-called myths, there—but so as not to mislead those who haven't worked with it before, it's not like you just go to the story category and then copy down the stories in a row. You look through frame after frame after frame, and you get headaches, and you feel like your eyes are burning in their sockets, and your back hurts, and you spend 25¢ a sheet to photocopy one page of something that's real important to you, and you spend maybe a year or so to learn how to read Harrington's handwriting, and you look through everything and find all the pieces, and eventually you hope that you can put it all together right. But there is just *so* much there… It's not just words on a piece of paper, but it's saving something from the past that connects with people now. (Linda Yamane, at the California Indian Conference, October 1992)

Harrington's work does not only inspire language study. The artwork of L. Frank Manriquez, Tongva-Ajachmem artist, has also been influenced by Harrington's notes and publications:

Coming from a background, as I did, where if you graduated from high school you were doing real well, drifting into Harrington's work is a real

Ernestine McGovran, 1992. Photo by Mary Bates Abbott.

stunning thing. I first picked up a book called *Encounter with an Angry God*. The illustration on the cover—well, I'm an artist, it caught my eye, and I thought, "This looks fascinating," and I opened it up, and it was about this man and this woman and their lives and, you know, tying her to the front of the car, and all these different stories. But at that point when I read that book, I didn't know I was California native. I knew I was native, because I'm the family throwback, so it's been pretty obvious my whole life. But I found out that I could be connected to this anthropologist, through my people, and that led me to the Morongo Reservation—Malki put out this book, *Chinigchinich*, [revised and profusely annotated by Harrington] and this is kind of my Bible. I use this to start off on just about any topic, mainly it's our language, but what I get from it—it's a connection back to my people. You know, you get so immersed—he writes about the cosmology, and the plants, and the village sites, and it's all in these bits and pieces, and it leads me to museums, and microfilms; just little bits and pieces, and then I meet this person over here, and they have this little piece, and then another person there, and they have a little piece. And then I try to put all these pieces together to see what rings true with what actually I dream and I feel.

I do, as I said before, artwork. In *Chinigchinich* I read about these steatite bowls, and Harrington goes on a little bit more about the steatite, and it was mined by our people off of the soapstone shelves off of

Catalina Island down south. That led me to museums and books of photographs, and museum basements, so that I could see actual soapstone cooking bowls. So two years ago I made the first soapstone cooking bowl in 200 years. And it was actually this book, and different anthropologists in different fields, that led me to making that bowl. And that bowl is one of the few arts that ever talked to me, where I felt something with it or it transcended time. In this book he talks about basket materials, about basket shapes, basket designs. That led me down another road to… weaving with the native materials, so that leads me to go out to gather, which leads me to ethnobotanists who tell me which twig, which tree, what time of year to choose. These are two examples of art which come basically from Harrington…

I work with Harrington's papers because I'm compelled to. He was just so esoteric, he's so hard to work with, but somehow it's kind of fitting to people who made stone bowls instead of clay pots, and made a canoe with planks sewn together instead of digging one out, a complex man for kind of a complex people. And I feel with Harrington it's kind of like what the basket people talk about, that baskets are all around us, we just have to go gather them together. And it takes a long time to do this; it takes a long time to make a basket. And so that's kind of how I feel with Harrington's work, I have to go out gathering all the materials to come together, and it will be a pretty good picture at the end. (L. Frank Manriquez, at the California Indian Conference, October 1992)

One cannot help but be fascinated by Harrington as a person; he was quite possibly the most eccentric man that most people who met him ever knew. But more importantly, he had a sure vision of something that transcended his individual life and his quirks, and he devoted his life to that vision. His gift to posterity was far greater than we can measure. To end in Ernestine McGovran's words:

If it were it not for him, all of you would not have your publications, and your stories, and your dictionaries or lexicons, and your theses, and whatever else you've done out there, were it not for this crazy man. Crazy like a fox. (Ernestine McGovran, at the California Indian Conference, October 1992)

In most works concerned with these mysterious markings, the term rock writing is seldom applied to them, in spite of the fact that this is the very term the Indians themselves have always used, and would thus seem to be the most appropriate one. (Tûm-'pe põ-'õp, for instance, means rock writing in Paiute. Other tribes have equally specific words.)

This omission is due largely to the fact that most scholars have never accepted the premise that these markings were indeed *writing*. The existence in the languages of many Indian tribes of a *word* for writing (in the sense of recording information for others to read) proves, at least, that picture writing was long accepted as writing by the Indian. And who but the American Indian himself is more qualified to say whether it is or not?

The existence of such a writing system among the Indians offers a solution to the mystery, so long ignored, of why tribes had their own words for reading and writing. Such words were not borrowed from English or Spanish, nor are they descriptive (as are many of their words denoting modern gadgets). They are retained from a recent time when the Indians practiced their own form of picture writing.

Although the idea that rock writing is indeed writing is in opposition to some theories set forth in modern publications on the subject, it does not disagree too drastically with others. The general feeling of most "experts" is that rock writing was meant to be understood, but only by the writer or local band.

—Martineau, *The Rocks Begin to Speak*, pp. 3-5

20

Writing Systems

Written history has a shallow time depth anywhere in the world. Human language could be half a million years old or more, in which case writing represents only one percent of human history anywhere in the world; and most languages of the world have *never* been written.

Traditionally, the languages of Native California were spoken, not written. But there were and are many other ways to record information: there were ways to keep accounts; ways to keep track of the passage of time and movements of the stars and moon; there were ways to mark trails and river crossings, and to tell travellers what to expect ahead. Dentalium shell beads, knotted ropes and notched sticks, rock carvings, calendar stones, and many other devices were used in the visual transmission of information. People recorded whatever they needed to record. The actual transcription of words was not necessary.

Take, for example, the presentation of a bill for some service. Instead of a written invoice with a description of the debt and how much is owed, the Wukchumne used to prepare short wooden sticks with bands of colored porcupine quills wrapped around them at one end. The creditor (in this case, a shaman charging for his services) would toss the appropriate number of these sticks into the debtor's home as a reminder of the indebtedness (Mallery 1893).

These ways of recording information visually can fulfill most of the functions that writing as we know it fulfills; but notice that none of them actually records *language*. The recording of actual words was not necessary or useful in traditional culture. Times change, however; and as European culture became dominant, the Native Californians learned to write—but in the languages of Europe. For most purposes in this country, writing goes along with English-speaking practices, and takes place in English-speaking contexts. Still, over time, more and more communities of Native California have found reasons to develop writing systems for their own languages. It may be as simple as wanting to write a word on a tribal insignia, or putting place names on a map. More importantly, writing is a way to preserve oral literature that may be about to disappear from memory. Writing is also used in the communities as an aid in teaching or learning languages. For some, the only access to the language of their heritage now is through written records.

When one looks for a way to write down a native language, there are many systems to choose from, but none of them is fully adequate for people's practical needs. The English spelling system, using the symbols of the Roman alphabet, can't work for Indian languages as is, mainly because it is too flawed itself. For example, take the **ee** vowel sound in the word "f**ee**d." That same sound can be spelled in so many different ways: as in "cl**ea**n," or "T**i**na," or "P**e**te," to name a few. And what about pronouncing the sound of any letter or letter combination? There is, for example, the **ou** of "tr**ou**t," "t**ou**gh," "thr**ou**gh," "b**ou**ght," "p**ou**r," and so on—in each case the **ou** is pronounced differently. And then there are all the silent letters—some of the **gh**'s in the words just cited; silent final **e**'s as in "lik**e**"; and it takes years for English-speaking kids to learn what vowel goes in front of **r**, in words like "f**er**n," "b**ur**n," and "f**ir**"—after all, they are all really just a drawn-out **r**! To quote Mark Twain, "The sillinesses of the English alphabet are quite beyond enumeration."

Systems from Spanish mission days: Ventureño

Unlike English, the alphabet used for Spanish is based on the *phonetic principle:* "one letter, one sound." That is, each sound in a language should have only one letter (or letter combination) to represent it; each letter should stand for only one sound. Because it adheres generally to the phonetic principle, words from other languages are fairly easy to spell in Spanish, unless of course the other language has sounds that are not in Spanish. During the mission era, many California languages were written down. There were hymnals, confessionals, and grammars written, using a Spanish-based alphabet.

For some languages, the mission writings are the only records left of them. One such language is Ventureño Chumash. A Father José Señán was at Mission San Buenaventura from 1797 until his death in 1823. While there, he wrote the Ventureño Confesionario, designed to help priests elicit confession from the Ventureño-speaking people at the mission. The written symbols used in the mission era matched Spanish

From the Ventureño Confesionario

Below is a page from the Ventureño Confesionario for questioning people about theft. Despite the insulting nature of such questions, the Confesionario is interesting in that it contains a list of what people were likely to own and to value at the time.

Yníp jono,nu huash paqueet l,uquí?	Have you ever stolen anything?
Qui uquí pal jono,nu huash?	What did you steal?
Yníp jono,nu huash alchúm, ca alcaputsh, ca chucuyash, ca lo sit sojoy uquí lo sicu?	Have you ever stolen beads, or a mortar, or a jar, or the other things that people own?
Majaquesh	Clothes*
Altacash	Big white beads
Chipé	White bone beads
Eshqueluóy	Colored bone beads, or sea shells
Yquémesh	Small spotted beads
Anmitmiti	Small beads
Sucupi	Garnets*
Tochó	Basketry tray*
Chuniec	Pestle
Ayuját	Seed beater (winnowing basket?)
Sutinét	Fiber rope
Chushtou,o	Fry pan
Estapá	Rush mat

---

* Translation uncertain.

pronunciation where possible, but special symbols were used where necessary to represent sounds different from Spanish. One unusual writing practice that Señán utilized was commas followed by small subscript letters. These were quite likely glottal stops* followed by "echo vowels," as short, whispered vowels are sometimes called.

Linguistic transcription of California languages

In the late 19th century, English-speaking scholars began to record California languages. Because of the "sillinesses of the English alphabet,"

---

* See Appendix for definitions of phonetic terms and symbols.

the scholars adopted or developed various versions of a phonetic alphabet. Europe was developing a phonetic alphabet at the same time, which is now known as the International Phonetic Alphabet, or IPA. (Interestingly, the early versions of this system were designed not to write non-European languages but rather for use by French students trying to learn English.)

But the United States, because of its isolation from Europe, developed

Preserving Shellfish
(Kashaya Pomo Using the Phonetic Alphabet)

1. ʔul duwení qan ya maʔa heʔén ƭʼoʔ ťin yoqʼocíʔbaˑ ʔama dúhšew ʔťin ʔacaʔ duwení qan ʔbakʰeˑ

2. mulídom- qʰhosʼamaˑdem ʔahqʰa daluyícedem- qʰal baʔabícʼkʰe ťin ʔiceˑduˑ mulídom mul waciˑdu yaʔ diyáˑduceˑdu ʔoʔ ʔahqʰa daluyíʔ waˑyiˇ "mayaʔkʰe maʔa ʔel dahsácʰmeʔˇ" cedúˑceduˑ mensʼíwem ʔul dicʼwácʼqacʼinˇ qʰaƭʰá wi pʰilaqaˑcinˇ mul noʔqʼó hcʰetaˑcʼinˇ sʼuqʰaˑduqʰáyaˑcʼinˇ qʰasíˑƭʼil cisaqaˑcinˇ miˑ ʔul ʔimo dáhalaˑcʼinˇ miˑ ƭʼáhyibiˑcinˇ ʔaƭʰaˑ cisáloˑqonˇ winaˑ ƭʼáhyaqanˇ qʰamosʼ ʔáhqʰa ƭʼahyibiʔˇ

3. mulidom mil ʔihcʰe dibúˑnati kihlaʔ sóh qʼoʔdi kʰhunuʔ ťin béƭʼbu ťin maci heˑ ku cápa qan yoqʼoyíˑtaʔ sʼuqʰaˑ pʰala menˇ men ídom mu ʔul duwení qan ʔbakʰe ƭʼo maʔa háʔdaˑ diʔkʼuʔ ťin men cícʼwacʼinˇ

4. mu ʔem méʔpʰi mil ʔbakʰe ƭʼoˇ

1. In the old days we could keep food without it rotting. There isn't anything that the people of the old days couldn't do.
2. When winter came and the sea ran high, [the Indians] could not go to gather food along the coast for long periods. Before the water had already become rough, the leader would command, "Store away your food." Having had him say when, they went up to the gravel beach, pried off mussels, gathered turban snails, packed them up the coastal cliffs, dug holes, poured [the shellfish] in there, packed up gravel, poured it on top, and poured ocean water [over all that].
3. Then even when it rained, [the mussels] were still good and unspoiled for several days or even one week—turban snails they kept the same way. Because they did that, the old time people did not die off from starvation.
4. That is all there is of that.

Essie Parrish, in Robert Oswalt's *Kashaya Texts*

a somewhat different phonetic system, known now as the Americanist system. These two major phonetic writing systems are still in competition today. The phonetic representation of languages in the Eastern Hemisphere tends to be in IPA, and languages of the Western Hemisphere are written with the Americanist system. As for California languages, there are many thousands of pages of texts and grammars written in the Americanist system. The example shown opposite is from the Kashaya language. The vowels are like Spanish; most of the consonants sound like English, but always have only one possible pronunciation—for example, **g** always has the sound of the "g" in **g**ood. A sound like the "sh" in **sh**all is a single sound and so would have a single letter in the phonetic alphabet, represented in the Americanist system as š. Similarly, the "ch" sound is represented as ç. The Americanist letter **q** stands for a sound somewhat like "k" but said further back in the throat. Kashaya has a set of glottalized sounds, and these are represented with an apostrophe over or immediately after the consonant symbol.

The phonetic alphabet can be adapted to any language in the world. A person who is well trained in the use of the phonetic alphabet can write down and pronounce the sounds of any language in the world—albeit with a strong foreign accent! But despite the excellent qualities of the Americanist phonetic alphabet, there are many reasons why it might not work as a practical system for Native communities. For one thing, typewriters and simple word processors would be incapable of reproducing the odd symbols. For another, many people are intimidated and repelled by the strangeness of the symbols. Third, some people are not attracted to the idea of a universal writing system—they want instead a writing system that symbolizes the uniqueness of their language. And finally, many people lack contact with the linguists who use the phonetic alphabet, and so have to follow some other available path to literacy.

Unifon: Tolowa

Several communities in northern California have experimented with a very different writing system, Unifon. Unifon is a phonetic alphabet that was developed about 30 years ago by Chicago economist John Malone. Based on Roman capital letters, it expands the English alphabet to 40 symbols, to more closely match the number of distinctive sounds

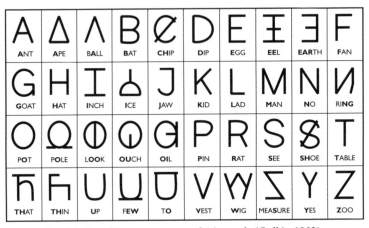

The Unifon alphabet of 24 consonants and 16 vowels (Culkin 1982).

English has. It is an alphabet that is closely matched to English spelling, so that, for example, Unifon letters that are designed to look somewhat like "A" are used for all the sounds that are typically spelled with an "a" in English.

In the lates sixties, Tom Parsons of the Center for Indian Community Development at Humboldt State University adopted Unifon to apply to Native Californian languages. Tolowa, Hupa, Yurok and Karuk students worked together to develop Unifon-based writing systems for their languages. Loren Bommelyn was one of those students. Loren and his family had been trying since the fifties to develop a writing system for Tolowa. Loren's mother, particularly, had been desperately trying to find a way to record their vanishing language: she had first attempted tape recording the elders, but they were reluctant to be recorded, so then she and Loren tried to work on the development of a writing system. They had no help from anywhere: linguists weren't working on Tolowa at that time, and there were no academics around who had the interest or the expertise to work with them. In 1969, they read a newspaper article about Tom's work on Unifon with the Hupa. Loren's mother immediately contacted Tom, and he readily started work with the family. Loren quickly saw that Unifon needed to be modified considerably before it would be able to represent all the distinctive sounds of Tolowa. He modified the vowels to suit the language, developed extra consonants to stand for the various consonants that aren't in English, and ended up with an excellent writing system, which has served the purpose of recording a great deal of Tolowa language over the years.

However, even a well-designed Unifon alphabet has problems. Over the last few years, the use of Unifon has been waning in favor of a modified English alphabet, for the languages of northern California. Tolowa, being the best-designed, lasted the longest. But as the years went by, Loren came more and more to realize that there are many practical issues that make Unifon problematic: for one thing, it can't be typed on a normal typewriter. It requires a computer with a specially-designed font. Most Tolowa people don't own computers, so it keeps them from being able to put anything into print. For another thing, it takes a long time to learn how to read Unifon, and that discourages many people from using it. Loren would like Tolowa people to be able to just pick up a book and sound out the words. He has just recently decided that at this time it would be best to switch over to a more familiar alphabetic system. Once he came to that decision, he went home to his family, and talked about it with his wife, Lena. She said, "Now hold on, Loren; are you going to throw away thirty years of work just like that?" He argued with her about the practicality of switching, but she was still skeptical—until Loren wrote a list of Tolowa words using the standard English alphabet, and called his 11-year-old son over to read it. His son had never seen this system of writing Tolowa before, but based on a combination of his speaking knowledge of the language and his knowledge of English writing, he read the list right off! "You've convinced me!" exclaimed Lena.

This is one way to write English.

ⴼIS IZ UNUⴼƎ ⲰΛ Tⵔ RΛT IⴹGLI8.

ðis iz stɪl ənʌðr wey to rayt ɪŋglɪš

A passage of English written in the Roman alphabet (English spelling rules), Unifon, and the phonetic alphabet.

From Let's Talk Iipay Aa: An Introduction to the Mesa Grande
Diegueño Language *(Couro and Langdon, 1975).*

Since then, Loren has already developed an excellent practical
writing system for Tolowa based on English letters, and is now working
on the transliteration of books and school curricula that were originally
written in Tolowa. And with the completion of that task, the reign of
Unifon in northern California will be over.

Writing systems based on the English alphabet: Diegueño

Most communities that have developed new writing systems for their
languages have found it practical to be able to utilize the knowledge and
writing technology that they already have available, just as Loren
decided for Tolowa. The majority of writing systems that American
Indian communities have developed over the last twenty years or so
have been based on the Roman alphabet, like English, but *not* using the
formidable spelling rules of English. The phonetic principle is generally
adhered to in these modern writing systems.

Diegueño is an example of a practical writing system based on the
Roman alphabet, but adhering to the principle of "one sound, one letter"
(or combinations of letters). For example, "ch" stands for the same sound
found in English words like "church." Combinations like "aa" and "uu"
stand for vowels that are lengthened slightly.

Like most California Indian languages, Diegueño has many sounds
not found in English. These can be written with letter combinations or
with new symbols. The glottal stop in Diegueño is written with an

apostrophe—"new" in the sense that it is not part of the English alphabet, but at the same time something that can be found on any typewriter. The combination "lly" stands for a sound not found in English. One way to describe it might be that it sounds like a combination of "sh" as in "**sh**arp" and "ly" as in "will **you**."

So by using symbols found on the typewriter, and combinations of symbols for the sounds that are not in English, a good representation of all the Diegueño sounds can be made. This is true for any language. But even though the symbols are familiar, it is difficult to take a language one has known orally all one's life and commit it to writing for the first time, or recognize the written form. To design a writing system that satisfies a community's needs takes enormous ingenuity and years of fine-tuning.*

Final remarks

As I have tried to show throughout this chapter, there are many possible ways to write a language down. No one way is the one and only "right" way. In fact, no standardized writing system would work well for all the languages of California. Not only do different solutions make good sense for different languages, but often communities choose different writing systems purposely, as a symbol of community identity. The Hualapais and Havasupais of Arizona, for example, could have had the same writing system for their two very similar languages, but made the official decision to design them differently as a symbol of their political separateness (Crook, Hinton and Stenson 1976).

Choosing a writing system has been controversial for many Native communities, leading to high emotions and intense disagreements. Like language itself, a writing system becomes a symbolic representation of a community and its values. But it cannot be forgotten that the heart and soul of California languages are in their speaking. Writing is at best a crude imitation.

---

* English had no standard spelling rules for centuries. We are told, for example, that William Shakespeare spelled his name in 14 different ways. Spelling was much more phonetic in early times, and there were many local variations in different parts of Great Britain. This variable spelling lasted until the 17th century, when the widespread availaility of printed matter encouraged standardization.

To the Lonely Hearts Language Club

At night
when the work is done
and the children are in bed
and the roar of the freeway is quieted
and the house cools and darkens and sighs into stillness,

She holds in her hands the pages
on which rest spidery symbols
of sounds whispered by dying grandmothers
and written down by a crazed linguist, long dead too,
of words spoken for the final time generations ago
entombed now in perpetual silence,
the last sound waves decayed into carbon traces
in a paper monument to the passing of a language from this earth.

Called each night by a power beyond her understanding
She lifts a page into her circle of light
and begins a ceremony of resurrection.
The pencil scratchings that encase the grandmothers' gifts
fall away and the words reawaken;
Her voice frees them one by one
and they fly into the night,
echoing into and out of corners.
The air vibrates with their saying.
The world resonates with their being.

by Leanne Hinton, for Cindy Alvitre,
L. Frank Manriquez, Ernestine
McGovran, and Linda Yamane

21

Keeping the Languages Alive

Language Action in California

As international economics and political structures spread and overwhelm the small traditional societies of the world, their languages spread with them, and the languages of small groups start to disappear. It has been estimated that half of the world's languages may die out in the next few generations; and in North America the situation is even worse. As linguist Michael Krauss says,

> For the whole USA and Canada together... of 187 languages, I calculate that 149 are no longer being learned by children; that is, of the Native North American languages still spoken, 80% are moribund. (Hale et al. 1992, 5)

California probably has the dubious distinction of having the most endangered languages of any part of North America. This is of course partly because there are so many Native Californian languages to begin with. Nonetheless, most Native Californian populations are small, and speakers are rarely in daily contact, because their communities seldom have a land base. These facts combine for a deadly situation: in California it is nearly *100%* of the Native languages that are no longer learned by children.

The loss of a people's cultural heritage and traditional values brings about great despair. And language is seen by many to be at the very root of culture, culture's vehicle, the means of expressing culture and values. Many Native Californians feel the loss of their language strongly. There are those who speak their language of heritage but have no one left to talk to. There are those whose ancestral language has not been spoken by anyone at all for a generation or more. Many people feel the loss of language as a loss of personal history, a loss of identity. There is a sense of loneliness, of yearning for lost meaning, lost values.

This yearning has led to action in Indian communities. People are doing whatever they can. They are forming tribal language committees, school and after-school programs, evening language classes; they are audiotaping and videotaping elders, and researching tapes and field notes from university archives. Along with these linguistic activities, there is also a resurgence of cultural and ceremonial activities. Basketmakers are organizing intertribally and negotiating with government agencies about the maintenance and harvest of plants that give basketmaking materials. New roundhouses and sweat lodges are being built; multi-generational singing and dancing groups are developing all over the state.

On the weekend of August 22 and 23, 1992, a group of Native Californians from every part of the state came together for a retreat at Walker Creek Ranch in Marin County, to share ideas and learn from each other about how to preserve their languages. The conference was funded by the Native California Network, a foundation dedicated to helping Native Californians save their cultures. Organized by Malcolm Margolin and foundation members Mary Bates Abbott and Robin Collier, the invitational conference hosted people who are dedicated to the task of teaching or learning or recording their languages. The energy and level of inspiration they generated have furthered greatly the task of saving the California languages.

Problems. There are a few major problems that all members of the conference had in common, and at the same time each community has its own unique problems. For all California languages, there is one basic problem: they are no longer the primary languages of the household, so the children are not learning them. Another common problem for the people trying to preserve their languages comes about because of the controversial nature of their task. People who believe that the preservation of Native American languages is a hopeless or even worthless task, or that it keeps people from assimilating to "mainstream" American culture have challenged their involvement. Those who would preserve their languages are criticized, embattled, ignored or ridiculed by various authorities, by the odd racist or superpatriot, and even sometimes by their own communities and families.

But beyond these fundamental issues, each language situation presents its own set of problems. Some communities are making an effort to teach the languages in schools or in after-school programs, and

The 1992 Tribal Scholars Language Conference. Front row, from left: Mary Bates Abbott, Jean Perry, Eric Elliott, Katherine Saubel, Martha Tapleras, Mary Jones, Vinna Smith, Berneice Humphrey. Middle: Bun Lucas, Ray Baldy, Brian Bibby, Betty and Mark Macarro, Maynard Gary, Nancy Richardson, Leanne Hinton, Susan Weese, Malcolm Margolin, Linda Yamane, Cindy Alvitre, L. Frank Manriquez, Laura Buszard-Welcher, Jeannine Gendar, Robin Collier, Sandra Camarena, Parris Butler, Ernestine McGovran. In the tree: Boss Wilson, Preston Arrowweed, Darryl Wilson, Carolyn Kuali'i, Darlene and Kowonash Franco, Hoss Wilson. Photo by Mary Bates Abbott.

are having to fight to have sufficient funding and sufficient hours of school time made available to the language learning process. Some languages are spoken by people who live far apart from each other, so that in-school or after-school programs cannot work. Some people fear that their educational programs actually undermine the language because it may lessen the parents' sense of responsibility. Parents may say, "Oh, I don't have to worry about it; the schools will take care of our language, so I'll just teach the kids English!" Some programs cannot find enough fluent speakers to be language teachers, and some have enough speakers but have to battle restrictions that don't allow the elders to teach without certification. Some people are trying to develop writing systems from scratch; some have more than one writing system in competition, and have to suffer factional struggles over which one should prevail. Some are trying to research and develop oral language teaching techniques, and get away from a dependence on writing. Some people are emphasizing the task of teaching adults the language, and are trying to develop language programs for them. And some are working with languages long dead, just trying to gather materials and learn what they can.

The Elders. Coming together at this conference were many Native Californians who share a common love and concern for their languages, including elders who have worked hard to pass on their languages to the next generations. There was Berneice Humphrey (Tolowa), who has been working on language programs for children since 1973. She brought a copy of an impressive book on the Tolowa language that she and other Tolowa tribal members created; the book was dedicated to her. There was Bun Lucas (Kashaya Pomo), who sings and tells stories in his language, and goes to schools all around him to spread his knowledge into the wider world. There was Mary Jones (Konkow Maidu), who works on language curriculum, and described how she feels now that there is no one left for her to talk to. There was Ray Baldy (Hupa), who has been teaching in the language programs at Hoopa for years. He described the approach he uses in language teaching, including games and songs he has developed, and showed us a video of a class. Vinna Smith (Karuk), one of the few fluent speakers left, is part of a team that has joined together to try to pass the language on to the next generation, and she is an important part of the Karuk language program in the public schools. Katherine Saubel (Cahuilla) is the director of the Malki Museum and the Malki Museum Press; she has published books on her language and other California languages and cultures, and has long worked with anthropologists and linguists to record her language and cultural knowledge. (Subsequent to this meeting, Ms. Saubel was inducted into the National Women's Hall of Fame.)

The younger generations. Inspiring too are members of younger genera-tions, most of whom did not learn to speak their languages as children but have made great efforts to do so as adults. There is Mark Macarro (Luiseño), who started his journey toward language learning when he decided to learn how to sing. Elders are very proud of him and his singing ability, but he tells the story of an elder who asked him one day how he thought he could ever be a singer without knowing the language. After some hard thinking, he began learning the language from the elders, studying language-learning materials, and gathering together everything he could find, published or unpublished, about Luiseño. Not satisfied with just learning the language himself, he has also started youth programs and has researched modern language teaching theory to help develop curriculum and teaching styles.

Then there are the members of the Wukchumne language program—present at the conference were Martha Tapleras, Susan Weese, and Darlene Franco. Darlene showed some of the materials they have developed: a lovely coloring book with Wukchumne words, and a lesson book. Susan says that when they began to try to get a language program together, it took a year or so before the elders would open up and share with the younger generation. The elders needed to be sure they were serious. She pointed out that people sometimes take too much from the elders without giving anything back. It is especially important to share the results of your study with them, to show them what is being done with the knowledge they have given.

Then there is Parris Butler, a Mojave artist and poet who is directing a language program at Fort Mojave. He has a background in creative writing, with a linguistic component, and is now working on developing a writing system with some of the fluent elders. Like Mark, Parris has researched modern language teaching techniques and applied them.

Another dedicated language activist is Brian Bibby, who is well known in California as a traditional singer and dancer, and also as a teacher. He has worked with Northern Sierra Miwok and Southern Maidu (Nisenan) elders to develop language curricula for children, and when it became obvious that people lived too far apart from each other to get the children together for language lessons, he began to develop curricula for computers and Language-Master machines, and put the machines in people's homes for the families to use. He points out that the main benefit of this technology is that it allows people to actually hear the language being spoken. Another benefit is that it gets whole families involved in the language teaching process.

Also present at the conference was Nancy Richardson (Karuk), the talented coordinator of the Indian language program at Humboldt State University, who works closely with the language teachers for Karuk, Yurok, Tolowa and Hupa. She has also worked with the Karuk Language Restoration Committee, an exciting committee that was founded to work out a plan to restore the waning Karuk language. Remembering when there were 150 native speakers, she illustrates the grave danger Karuk is in by pointing out that now there are only 12.* She stresses that a language plan has to be done by the community itself. One could hire a talented expert to create one, but no one would ever use it! It must be created through the deepest thought, hardest work, and best intentions of the people themselves.

Working on a more individualized project is Darryl Babe Wilson, Achumawi-Atsugewi writer, now completing a master's degree at the University of Arizona. While anthropologists like Harrington (Chapter 19) worked hard to discover elderly speakers of California languages, Darryl did a turnabout and discovered an elderly anthropologist instead. Susan Brandenstein (Park), when she was a student of A.L. Kroeber and Robert Lowie at Berkeley in 1930, was sent by them to Atsugewi country. She never published the results of her field work, and Darryl, with her cooperation, has been working for a couple of years now to make sure that her notes are copied and safely deposited. Darryl is basing his graduate work on the study of the linguistic and cultural information contained in the notes.

By no means was every language activist in California present at that meeting. Among the other people doing important work are Loren Bommelyn (Tolowa) and Julian Lang (Karuk). Loren Bommelyn has been discussed frequently in this book (see especially Chapters 20 and 22). Julian Lang also learned his language fluently as an adult, through hard work and sheer talent, and is active in language development and teaching as well as in song, literature, visual arts, and an astonishing number of other pursuits.

---

* Recently Jeanerette Jacups-Johnny, Karuk medicine woman, told me that in 1910, the Karuk people successfully fought off an attempt to build a dam on their river, even though none of them knew English. So we see that in only 80 years, Karuks have shifted from monolingual Karuk speakers to monolingual English speakers.

Languages with no speakers. The person mentioned most often at this conference was the early 20th-century linguist J.P. Harrington, who devoted his life to gathering linguistic data of the languages of the West, especially California (see Chapter 19). His unpublished field notes are a great resource now for many languages, and for some languages, his notes are all that remain. Several people who attended the conference work with Harrington notes, trying to understand as much as they can about the now-unspoken languages of their heritage.

Cindy Alvitre (Tongva, also known as Gabrielino) lived in Inuit villages through her teens and early twenties and was inspired by their living language. When she went home she devoted herself to revitalizing her own culture and language. She works with Harrington field notes, and has dreams of resurrecting Tongva to spoken status. Chair of her tribe, she tries to bring in a few words of her language at each meeting. She is also heading a project to build a plank canoe and paddle with a team of her people to the islands they once inhabited.

L. Frank Manriquez (Tongva and Ajachmem), artist and carver of stone, and cartoonist for *News from Native California*, years ago also caught the language bug, and surrounds herself each day with thousands of slips of paper filled with words taken from Harrington's field notes on her ancestral languages.

Linda Yamane (Ohlone) spent years gathering together the voluminous notes of Harrington on the Rumsen language, and teaching herself to understand his peculiar handwriting and special characters. Now, from his notes and from old recordings in archives such as the Hearst Museum at the University of California, she is learning the old words and stories, and recreating as well the song traditions of her ancestors.

Ernestine McGovran (Chumash), whose family worked closely with Harrington for many years, has a particularly interesting mission. Her mother, Mary Yee, learned to write her language fluently, and kept notebooks of her sessions with Harrington. Ernestine (in the small amount of time left to her each day after her demanding job as an intensive-care nurse) is working on her mother's notebooks.

Some language teaching ideas. The most popular language teaching method among the members of the conference was TPR, short for "Total

Physical Response," a method that involves teaching words, phrases and discourse accompanied by gestures and activities, and gets the students to join in on these activities. Nancy Richardson gave an exciting demonstration lesson, teaching Karuk. She began with a set of commands, such as "Stand up!" and "Sit down!" showing us by gestures what she wanted the learners to do. As is the case when children learn their primary language, we all learned to understand these words long before we could say them; that period is called the "silent period," and is every bit as important as the later stages when one can actually utter the words. Nancy also taught the audience the words for some body parts (head, shoulder, knees, feet), and then told us (in Karuk) to point to each part when she said the word. She taught us how to say "yes" and "no," and then asked us, "Is this the shoulder?" (etc.) while pointing to a body part. She taught a song (based on an English song "Head and Shoulders, Knees and Toes") which the audience had to sing with the appropriate gestures, and this allowed them to learn how to say the words out loud. Since everyone was singing together, forgetting the words didn't embarrass anyone. She went on to teach words for basketry materials in the same general way. The delight of TPR and related methods lies in their naturalness. Language learning is no longer a task of grueling drill and memorization, but something that actually seems easy, and certainly fun!

School language programs and after-school programs in the United States never give students enough time to become proficient. As one language-teaching specialist recently told me, it almost doesn't matter what method is used in language teaching, so long as students get regular and well-structured instruction. And what really matters is that it takes about five hundred hours of such instruction to reach basic proficiency. Thus it was with great delight that the conference attendees heard Nancy Richardson tell about the summer language immersion camps for Karuk children and their families that took place in 1992 in northern California. Such camps give great hope for the survival of California languages. In summer 1993 the same pattern was used for language immersion camps in the Hupa language.

Carolyn Kuali'i is an emissary from her people in Hawaii to the people of Native California. She brought with her an inspiring message about language teaching in Hawaii. Twenty years ago, Hawaiian would have been defined as "moribund," because the children were not learning it. But now there are several elementary schools where the primary language of instruction is Hawaiian all the way through sixth grade, and the ultimate goal is to have bilingual schools up through high school. These schools have not only saved the language from dying by creating a new generation of fluent speakers, but they have also increased the scholastic success of the children. Native Hawaiians used to have a very high dropout rate from school, but the Hawaiian language schools have reduced the dropout rate significantly. Of course given that the previous generation had not learned Hawaiian, finding a sufficient number of teachers to staff the schools has been difficult. Helping solve this problem is the Hawaiian language program at the University of Hawaii, which is good enough to teach a person to speak fluently. Hawaii developed its school program through the inspiration of the Maoris of New Zealand, who have developed one of the best indigenous language programs in the world.

Despite the inspiring nature of the Hawaiian program, the number of speakers and even of people who might ever be interested in speaking a given language is so small for each of the California languages that the idea of training hundreds or thousands of children to speak one seems unthinkable. In California, teaching even *one* child to speak is a great feat.

This chapter began with the statement of the basic problem leading to language death: that the children are not learning to speak their language of heritage at home. Schools can never teach a language as well as a child could learn it as the primary language at home, so one problem of great interest is how to make a language important enough at home to allow the children to learn it. At home, specific teaching techniques don't need to be considered; if the parents speak a language constantly to each other and to the children, the children will learn that language. But this seemingly simple solution is fraught with problems. For one thing, few Californians of parenting age know their ancestral language well enough to use it dominantly in the household; and even more rarely do both parents know the language well enough to use it as the primary language of communication with each other. Also, the child herself (or himself) may well have experiences that lead her to reject the language. Once she realizes that none of her friends, schoolmates or teachers speaks it, and once she gets teased about it a few times, she may refuse to speak the language again. This problem is prevalent in all types of bilingual households. There are many families where the adults speak the language of heritage, while the children refuse to reply in any language but English.

Jean Perry had some wise suggestions about language teaching in the home, and talked about her efforts to teach Yurok to her daughter, Orowi (from the Yurok word for "dove"). Jean, who has a background in linguistics and has started to learn Yurok over the last few years, and her husband Merk Oliver, a semi-fluent speaker, have worked at speaking Yurok to each other and to their daughter at home. At three and a half years old, Orowi knew a lot of Yurok words, and was just beginning to form sentences. Her Yurok probably lagged behind her English by a couple of years. Her most important language crisis came about when she entered preschool, where no one else spoke Yurok. At that point, she discovered that many things for which she only knew Yurok names had English names too. After a few experiences of being misunderstood, she decided that her parents had played a very dirty trick on her, and after three or four months simply refused to speak Yurok at all. Jean recalls a moment that seemed like a death knell for Yurok in her family, when during a conversation about her stuffed bear, Orowi said with finality, "That's *not* a **chir'ery**, that's a teddy bear!" But the lesson here is that a committed family must not give up hope, but must work through the problems as well as they can. Jean and Merk kept on trying, and several things happened that helped Orowi understand the value of Yurok. She found several friends at preschool who were bilingual—one in French, for example, and one in Japanese. And with the help of the teachers, who asked them to share their special language knowledge with the class, all the bilingual children, including Orowi, began to realize the importance of knowing different words for things. Even more importantly, Orowi began to take her place in traditional Yurok cultural activities, fishing with Merk and Jean, and participating in Brush Dances. In 1992, a Brush Dance was held for Orowi herself; she was ceremonially purified through a night of fasting and bathing and dancing, and was given a new set of clothes to begin life anew. These events showed her the value of being Yurok and of speaking the Yurok language, which is probably the most important lesson a child can learn about her language and culture. The future of Orowi's relationship to Yurok cannot be predicted, but as of now she is taking great pride in her language.

Steps toward the future

The final parts of the conference were devoted to the question of what should happen next. Here are just a few of the many exciting ideas that people put forward.

A master-apprentice language program. This program emphasizes teaching the languages to highly motivated young adults (see Chapter 22). The idea is to fund the living expenses of teams of elders and young people with grants, so that they do not have to work for several months, and can thus isolate themselves from English-speaking society and become immersed in traditional culture and language. It was estimated that three to four months in an immersion situation would go a long way toward the development of proficiency, especially for people who already have some passive knowledge.

Stipends for scholarly efforts by Native Californians trying to research their languages of heritage.

A language learners' retreat, modelled after writers' retreats, where people trying to learn their languages can come with their materials for a week or two and spend full time at it, coming together during breaks for discussion and mutual support.

A newsletter for the California languages.

Lobbying for relevant legislation and funding.

Help in credentialing or certification of elders, or in finding ways to get schools to allow elders without teaching certificates to teach in the classrooms.

Developing centers where linguistic and educational materials on California languages can be found, or help in finding the materials.

Videotapes on the California languages.

Language restoration plans, to be produced by each interested tribe.

Workshops on how to teach languages, how to develop writing systems or written materials, how to find and study linguistic materials, and how to record the elders.

Setting up a California language committee that will develop plans and proposals in cooperation with Native California Network. This idea was implemented on the last day of the conference, and a committee was formed, consisting of people from all over the state, and from all sorts of language situations. The committee, in cooperation with the conference group as a whole, came up with this statement of overall purpose: "To empower the diverse native population of California by creating a network that will support and provide necessary resources to maintain and regain the native languages that are the vital link to our culture."

The language committee, known as the Advocates for Indigenous California Language Survival, is now well-established, and has been active in assessing needs and implementing programs. One important program in progress right now is the Master-Apprentice Language Learning Program; the first six language teams began their work together in summer 1993 (see Chapter 22).

A number of people who attended the 1992 conference went to the NALI (Native American Languages Issues) conference in May 1993 in Hawaii and saw firsthand the result of language revival work there. As they listened delightedly to grownups and children making speeches and chattering to each other without self-consciousness in the Hawaiian language, they remembered that a generation ago there were no children speaking the language at all. It is a fine model to aspire to.

Some Final Thoughts

Looking back, many vivid moments of the 1992 conference take shape in memory. The Wukchumne talked about the importance of ceremonies to validate one's membership in a culture, and said that they have brought back naming ceremonies as a meaningful part of their culture. Names came up often in the conference: knowing your own name is an important part of realizing your membership in a culture, and understanding your place in it.

Katherine Saubel told of an old woman of her tribe who said that

Parris Butler, first chairperson of the Advocates for Indigenous California Language Survival. 1993 photo by Mary Bates Abbott.

when the white man came he wanted to destroy them and their culture. Speaking the language and doing the ceremonies just reminded her of this, and the pain was too great. She just wanted to forget. But Katherine's response was, "We're still here and I want to *stay* here. We survived."

Mark Macarro related a story of someone who said to him, "Why are you bothering to try so hard to learn the language? You don't have anyone to talk to, and in ten years the language will be dead anyway. No one will know or care." When Mark told this to an elder, she said, "How could he say that? Doesn't he know that the spirits will know?" Mark took this to heart, and it gave him a respite from the loneliness of his work. As Mark says, "You aren't really doing this alone. The spirits are there watching; the spirits know."

And then there was the time I was talking with L. Frank and Cindy. Cindy said she yearned for the recreation of a Gabrielino-speaking community, but has been told by many—and sometimes believes herself—that it is hopeless.

"Sometimes I think it is hopeless, too," I said. "But then this conference has been so inspiring..."

"Yes," said L. Frank, crystalizing the thought. "How can it be hopeless when there is so much hope?"

Okay, you children listen. If he won't tell you, then I must. You must know your language first. Yes, we must know the white man language to survive in *this* world. But we must know our language to survive *forever*.

—Darryl Babe Wilson quoting his aunt Gladys,
in "Salila-ti Mi-mu d-enn-i-gu,"
News from Native California 7:2, p. 38

22

Rebuilding the Fire

We are in the early stages of a renaissance of native language and culture revival the world over. New Zealand and Hawaii are two examples of places where endangered languages have been restored to a flourishing status in the last ten years. Before the revival began, the Maori and Hawaiian languages were threatened with extinction because, just as in California and so many other places, the younger generation no longer spoke them. But a language immersion program that involved schools from preschool to the university turned the situation around.

These models provide hope to California Indians who are striving to save their own languages from extinction. But can California emulate these inspiring programs? One difference between California and the New Zealand-Hawaii model is that the latter two areas focused their energies on a single language. California, in contrast, has no single major Indian language, but instead has fifty or so languages spoken by individuals or small groups. Second, Maori and Hawaiian, even at their lowest points, were still spoken by thousands of people. California languages nowadays may be spoken by only a few dozen, or even as few as one or two individuals, almost always of an advanced age.

For years, now, Native Californians have been working to save their languages. As we saw in the previous chapter, elders who speak their language of heritage have teamed up with younger tribal members who are trained in education, along with other educationists and linguists, to develop teaching curricula and programs that will give children an appreciation and beginning knowledge of their languages and cultures. People have developed tribal writing systems; they have collected materials, made tape recordings, dictionaries, and collections of stories. Yet still they have to watch the languages erode, and the number of speakers diminish. And notwithstanding these wonderful programs, given that the languages are not being taught in the home, there are no new fluent speakers growing up. Is it too late for the California languages?

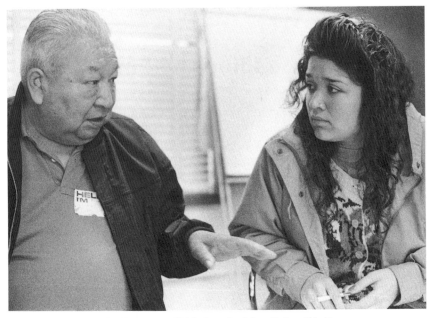

Ray Baldy and Melodie Carpenter. 1993 photo by Mary Bates Abbott.

A new program is now being piloted that is designed to suit the particular needs of Native Californian communities. Right now it is of great importance simply to produce new fluent speakers to carry on these languages in crisis. Many other steps are also necessary if the complete loss of California languages is to be averted, but this one is crucial. To this end, twelve talented people, supported by many others just as committed, are embarking on a program of intensive language work: six native speakers and six of their young friends or relatives who are committed to learning the language of their heritage fluently. Funded by grants from public and private sources that were gathered together by the Native California Network, the teams were selected from a pool of highly talented applicants and invited to a training workshop in June 1993. The members of each team committed themselves to spending approximately 20 hours per week for a period of four months or so speaking their language together, so that the younger member could gain proficiency. All the younger team members are people who have already had some experience with the language, so none of them is starting from scratch.

The Teams

Hupa. Ray Baldy, speaker of Hupa, talented story teller and talented teacher, works with elementary school children in the Hupa Language Program. His imaginative lessons, his patience with students, and his overall dedication to passing on his knowledge of language and culture to future generations make him an ideal elder team member.

Winnie Baldy-George, Ray's sister, a medicine woman for ceremonial dances, is fluent in the Hupa language, and has great knowledge of Hupa lore. She is helping the team.

Melodie Kay Carpenter, Ray's niece, is the youngest team member. She is an eighth grade teacher at Hoopa Elementary School and teaches Hupa after school on Tuesdays and Thursdays with Ray. Melodie wants to become proficient in Hupa so that she can participate more effectively in the teaching and restoration of Hupa language and culture.

Karuk. Violet Super is an elder of the tribe, and a fluent Karuk speaker and story teller; her work with linguists has helped define the way Karuk is characterized in the linguistic literature today.

Terry Supahan, Violet's grandnephew, is the younger member of this team. He is a member of the Karuk tribal council and also a member of the Karuk tribe's Language Restoration Committee. He is the Karuk language program facilitator and a teacher at Orleans Elementary school. He also teaches a community Karuk language class to regular classroom teachers and adult tribal members; he has helped plan and teach at the tribe's language immersion camps. Increasing his Karuk to fluency has long been a goal for Terry, but when his great-uncle died two years ago he really began to realize how little time he had left to learn it. It was that impetus that led him to step up his efforts and commit himself to this program.

Terry's wife, Sarah Supahan, is also a teacher and also involved in Karuk cultural and linguistic preservation and restoration. She is supporting Terry in his project with Violet, and learning along with him.

Mojave. Claude Lewis, the elder member of this team, has been a member of the Mojave tribal council for twenty years. He is a fluent speaker of Mojave and has much knowledge of traditional culture, Mojave geography, and tribal history. A kind and generous man, he is willing to devote a great deal of his time to working with the younger generations.

Parris Butler is the director of the Aha Makav Language Education Program, and has been working for years on documenting his language and perfecting a new writing system for it. He has a background in linguistics and art. Parris is also the current chair of the Advocates for Indigenous California Language Survival. He wants to become fluent in Mojave for his own deeper understanding and participation in his culture, and also to be more effective in his language teaching efforts.

At the workshop with Parris and Claude was Sylvia Arteaga, who also works in the language program, and is benefitting from the summer's language learning project.

Wintu. Florence Jones, an Indian doctor, is the elder member of this team. Emmerson Miles, Florence Jones' interpreter while she is doctoring, is helping Florence and her apprentice and granddaughter, Caleen Sisk-Franco, in the language project. To quote Caleen:

> Florence Jones was born at the turn of the century in a mountain home near a place called Baird, California which is now under Lake Shasta. The youngest of fourteen children born to William and Jenny Curl, at age five she was caught by white men and taken to an Indian school in Greenville, California some 300 miles away. Within two years the school burned down and Florence returned home to the McCloud River. Her mother, Jenny, was a very respected and powerful medicine woman for the Wintu. Her father, Bill, [was] a speaker and leader of the people. Florence began her official training to become an Indian doctor at age ten. When she was born, six Indian doctors came to doctor her and announced that she was a "spiritual child." (They believed when a child is born to a woman of her mother's age that the child is either evil or spiritual.) Tildy Griffith, a medicine woman (Florence's aunt), was her coach into the spiritual doctoring of the Wintu. She is now the last Wintu doctor. She and Emmerson are the last two speakers. She is the last one who knows the higher language of the Wintu, the "doctoring language." (Caleen Sisk-Franco, at the Master-Apprentice training workshop, June 1993)

Caleen is trying to learn doctoring practices and philosophy, as well as the language. Despite a heavy workload and a big family, she drives the

Florence Jones and Caleen Sisk-Franco. 1993 photo by Mary Bates Abbott.

95 miles to Florence's house about four times a week to work with her and learn the language. At 18 months, Caleen's youngest daughter is just starting in on language learning, and Caleen hopes the two of them will learn Wintu together.

Yowlumni. Agnes Vera, the elder member of the team, grew up speaking Yowlumni, a Yokuts language, and knows tribal history, legends, customs and spiritual traditions. She is looked up to in the community as a wise elder who can give guidance and support.

Her son Matt Vera, the younger member, participates strongly in spiritual gatherings. Matt is involved with many traditional cultural activities. He is currently working on the development of a tribal orthography, and has been working on a dictionary, a collection of common phrases, and stories. His goal is to carry on tribal traditions, and he wants to know his language of heritage fluently as a part of that goal.

Matt and Agnes lead sweat house ceremonies together and also, at their lovely ranch, host people who are fasting and purifying themselves. Their spiritual strength provides great inspiration to members of their community and to guests like me as well.

Present at the workshop with Agnes and Matt was Darlene Franco, Wukchumne, who will be participating in language learning with them when she can.

Yurok. Jessie Exline has been teaching the Yurok language for twenty years. She received a Lifetime Eminence Credential from the state of California for her teaching of language and culture. She wrote a Yurok dictionary. It is her life's dream, as Carole Korb says, to produce fluent speakers in the younger generations.

Carole Korb, a teacher, has taken Yurok classes from Jessie and has taught as a substitute in Jessie's place when needed. By herself and together with Jessie she has given presentations on the Yurok language to teachers and others. Today there are no more than about twenty fluent speakers of Yurok, all in their seventies or older. Among other things, the language is necessary for tribal ceremonies, so vital elements of the culture will be lost along with the language if it dies.

The Method

On the weekend of June 4–6, 1993, the teams gathered at Walker Ranch in Marin County for two days of training in special techniques for teaching and learning second languages, to guide them in their quest for language fluency. A six-person professional staff handled the training:

Mary Bates Abbott, Director of Native California Network, administrator of the program;

Leanne Hinton (this author), designer of the training component;

Nancy Richardson, Language Program Director for the Center for Indian Community Development at Humboldt State University;

Martha Macri, linguist and Assistant Professor in the Native American Studies and Anthropology departments at the University of California at Davis);

Jean Perry, linguist and Coordinator for Sponsored Projects at Humboldt State University;

Claire Kramsch, an expert in second language learning and teaching, and a professor in the Department of German Language and Literature at the University of California at Berkeley.

The Master-Apprentice Language Learning Program is based on the theory that adults can learn language informally, through listening, practicing, and eliciting language from a native speaker. We can take many lessons in language learning by observing the natural way in which children learn their first languages. They do not need to be consciously taught, even though their parents enhance their learning in many ways. So long as their environment is rich with language, they cannot *help* but learn it. Through the context of activities and actions and gestures and objects, they manage to unconsciously sort out what words mean; and through constant hearing and practicing and experimenting, they figure out the grammar of their languages.

In much the same way, when adults move to a country where another language is spoken, even if they don't take any formal classes they tend to learn the language, *if* they are exposed to it enough. Among immigrant families, the children learn the new language fastest and best, primarily because they are exposed to it and practice it more than their parents, through their schools and friends. Adults tend to be more restricted in their social networks, and often have less exposure to the new language than their children.

So what we want is a kind of *language immersion* program, where the student can gain many hours of exposure to the language. The major challenge is to find a way to get that exposure. We cannot simply send them off to a community where their language is spoken all the time, for such a community does not exist. Instead they must *create* the immersion situation. The habits of speaking the traditional language are gone, even for the fluent speakers, in all but a few restricted events. Even people who speak the same Indian language fluently tend to use English together in everyday communication. So the Master-Apprentice program requires the development of new language habits in order to create the desired immersion situation.

The model for the Master-Apprentice program is Loren Bommelyn, Tolowa educator, dancer, basketmaker, and overall creative force. He has been extremely successful in learning his ancestral language as an adult. When I first met Loren in 1982, we shook hands and I said something like, "Glad to meet you." Loren responded with a stream of Tolowa, and then went on in English, "How do you do?"

"Gee, what was that you said before?" I asked. Loren spoke in

Tolowa again, and then explained, "I'm learning to speak Tolowa, and so I try to say everything in Tolowa first. Then if I don't know it, I'll ask my teacher next time I see him." Loren spoke this way to friends, family and strangers for a few years; and he now speaks Tolowa fluently.

One of the reasons that his technique of self-teaching is so ingenious is that he has created his own immersion situation. Realizing there was nowhere to go where the language was spoken all the time, Loren created a fantasized speech community for himself, by translating whatever anyone said into Tolowa as he went about his day. He lived in the language by making the language live in him.

The desire to speak in the language of mutual understanding can be overwhelming, and leaving English behind while developing the habit of speaking in the language of heritage is the single biggest challenge the pioneering Master-Apprentice teams have to overcome. For everything they do together they try to develop habits of speaking to each other in their language. In many of their activities, the language can be used readily. For example, when I called Parris and Claude to see how things were going, they were making bows and arrows together. Claude can speak in Mojave to Parris while doing this, and the actions he performs and the objects he manipulates while talking provide the context for Parris to understand what is being said, even if he does not recognize all the words.

The teams try to use their language in non-traditional settings as well. If they are fixing a car together, or going to a store, they try to speak in their language. The lack of words for non-traditional concepts, which some people might think is the main difficulty in using the language in these situations, is in fact the least of their problems. If the team doesn't know a word in their language for some non-traditional item, they can borrow a word from English, or they can make up a descriptive term. But many terms for new items already exist in Indian languages. For example, Jaime deAngulo noted in his writings that the Achumawis had words for all the car parts based on animal body parts—the engine was the heart, the headlights were the eyes, and so on.

Eight rules of teaching and learning were given to the teams at the training workshop. In general, these rules are simply reminders of how to recreate the sort of environment that allows children to learn language. The rules are as follows:

Claude Lewis. 1993 photo by Mary Bates Abbott.

Eight Points of Language Learning

Teachers

1. Be an active teacher. Find things to talk about. Create situations or find something in any situation to talk about. Tell stories. Use the language to tell the apprentice to do things. Encourage conversation.

2. Don't use English, not even to translate.

3. Use gestures, context, objects, actions to help the apprentice understand what you are saying.

Apprentices

1. Be an active learner. Ask about things. Create situations, bring things to ask your teacher to tell you about; find things in the environment to ask about; ask him/her to tell you stories.

2. Don't use English, not even when you can't say it in the language. Find other ways to communicate what you want to say.

3. Use gestures, context, objects, actions to help in your communication when you don't know the words.

4. Rephrase for successful communication. Rephrase things the apprentice doesn't understand, using simpler ways to say them.

5. Rephrase for added learning. Rephrase things the apprentice says, to show him correct forms or extend his knowledge to more complex forms. Encourage communication in the language, even with errors.

6. Be willing to play with language. Fantasize together; make up plays, poems, and word games together.

7. Understanding precedes speaking. Use various ways to increase and test understanding. Give the apprentice commands to follow. Ask him/her questions. It is not necessary to focus on speaking each new word right away; that will come naturally.

8. Be patient. An apprentice won't learn something in one lesson. Repeat words and phrases often, in as many different situations and conversations as possible.

4. Practice. Use new words and new sentences and grammar as much as possible, to yourself, to your teacher, to other people.

5. Don't be afraid of mistakes. If you don't know how to say something right, say it wrong. Use whatever words you know; use gestures, etc. for the rest.

6. Be willing to play with language like children do. Name things you see, count them, talk about what color they are. Make up stories.

7. Understanding precedes speaking. You may recognize and understand many things you cannot say. Focus on understanding: that is the most important step toward language learning. After you understand an utterance fully, learning to speak it will not take long.

8. Be patient with yourself. It takes a long time to learn a language well. You are doing a heroic task; forgive mistakes.

The teams were given pointers on how to communicate successfully without using English. The use of context and gestures and rephrasing was suggested; the learners were also instructed to ask the elders how to ask for information in their language; they need to be able to ask things like this in their language:

"How do you say .... ?"

"What is this?"

"What are you doing?"

Learning how to ask "How do you say..." in the Indian languages was not easy. Some teams feared there was no way to ask it at all in their languages! (But have faith, there is *some* way to communicate the idea, *any* idea, even if it has to be said in a completely different way from English.)

Over the weekend, the teams did exercises in which they had to spend anywhere from half an hour to two hours at a time together without speaking a word of English. At first, this sort of task is nerve-wracking; the effort to communicate and understand without using the language we know best results in frustration, headaches and exhaustion! If you have ever been to a foreign country, you may remember this feeling: I once spent a year in South America, arriving with only the most rudimentary knowledge of Spanish, and for the first few weeks I felt sick by the end of every day. But learning was taking place, and eventually it all fell together and I found myself understanding and communicating; no more headaches.

The staff focused on many other aspects of language learning: Jean Perry discussed the use of the tape recorder in language learning, and I discussed the use (and misuse!) of writing in the language learning process and in analyzing the grammar of sentences. Nancy Richardson showed how people can structure language lessons together, and demonstrated a lesson. Claire Kramsch talked about *functional* learning— one does not learn to speak fluently by simply learning words and grammar; language is also a series of social customs. How do people greet each other in a particular language? How do they say goodbye? How do they ask for something? How do they make a complaint, or show appreciation? How are conversations structured? When people converse, do they tend to talk fast or slow? Are there long pauses between utterances, or is silence shunned? All these things are done in very different ways in different languages, and it is that sort of under-standing that makes a person able to use a language in everyday communication. As an example of how different customs can be, Havasupai people did not traditionally express anger in words. Instead, they would go off alone and make up a song about the incident, and when they returned, they would sing the song where the person they were aggrieved by would hear it. Another example: Nancy Richardson mentioned that in Karuk, one never apologizes verbally. Apologies are unacceptable; one makes reparation instead. And Terry Supahan pointed out that when the elder Karuks are conversing, they speak extremely rapidly, and they tend to use a great many contractions and abbreviated forms that make the language very different from formal Karuk.

Martha Macri brought out some of the emotional difficulties surrounding language learning. For example, the discrimination that elders have had to face during their lives for speaking their language; these unpleasant memories can be dredged up again when they use the language now. There is also the humility that some elders feel in the face of what is being asked of them; they think about how much more *their* elders knew, and they may balk at passing on what they believe to be a small and partial understanding of their language and culture. Sensitivity to criticism and ridicule is an issue for some of the younger team members, especially, because they might be told they aren't speaking the language right. Team members have experienced all of these problems and others in the past, and it is good for them to air the problems and understand that they are not alone in having to face them.

The guidelines presented to the teams are loose enough to allow for individual situations, learning styles and activities. The teams are really designing their own means of learning, within the contexts of their own lives and their own communities.

As I write this last chapter, the six teams are at work in their communities. Martha Macri, Nancy Richardson and I recently travelled around the state together to visit them, and found that they were making excellent progress in their languages and doing wonderful projects. Two different learning styles have emerged among the six teams: the "intuitive" and the "analytical" styles, I call them informally.

The apprentices who are learning by the "intuitive" style have taken to heart the idea that children are the ideal language learners, and are learning and speaking their languages much in the same way children do. Nancy Richardson points out that they are good at taking risks: they are not afraid to make mistakes, and they are willing to make grammatical errors. They have the courage to launch into long statements in their languages even though they know they will have to ask for words along the way and get corrected by the elders afterwards. This style means they get lots of practice and have developed a great deal of communicative competence along the way.

The apprentices who learn by the "analytical" style focus on understanding the rules of grammar, and tend to develop word lists and ask for paradigms of new verbs. While the intuitive teams talk about their activities and the world around them, the analytical teams also talk a great deal about language itself. The analytical apprentice is slower to develop communicative competence, but quicker to develop grammatical accuracy, and his speech contains very few errors. Both sorts of teams will come to proficiency, but they become good at different language skills at different rates.

None of the teams works in a social vacuum; the elders and apprentices are all sharing their knowledge with relatives or other people around them. The Karuk, Yowlumni, and Wintu teams are involving their whole families in the language learning process. The Karuk, Hupa, Mojave and Yowlumni teams have all been teaching language classes either to children or to families during this summer. Two teams have produced excellent videos: the Karuk team did a video about their language immersion camp, and the Hupa did a wonderful series of instructional videos all in Hupa, teaching language by the "direct method" where English is not used at all. Parris Butler of the Mojave team finalized the writing system he designed and it was approved by the tribal council. And all the teams have been using their languages in religious ceremonial activities—down south in the sweat house or memorial ceremonies; up north in the Deerskin Dance and Brush Dance and other important ceremonies.

There couldn't possibly be more dedicated and qualified people than these. Their successes and failures alike will form the basis for fine-tuning this model for language learning that we all hope will help rescue the California languages from their downward spiral into extinction, and restore the activities and values that are so important to the cultures of Native California. Is it too late for the California languages? No. How can it be when people like these bend their efforts to saving them?

Afterword

Linguistics and the California Languages

Explorers, mission priests, anthropologists and linguists have all done a great deal to record words, grammar, texts and cultural context of the California languages. This activity increased dramatically when the Anthropology department at the University of California at Berkeley, headed by A.L. Kroeber, provided a center for teams of anthropologists who all focused on the languages and cultures of California. In this climate, such anthropologists as Kroeber, Dixon, Gifford, Sapir, and Harrington were able to collect vast amounts of linguistic material on many different languages. Later, in the 1950s and also at the University of California at Berkeley, Mary Haas and Murray Emeneau founded the Department of Linguistics and the Survey of California and Other Indian Languages, with the result that, for many years, linguists receiving their training there usually focused their primary research on California languages. As other University of California campuses were founded, linguists in other parts of the state also did a great deal of research on California languages. Big archives of field notes, tapes and film made by these people now exist in many places. These materials are put to good use by Native Californian communities; publications, field notes and audiotapes made by these field workers have all been gone through by tribal members who are seeking to study, retain, or renew their languages of heritage.

Conflicts between the goals of linguists and the goals of communities. Despite the tremendous usefulness to the native communities of the linguists' work, conflicts in the motives and goals of linguists and Native Californian communities have sometimes made the relationship between the two groups less than ideal.

(1) Who is the audience? Linguistic field work and publication is usually done for the sake of an audience of linguists rather than an

audience of tribal members. The primary interests of the linguistic audience are in such matters as linguistic theory and language comparison, while the community audience is interested in language learning and preservation. Linguistic jargon and a highly technical writing style are preferred by the linguistic audience, but such an approach may make a document unintelligible to the general public, thus lessening its potential value to the community. On the other side of the coin, occasional reluctance on the part of native communities to allow language materials to be disseminated outside the tribe comes into conflict with the linguists' charge to make materials publicly available.

(2) *Authorship vs. Application.* The linguist depends for his job on the approval of colleagues and superiors. In the university setting, publishing academic papers is the most important way for a scholar to show worthiness for tenure and promotion. The language community usually has no interest in publication per se, but rather in the development of materials and programs that lead to language learning and the retention of traditional knowledge.

(3) *Theory vs. Data.* Over the last 40 years or so, linguistics has become more technical than it was during the first half of the century, with the result that scientific jargon and theories have made linguistic publications less intelligible to the public than when Sapir and Kroeber were doing their great work. The modern linguist is frequently defined by his contribution to linguistic theory, which often means the creation of or contribution to new models of the mental representation of language. The language community is interested in the data that linguists have collected, not in the theories they have expounded. Frequently linguists have collected only the data that is relevant to the particular theoretical point they are trying to make, so that the more theory-oriented a linguist is, the less relevant his work is to the goals of the language community.

(4) *Who's in charge?* Linguistic tradition has evolved around an asymmetrical relationship between the "expert" and the "informant," where the latter is expected to answer questions asked by the former. The linguist, in this situation, decides what to study and what to do with the results. This relationship is now being redefined by language communities, who want a say in what is studied and what is done with the results. (Within communities, there is an internal conflict as well: is it the

individual member or some community-wide authority that decides what knowledge is transmitted to the scholar and what is done with it?)

The conflicts in expectations and goals have led to some rifts between academics and the communities they desire to study. It is important that both groups understand each others' goals and take them into account in their decisions on whether to work together and how to focus that work. New generations of linguists being trained at universities must be taught to understand and respect the needs and goals of the communities in which they will work. And it is also important for the members of the communities who can find use for linguists to understand what it is that linguistics students must accomplish before they can get jobs. I believe it is possible for the goals of both groups to be met in joint endeavors.

Linguistics for the community. The new collaborative relationship that is developing between speakers and linguists has sent language work in new directions that have been beneficial for everyone. In the past 25 years or so, linguists have focused much more of their attention on applying their skills to community needs. This has been useful not only to the communities, but has also resulted in a greater depth of linguistic understanding by the scholars themselves.

I will name here a few joint endeavors between linguists and communities in California. In the 1970s, Margaret Langdon and some of her graduate students worked with Mesa Grande Diegueños, especially Ted Couro, to produce and publish language learning materials for use in the community, including the pedagogical grammar *Let's Speak Iipay 'Aa* (Couro and Langdon 1975). In the same vein, Ronald Langacker worked with Villiana Hyde to produce a useful learning-oriented grammar of Luiseño (Hyde 1971). Eric Elliott, who is presently a graduate student at the University of California at San Diego (where Ron Langacker and Margaret Langdon teach), is working with Villiana Hyde to extend the materials on Luiseño further. They are finishing up a collection of advanced lessons that are intended as a sequel to the Hyde/Langacker grammar, and have compiled an impressive dictionary and set of texts. Eric is also working on Cahuilla with Katherine Saubel.

Pamela Munro has been very active in joint ventures with Mojave and Yavapai speakers to produce some of the most complete dictionaries ever done for this region, and, like many linguists trained under Margaret Langdon, has insisted on using a practical orthography in most of her writings. She is representative of the newer breed of linguists who think of their audience as twofold—not linguists only, but both linguists and Native Californians.

In the north, linguist Bill Bright has been collaborating with Karuk language activists Julian Lang and Nancy Richardson to develop curriculum and other useful materials for that language. Victor Golla works with Hupa speakers on language preservation, and also publishes two newsletters that are tremendously useful to linguists and Native Americans alike, the *SSILA* Newsletter* and the more irregular *J.P. Harrington Newsletter*. Martha Macri is another linguist who is doing useful work: she has been working with Native American students at the University of California at Davis to help them learn ways of actively teaching themselves their language of heritage. Linguists such as Catherine Callaghan, Paul Kroskrity, Sally McLendon, Marianne Mithun, Robert Oswalt, Bill Shipley, Shirley Silver, and others have all focused much of their work on projects of community interest in California.

Further afield, linguists like Akira Yamamoto have done a great deal for Native American language retention in general. Akira has been an organizer and constantly popular teacher at summer workshops, teaching linguistics and language teaching methodology to Native Americans who are working on their languages. His work in recent years at NALI** conferences has been especially helpful to Native Californians who have attended. Akira has also been involved in planning for funding priorities and provisions for the grants to be administered under the Native American Languages Act (see Chapter 18).

These are just a few of the linguists who have been working collaboratively with Native Californians to meet the needs of the language communities. Of course the most useful linguists of all would be those who are actually members of the community. People like Loren Bommelyn and Julian Lang have become extremely skilled at linguistic analysis; but as of yet, we have no Native Californians who have become

---

*   Society for the Study of the Indigenous Languages of the Americas
** Native American Language Issues

professional linguists. A fine model is Ofelia Zepeda at the University of Arizona, a linguist, poet, and member of the O'odham (Papago) Nation, whose work on O'odham language preservation and maintenance has been of tremendous value.

New skills for the new California linguist. Linguists are being shaped by the needs and goals of language communities; we are educated as much by the community members as we are by the universities. The new generation of linguists realizes that in some ways their university education has been deficient in teaching them how to do the sort of applied work that is asked of them. Linguistics tends to focus on writing and analysis, words and sentences, which are not the most important aspects of language maintenance and learning. In the California communities, the needs focus more on language learning than language analysis. Writing is important to language preservation, but not to learning how to speak and understand language. Learning words and sentences does not teach someone how to hold a conversation, how to be polite to elders, or how to pray. The new California linguist should be well-educated in such fields as discourse, and the psychology and sociology of first-language learning, and the theories and methods of second-language learning. The old field of Language and Culture, once but no longer seen as central to linguistics, needs to be learned by the new California linguist as much as ever.

New goals for the new California linguist. One reason that so many linguists are interested in doing work of the sort that language communities want done is because, despite the professional conflicts, this work is so fulfilling. All of us want to do something meaningful with our lives. When I had my first faculty position at the University of Texas back in the 1970s, I had a hard time finding a sense of meaning and fulfillment in many of the requirements of my job; what kept me sane and happy were my biweekly treks to the Havasupai and Hualapai communities in Arizona, where I was working with teams of Havasupais, Hualapais, and other linguists to develop writing systems, literature, and bilingual education curricula for their schools. My experience and feelings are probably very close to those of other linguists who have been honored to apply their skills to community needs: the opportunity to be in the language communities, to develop and maintain ties to the people there, and to do something of use gives great personal joy. Despite the conflicts in goals and style that are built into the cultures of linguistics and Native American communities, there is more that binds us together than separates us. We our bound by our love of language, the goal of documenting endangered languages, and the fervent hope that the languages will survive.

In helping to preserve and restore the languages of California, community members and linguists alike are not just helping isolated small communities achieve goals they have set for themselves. We are creating something within the larger American community as well; we are helping to change our nation's viewpoint toward an acceptance of cultural and linguistic pluralism—toward a sense of unity in diversity, where there is room for all to practice their cultures of heritage while at the same time participating in the larger society. We are helping our state develop joy in the infinite mosaic—the complex pattern of languages and cultures that has always been the human pattern of California.

APPENDIX

Reference Guide to Linguistic Symbols

In this book I frequently use a general writing system adapted from the Roman alphabet, and modelled on the newer practical writing systems in use today in California and elsewhere. For purposes of this book, I try to write words from any given California language in its the practical writing system of that language if one exists, if I know it, and if it makes sense to use it in that context. Otherwise, I will usually use the symbols shown in the chart below, and if I have to add any more, I'll explain them as I go along.

'	glottal stop*
a	as in father
a:	drawn out a, as in fall
ay	as in fine
b	as in boy
ch	as in child
d	as in dove
e	as in hello
e:	drawn out e
ə	lax vowel as in sofa
f	as in fish
g	always the hard g, as in girl
h	as in help
i	as in Tina
i:	drawn out i
ɨ	part way between u and i
j	as in jump
k	as in skate (unaspirated)

---

* A glottal stop is not actually a sound at all, but rather a cessation of sound. It is what separates the two parts of the English exclamation "Uh-oh."

kʰ	as in **k**ite (aspirated)
k'	glottalized k
l	as in **l**emon
ly	as in Co**ll**ier
ł	whispered, "slurpy" l
m	as in **m**innow
m'	glottalized m
n	as in **n**ails
n'	glottalized n
ng	as in si**ng**
ny	as in ca**ny**on
o	as in **o**ver
o:	drawn out o
pʰ	as in **p**uff (aspirated)
p'	glottalized p
q	like k, but tongue further back
qʰ	aspirated q
q'	glottalized q
r	in some languages, like English r; in others, like Spanish r
s	as in **s**ame
ṣ	like s, but with tip of tongue further back in mouth
sh	as in **sh**eep
t	as in s**t**ick (unaspirated)
tʰ	as in **t**ime (aspirated)
t'	glottalized t
ṭ	like t, but tongue further back
ṭʰ	aspirated ṭ
ṭ'	glottalized ṭ
th	as in **th**in
ts	as in ca**ts**, or the Japanese loan word **ts**unami
u	as in h**u**la
u:	drawn out u
v	as in **v**ase
w	as in **w**ait

w'	glottalized w
x	as in Spanish **j**unto
y	as in **y**es
y'	glottalized y
z	as in **z**ebra
zh	as in **Zs**a **Zs**a

Other common symbols

In direct quotations, I sometimes use alternative symbols commonly employed in linguistic writings. Below are the most common symbols encountered in the literature on Native Californian languages, along with their equivalents from the list above.

Linguistic Symbol	Equivalent
ŋ	**ng**
š or ʃ	**sh**
č or tʃ	**ch**
c	**ts** or **ch** (used different ways in different languages; and in some languages the sound varies between the two)
ž or ʒ	**zh**
ǰ or dʒ	**j**
θ	**th** (as in **th**in)
ð	**th** (as in **th**en)
ñ or ɲ	**ny**
ʔ	**'** (glottal stop)
ṕ, t́, ḱ	**p', t', k'** (glottalized consonants)
æ	sound of vowel in English 'bad'
á, é, í, ó, ú	Accent mark over a vowel means that vowel is accented—that is, a bit louder or fuller than the other vowels; examples of accented vowels in English words are: térrify, terrífic, combinátion, combíne.
a·, e·, i·, o·, u·	These are alternative ways of representing
aa, ee, ii, oo, uu	the long (drawn out) vowels.

BIBLIOGRAPHY

Allen, Elsie. 1971. *Pomo Basketmaking*. Happy Camp, Calif.: Naturegraph.

Annals of America. 1968. 14:1916-28. Chicago: Encyclopedia Britannica.

Aoki, Haruo. 1979. *Nez Perce Texts*. University of California Publications in Linguistics, Vol. 90. Berkeley: University of California Press.

Barrett, S. A. 1908. *The Geography and Dialects of the Miwok Indians*. University of California Publications in American Archaeology and Ethnology, Vol. 6, No. 2. Berkeley: University of California Press.

— 1908. *Pomo Indian Basketry*. University of California Publications in American Archaeology and Ethnology, Vol. 7, No. 3. Berkeley: University of California Press.

Beeler, Madison S. 1964. Ventureño Numerals. In *Studies in Californian Linguistics* ed. William Bright. University of California Publications in Linguistics, Vol. 34. Berkeley: University of California Press.

— 1961. Senary Counting in California Penutian. *Anthropological Linguistics* 3:6.

— ed. 1967. *The Ventureño Confesionario of José Señán, O.F.M.* University of California Publications in Linguistics, Vol. 47. Berkeley: University of California Press.

Boas, Franz. [1911] 1966. *Handbook of American Indian Languages*. Smithsonian Institution: Bureau of American Ethnology. Reprint. University of Nebraska Press.

Bright, William. 1957. *The Karok Language*. University of California Publications in Linguistics, Vol. 13. Berkeley: University of California Press.

Bright, William, and Jane O. Bright. [1965] 1976. Semantic Structures in Northwestern California and the Sapir-Whorf Hypothesis. In *Formal Semantic Analysis*, ed. Eugene Hammel. *American Anthropologist* (special publication) 67:5, pt 2: 249-58. Reprint. in *Variation and Change in Language: Essays by William Bright*. Selected and introduced by Anwar S. Dil, 74-88. Stanford University Press.

Broadbent, Sylvia M. 1964. *The Southern Sierra Miwok Language*. University of California Publications in Linguistics, Vol. 38. Berkeley: University of California Press.

Callaghan, Catherine A. 1977. Coyote the Imposter (Lake Miwok). In *Northern California Texts*, Victor Golla and Shirley Silver. Chicago: University of Chicago Press.

— N.d. Encounter with J.P. Harrington. *Anthropological Linguistics*. Forthcoming.

Campbell, Lyle and Marianne Mithun, eds. 1979. *The Languages of Native America: Historical and Comparative Assessment*. University of Texas Press.

Chafe, Wallace. 1962. Estimates Regarding the Present Speakers of North American Indian Languages. *International Journal of American Linguistics*. 28(3): 162-171.

Couro, Ted and Margaret Langdon. 1975. *Let's Talk 'Iipay Aa: An Introduction to the Mesa Grande Diegueño Language*. Malki Museum Press & Ballena Press.

Crook, Rena, Leanne Hinton and Nancy Stenson. 1976. The Havasupai Writing System. *Proceedings of the 1976 Hokan-Yuman Languages Workshop*. ed. James E. Redden. University Museum Studies, No. 11:1-16. University Museum: Southern Illinois University at Carbondale.

Culkin, John. 1982. Alphabet for the Computer Age. *Science Digest* 9(8): 26–27.

de Angulo, Jaime. [1950] 1990. *Indians in Overalls*. In *The Hudson Review*. (Autumn) Reprint. San Francisco: City Lights Books.

de Angulo, Jaime, and William Ralganal Benson. 1932. Creation Myths of the Pomo Indian. *Anthropos* 27:264.

Densmore, Frances. [1932] 1972. *Yuman and Yaqui Music*. Smithsonian Institution, Bureau of American Ethnology Bulletin No. 110. Reprint. New York: Da Capo Press.

Dixon, Roland B. and A.L. Kroeber. 1919. *Linguistic Families of California*. University of California Publications in American Archaeology and Ethnology, Vol. 16, No. 3. Berkeley: University of California Press.

Egli, Ida Rae. 1992. *No Rooms of Their Own: Women Writers of Early California*. Berkeley: Heyday Books.

Fredrickson, Vera Mae, ed. 1989. School Days in Northern California: the Accounts of Six Pomo Women. *News from Native California*, 4(1): 40 ff.

Gifford, Edward Winslow and Gwendoline Harris Block. [1930] 1990. *Californian Indian Nights*. Reprint. Lincoln and London: University of Nebraska Press.

Goddard, P.E. 1912. *Elements of the Kato Language* . University of California Publications in American Archaeology and Ethnology, Vol. 11, No. 1. Berkeley: University of California Press.

Golla, Victor. 1984. *The Sapir-Kroeber Correspondence*. Survey of California and Other Indian Languages, Report 6. Dept. of Linguistics, University of California, Berkeley.

Golla, Victor and Shirley Silver. 1977. *Northern California Texts. International Journal of American Linguistics*. Native American Texts Series, Vol. 2, No. 2. University of Chicago Press.

Greenberg, Joseph H. 1987. *Language in the Americas*. Stanford University Press.

Grimes, Barbara, ed. 1988. *Ethnologue: Languages of the World*, 11th ed. Arlington, Texas: Summer Institute of Linguistics.

Gudde, Erwin G. 1969. *California Place Names*. 3d ed. Berkeley: University of California Press.

Hale, Kenneth, Michael Krauss, et al. 1992. Endangered Languages. *Language* 68(1): 1-42.

Harrington, J.P. [1933] 1978. *Chinigchinich*. A revised and annotated version of Alfred Robinson's translation of Father Geronimo Boscana's historical account of the belief, usages, customs and extravagencies of the Indians of this mission of San Juan Capistrano, called the Acagchemem tribe. Santa Ana, Calif.: Fine Arts Press. Reprint. Banning, Calif.: Malki Museum Press.

Heizer, Robert F. 1978. *Handbook of North American Indians. Volume 8: California*. Smithsonian Institution.

Heizer, Robert F. and M. A. Whipple. 1951. *The California Indians: A Source Book*. Berkeley: University of California Press.

Hickman, James C., ed. 1993. *The Jepson Manual: Higher Plants of California*. Berkeley & Los Angeles: University of California Press.

Hinton, Leanne. 1980a. Vocables in Havasupai Songs. In *Southwestern Ritual Drama*, ed. Charlotte J. Frisbie, 275-305. University of New Mexico Press.

— 1980b. When Sounds Go Wild: Phonological Change and Syntactic Re-Analysis in Havasupai. *Language*. 56(2): 320-344.

— 1984. *Havasupai Songs: a Linguistic Perspective*. Berlin: Gunther Narr Press.

— 1987. *Yana Morphology: a Thumbnail Sketch*. Southern Illinois University Occasional Papers on Linguistics: papers from the 1987 Hokan-Penutian Languages Workshop, 7-16.

— 1991. Takic and Yuman: A Study in Phonological Convergence. *International Journal of American Linguistics* 57(2): 133-157.

— 1992. *Ishi's Tale of Lizard*. New York: Farrar, Straus and Giroux.

Hinton, Leanne, and Lucille Watahomigie. 1984. *Spirit Mountain: An Anthology of Yuman Indian Oral Literature and Song*. Suntracks: University of Arizona Press.

Hyde, Villiana. 1971. *An Introduction to the Luiseño Language*. ed. Ronald W. Langacker in collaboration with Pamelo Munro et al. Banning, Calif: Malki Museum Press.

Kroeber, A. L. 1916. *California Place Names of Indian Origin*. University of California Publications in American Archaeology and Ethnology, Vol. 12, No. 2. Berkeley: University of California Press.

— [1925] 1976. *Handbook of the Indians of California*. Bureau of American Ethnology, Bulletin 78. Washington, D.C.: Government Printing Office. Reprint. New York: Dover Books.

— 1948. Seven Mohave Myths. *Anthropological Records*. 11(1): 1-70. University of California Publications. Berkeley: University of California Press.

Kroeber, A.L. and George William Grace. 1960. *The Sparkman Grammar of Luiseño*. University of California Publications in Linguistics, Vol. 16. Berkeley: University of California Press.

Ladefoged, Peter. 1992. Another View of Endangered Languages. *Language*. 68(4): 809-111.

Laird, Carobeth. 1975. *Encounter with an Angry God*. Banning, Calif.: Malki Museum Press.

Lakoff, Robin. 1975. *Language and Women's Place*. New York: Harper & Row.

Langdon, Margaret. 1978. Animal Talk in Cocopa. *International Journal of American Linguistics*. 44(1): 10-23.

Langdon, Margaret and Pamela Munro. 1980. Yuman Numerals. In *American Indian and Indoeuropean Studies: Papers in Honor of Madison S. Beeler*, ed. K. Klar, M. Langdon, S. Silver. The Hague: Mouton.

Le Guin, Ursula K. 1968. *A Wizard of Earthsea*. Ace Books edition.

Lee, Dorothy. 1959. *Freedom and Culture*. Prentice-Hall.

Lucy, John A. 1992. *Language Diversity and Thought: A Reformulation of the Linguistic Relativity Hypothesis*. Cambridge University Press.

Luthin, Herb. 1991. *Restoring the Voice in Yanan Traditional Narrative: Prosody, Performance and Presentational Form*. Ph.D. diss., University of California, Berkeley.

Mallery, Garrick. 1893. Picture-writing of the American Indians. In *Tenth Annual Report of the Bureau of Ethnology to the Secretary of the Smithsonian Institution, 1888-89*, J. W. Powell.

Margolin, Malcolm, ed. [1981] 1993. rev. ed. *The Way We Lived: California Indian Reminiscences, Stories and Songs*. Berkeley: Heyday Books.

Marr, Jack, ms. Letters from J.P. Harrington.

Martineau, LaVan. 1973. *The Rocks Begin to Speak*. Las Vegas: KC Publications.

Nichols, Johanna. 1992. Linguistic Diversity and First Settlement of the New World. *Language* 66(3): 475-521.

Oswalt, Robert L. 1960. Gualala. *Names*. 8(1).

— 1961. *A Kashaya Grammar*. Ph.D. diss., University of California, Berkeley.

— 1964. *Kashaya Texts*. University of California Publications in Linguistics, Vol. 36. Berkeley: University of California Press.

— 1980. Ukiah: Yokaya. In *American Indian and Indoeuropean Studies: Papers in Honor of Madison S. Beeler*, ed. K. Klar, M. Langdon, S. Silver. The Hague: Mouton.

Peattie, Donald Culross. 1953. *A Natural History of Western Trees*. Houghton Mifflin.

Pitkin, Harvey. 1984. *Wintu Grammar*. University of California Publications in Linguistics, Vol. 94. Berkeley: University of California Press.

Powers, Stephen. [1877] 1976. *Tribes of California*. Contributions to North American Ethnology, Vol. 3. Washington, D.C.: Government Printing Office. Reprint. Berkeley: University of California Press.

Press, Margaret L. 1979. *Chemehuevi: A Grammar and Lexicon*. University of California Publications in Linguistics, Vol. 92. Berkeley: University of California Press.

Pullum, Geoffrey. 1991. *The Great Eskimo Vocabulary Hoax, and Other Irreverent Essays on the Study of Language*. University of Chicago Press.

Robins, R.H. 1958. *The Yurok Language: Grammar, Texts, Lexicon*. University of California Publications in Linguistics, Vol. 15. Berkeley: University of California Press.

Sapir, Edward. 1910. *Yana Texts*. University of California Publications in American Archaeology and Ethnology, Vol. 9, No. 1. Berkeley: University of California Press.

— 1917. Unpublished field notes of Yahi with Ishi. Bancroft Library, University of California, Berkeley.

— 1921. *Language: An Introduction to the Study of Speech*. New York: Harcourt, Brace.

— [1929] 1970. The Status of Linguistics as a Science. *Language*. 5:207-14. Reprinted in *Culture, Language and Personality*, ed. David G. Mandelbaum, 65-77. Berkeley: University of California Press.

— 1985 Abnormal Types of Speech in Nootka. In *Selected Writings of Edward Sapir in Language, Culture and Personality*, ed. D. Mandelbaum, 179–196. Berkeley: University of California Press.

— 1985. Male and Female Forms of Speech in Yana. In *Selected Writings of Edward Sapir in Language, Culture and Personality*, ed. David G. Mandelbaum. Berkeley: University of California Press.

Schlichter, Alice [Shepherd]. 1981. *Wintu Dictionary*. Survey of California and Other Indian Languages, Report 2. Dept. of Linguistics, University of California, Berkeley.

Shepherd, Alice. 1989. *Wintu Texts*. University of California Publications in Linguistics, Vol. 117. Berkeley: University of California Press.

Sherzer, Joel. 1976. *An Areal-typological Study of American Indian Languages North of Mexico*. Amsterdam and Oxford: North-Holland Publishing Company; New York: American Elserier Publishing Company.

Shipek, Florence Connolly. 1991. *Delfina Cuero: Her Autobiography: An Account of Her Last Years and Her Ethnobotanic Contributions*. Anthropological Papers, No. 38. Ed. Sylvia Brakke Vane. California: Ballena Press. Orig. printed as *The Autobiography of Delfina Cuero*. Malki Museum Press (1970).

Shipley, William, ed. 1992. *The Maidu Indian Myths and Stories of Hanc'ibyjim*. Berkeley: Heyday Books.

Stewart, George. [1936] 1960. *Ordeal by Hunger*. Houghton Mifflin. Reprint. Ace Star.

— 1962. *The California Trail*. McGraw-Hill.

— 1967. *Names on the Land; A Historical Account of Place-Naming in the United States*. 3d ed. Boston: Houghton Mifflin.

Strankman, Gary, 1993. The Power of Names. *News from Native California*. 7(3): 38-41.

Teeter, Karl V. 1964. *The Wiyot Language*. University of California Publications in Linguistics, Vol. 37. Berkeley: University of California Press.

Vera, Matt. 1993. The Creation of Language, a Yowlumni Story. *The Advocate*. 1(3) In *News from Native California*: 7(3): 19-20.

Wagner, Henry R., ed. 1924. California Voyages, 1539-1541: Translations of Original Documents. *California Historical Society Quarterly* 3(4).

Walsh, Jane MacLaren. 1976. *John Peabody Harrington: the Man and his California Indian Fieldnotes*. Ballena Press & Malki Museum Press.

Whistler, Kenneth W. 1977. Wintun Prehistory: An Interpretation Based on Linguistic Reconstruction of Plant and Animal Nomenclature. *Proceedings of the Third Berkeley Linguistic Society Meeting*. Dept. of Linguistics, Berkeley Linguistic Society 3:157-174, University of California, Berkeley.

Wilson, Darryl Babe. 1993. Salila-ti Mi-mu d-enn-i-gu. *The Advocate*. 1(2). In *News from Native California*. 7(2): 38.

Woiche, Istet. [1928] 1992. *Annikadel: the History of the Universe as Told by the Achumawi Indians of California*. Tucson: University of Arizona Press. Orig. printed as *An-Nik-A-Del: The History of the Universe*. Stratford Company.

Index
Languages and Individuals*

---

* Works of individual authors are quoted throughout this book; these references are included in the bibliography, but not in this index.

Titles of related interest from Heyday Books:

The Way We Lived: California Indian Stories, Songs and Reminiscences (Edited with Commentary by Malcolm Margolin)

Life in a California Mission: Monterey in 1786 (Jean François de La Pérouse)

To the American Indian: Reminiscences of a Yurok Woman (Lucy Thompson)

The Maidu Indian Myths and Stories of Hanc'ibyjim (Edited and Translated by William Shipley)

It Will Live Forever: Traditional Yosemite Acorn Preparation (Beverly R. Ortiz, as told by Julia F. Parker)

Indian Summer: Traditional Life Among the Choinumne Indians of California's San Joaquin Valley (Thomas Jefferson Mayfield)

Flutes of Fire: Essays on California Indian Languages (Leanne Hinton)

Ararapíkva: Traditional Karuk Indian Literature from Northwestern California (Edited and Translated by Julian Lang)

Adopted by Indians: A True Story (Thomas Jefferson Mayfield, Edited by Malcolm Margolin)

Native Ways: California Indian Stories and Memories (Edited by Malcolm Margolin and Yolanda Montijo)

Quarterly magazine:

News from Native California: An Inside View of the California Indian World

For more information, visit www.heydaybooks.com